Like Them That Dream

Like Them That Dream

The Maori and the Old Testament

Bronwyn Elsmore

Published by Libro International, an imprint of Oratia Media Ltd, 783 West Coast Road, Oratia, Auckland 0604, New Zealand (www.librointernational.com).

Copyright © 1985, 2000, 2011 Bronwyn Elsmore

The copyright holder asserts her moral rights in the work.

This book is copyright. Except for the purposes of fair reviewing, no part of this publication may be reproduced or transmitted in any form or by any means, whether electronic, digital or mechanical, including photocopying, recording, any digital or computerised format, or any information storage and retrieval system, including by any means via the Internet, without permission in writing from the publisher. Infringers of copyright render themselves liable to prosecution.

ISBN 978-1-877514-26-5
Ebook ISBN 978-1-877514-27-2

First published 1985 by Moana Press
Second edition 2000 by Reed Books
This edition 2011 by Libro International

Printed in New Zealand

Dedication

In memory of my father
Bernard Henry Norris Teague
Who passed away in May 1982 before
this could be written, but without
whose influence over many years it
would probably not have eventuated.

POROPOROAKI
E taku Koro, haere, haere,
Ka karanga a Hine-nui-te-po;
Papatuanuku has bared her breast
reclaimed you as her own.
The hands are washed, the fast broken,
Kawakawa now removed —
curling leaves a mute reminder
of transitory life.
Not for you the korowai,
Te iwi whanau your only claim,
But to me, bereft, lamenting,
One of Tane's totara fell.

- B.M.E. -

Contents

List of Illustrations	8
List of Abbreviations	9
Preface	11

Part One: The Early Picture
1.	Maori and Missionary	17
2.	Politics and Problems	33
3.	Disease and Decline	42
4.	Principle and Practice	53

Part Two: The Maori Response
5.	Jesus or Jehovah?	71
6.	Indigenous and Imported	87
7.	Rejection and Reformulation	100

Part Three: The New Religions
8.	The New Religions	107
9.	Papahurihia, or Karakia Nakahi	109
10.	Other Early Movements	116
11.	Pai Marire	123
12.	Ringatu	132
13.	Parihaka Movement	140
14.	Tariao	150
15.	Arowhenua Movement	154
16.	Tekau-ma-rua	161
17.	Maketu Movement	165
18.	Upper Waihou Movement	171
19.	Kohititanga Marama	175
20.	Iharaira	182
21.	Ratana	190

Conclusion	197
Glossary	201
Bibliography	203
Index	211

List of Illustrations

Map: Location of places mentioned	14
The 'Flying Dragon'	120
Te Ua Haumene	128
Te Kooti	133
Te Whiti-o-Rongomai	141
Te Whiti and Tohu Kakahi	147
King Tawhiao	152
Te Mahuki Manukura at Te Kumi	162
Himiona Te Orinui	166
Rihara Te Reke	169
The pillars for the Kohiti temple	179
Rua Kenana	183
Zion at New Jerusalem	186
Tahupotiki Wiremu Ratana	193

List of Abbreviations

AJHR — Appendices to the Journals of the House of Representatives
AML — Auckland Institute and Museum Library
APL — Auckland Public Library
ATL — Alexander Turnbull Library
BOPT — Bay of Plenty Times
CMS — Church Missionary Society
HL — Hocken Library
JPS — Journal of the Polynesian Society
MS — Manuscript
NML — Napier Museum Library
NZH — New Zealand Herald
NZJH — New Zealand Journal of History
NZPD — New Zealand Parliamentary Debates
PBH — Poverty Bay Herald
SJC — St John's College
TPNZI — Transactions and Proceedings of the New Zealand Institute
TS — Typescript
WMS — Wesleyan Methodist Missionary Society

When the Lord turned again the captivity of Zion, we were like them that dream.

Then was our mouth filled with laughter, and our tongue with singing: then said they among the heathen, The Lord hath done great things for them.

The Lord hath done great things for us; whereof we are glad.

Turn again our captivity, O Lord, as the streams in the south.

They that sow in tears shall reap in joy.

He that goeth forth and weepeth, bearing precious seed, shall doubtless come again with rejoicing, bringing his sheaves with him.

- Psalm 126 -

Preface

From any study of the history or the beliefs and practices of Maori religious movements in New Zealand, it is immediately obvious that great emphasis is placed on the Old Testament scriptures. This was first noted in the journals of missionaries more than a century and a half ago, and has been pointed out by other writers since.

Such references, however, have generally been brief, and usually restricted to consideration of one particular movement or period only. Yet to fully appreciate this aspect of the response in any one movement or time, it is essential that the whole topic be looked at. To view a small part of the picture only is to miss the full context and therefore the pattern evident in the development of the phenomenon.

In writing this book I have tried to keep in mind at all times the general reader — in New Zealand or elsewhere — in an effort to ensure its readability by those with even little prior knowledge of the topic. At the same time I have been aware of those who will be reading with an academic interest in the subject. To satisfy both groups fully is no doubt an impossible task, and I can only hope that the result will be acceptable to most.

The very scope of the subject has imposed upon me the regrettable necessity of having to view the Maori as an homogenous race, with each tribe and subgroup adhering to unified views, beliefs, traditions and practices. In fact, while overall tendencies were similar, there was variation in many areas of thought and practice. It would, however, be tedious, unwieldy, and probably almost impossible to try to distinguish between the views of different groups, or even between members of one tribe. The alternative — to speak generally of trends which recurred or were common to a number of peoples — should not, therefore, be taken as a statement that any one motivation or reaction was universal among the Maori. While in each area there were those who rejected the message of the missionaries (and this was sufficiently frequent to allow references to general reactions), there were also members of Maori communities who adopted the beliefs taught by the churches, and not only remained firm believers for the rest of their lives but also at times took the side of the missions against their Maori brethren.

Similarly, some generalisation must occur concerning the missions and the missionaries. There was much variation among different members of the clergy in their attitudes towards the Maori. The missionaries themselves were aware of this, and conscious that they did not present a united front to those they were teaching. Consequently, it was often the clergy who were the strongest critics of the New Zealand missions. But the fact remains that many of the missionaries were tireless workers for the benefit of the Maori, and in return were regarded with great love and affection.

This work is organised into three parts, followed by a brief conclusion. Part One outlines the background to the Christian mission in New Zealand, colonisation, and the effects of these on the Maori. Part Two considers the cultural reasons why the Maori very often chose to identify with the Israelites of ancient times, and therefore based their religious response on the Hebraic scriptures. Part Three examines the religious aspects of a number of the Maori movements, showing how that identification manifested itself within them, according to the context of the time.

Part One is included in order to give those with little previous knowledge of this country's history a necessary background to the times and conditions of the early European contact period and colonial New Zealand. It is a basic introduction dealing only with the matters which are relevant to this specific topic, and should not be considered to be any more than this. Readers interested in any particular matter mentioned should consult more detailed studies in that field for further knowledge.

The purpose of this book is to examine particularly the 'Hebraist' aspect of Maori religious movements and to explain the several reasons why this emphasis occurred within them. It should not be taken that they were therefore totally inspired in this manner and so constituted a complete rejection of Christianity — indeed they were all a synthesis of traditional, Christian and Hebraic elements in varying degrees.

During my years of research on this topic I have been helped by numerous people to whom I must express my sincere gratitude.

Special thanks to the tangata whenua in several parts of Aotearoa who have shared their knowledge with me — Mr Ronnie Bell (Mahanga), Mr Rua Niania, and Mr and Mrs J. Robinson (Iwitea), Mr Teti Peka (Kihitu), Mr and Mrs Mac Whaanga (Mahia), Mr Apirana Te Rauna Hape, Mrs Maria Thompson, Mr Turi Tipoki, Mr Horace Whaanga (Wairoa), Mr M. Delamere (Opotiki), Mr Anaru Kohu, Mrs Meri Lucas, Mrs Pera Nuku (Tauranga), Mr Hawiki Ranapia (Motiti), Mr William Pakeha (Te Teko).

Ka whakapai ahau ki a koutou mo ta koutou atawhai. Kia ora koutou.

The staff of New Zealand Government Departments have invariably been very helpful — particularly those of National Archives (Department of Internal Affairs), and the Department of Statistics. The friendly assistance of the librarians and staff of the Auckland Institute and Museum Library, Alexander Turnbull Library (Wellington), Hocken Library (University of Otago), Napier Museum Library, and the Bernard Sladden Library (Tauranga Public Library) has been much appreciated.

I am also grateful to members of the staff of several universities with whom I have discussed ideas — Dr Brian Colless, Dr Peter Donovan, and Dr John Owens (Massey University), Dr James Veitch (Victoria University of Wellington), and Dr Harold Turner (Director of the Study Centre for New Religious Movements in Primal Societies, Birmingham, England).

A number of other people have helped in a variety of ways and this is acknowledged with thanks. Mr D.H. Maxwell, Mr A.H. Matheson (Tauranga), the late Frank Davis (Palmerston North), Mr Bill Dacker (Dunedin), Mr A. van der Wouden (Whakatane), Mr H.G.D. White (Opotiki), Mr Robert de Roo of The Tauranga Moana Press, and Mr Stephen Kale of Design Com.

My sincere and loving thanks to my family who have cheerfully coped during my periods away from home in the course of my research, and to my mother, Thelma Teague (Wairoa).

1985

Regrettably, in the past fifteen years many of the above-named people have passed away.

He mihi ki a koutou. Hoki atu ki te Kaihanga; takoto rangimarie i runga i te aroha.

2000

Location of places mentioned in the text.

Part One

The Early Picture

1. Maori and Missionary

It is perhaps a popularly held belief among New Zealanders that from the arrival of the Christian missionaries in 1814, the 'Christianisation' of these islands was inevitable, almost immediate, and total. In fact, it proved to be none of these three.

From the time of contact with Europeans, the Maori culture which had evolved over many centuries was set against another which was the product of long development in a very different environment — geographically, historically and ideologically. As the customs and practices of the two met, the belief systems which underpinned the structure of each society proved to be the area where the real tensions would be felt. This was especially so as it was the express purpose of the missionaries to convert the Maori to Christianity through a process of 'civilisation' into European ways, and religious instruction.[1] Though those first settlers knew the task would not be easy, they could not have dreamed of some of the effects of their endeavours.

From 1814 to the 1830s, the period of early missionary contact, Christian influence on Maori was minor. The first baptisms were not recorded until after 1825, and even then they were few and occasional for several more years. In this early period the missionaries felt they were like prophets crying in the wilderness, and farmers sowing their seeds on rocks. In 1829 the Wesleyan mission, discouraged by lack of success, considered withdrawing from the field.

From the 1830s, however, a great rush of conversions began. While the reasons for this development may be many, at the basis appears to be the early attitude of Maori as the 'protectors' of the Europeans. Maori were a proud people with a background of identity and belief which was not to be easily replaced or transformed, and they did not see the new religion as at all relevant to their way of life. The Rev. John Butler found an example of this when he visited a village and explained to the chief the Christian teaching of monogamy. In reply to the missionary's statement that God was angry with all men who had many wives, the chief replied, 'Our God is not angry with us, and your God does not live in New Zealand'.[2]

Indeed, early missionaries were very much at the mercy of Maori, with their lives dependent upon the goodwill of the chiefs of the area in which the mission stations were placed. In the Bay of Islands, for instance, their well-being was guaranteed by the chief Hongi Hika, who had seen the material advantages of friendly relations with the newcomers after his very successful visit to England. But the missionaries were not in any doubt that this policy was based on the chief's own interests rather than on any devotion to the message of the mission. Five Maori youths living at the Bay of Islands mission station around 1819–20 and being educated by missionaries were also appreciated by the Rev. John Butler as 'hostages for our security'.[3]

During this early period, then, Maori took what aspects of the introduced culture suited them, and disregarded the rest as inappropriate and unnecessary to their way of life. Missionaries were not regarded as possessing great mana, but were valued rather as suppliers of material goods. It was in this capacity that they were accepted and protected.[4] By 1830,[5] however, in this second phase of contact, Maori began to realise that the tide had turned and the race was being more and more influenced by European culture.

With the spread of the new religion came an inevitable response characterised by the rise of religious movements which attempted to reconcile the new beliefs with the old. In mission areas, movements very often included some aspect of opposition to the Christian message, and it was not until the following century that the conversion of the Maori to Christianity was anywhere near total.

It is often supposed that the motivation for conversion was usually inspired by material considerations, with such lines as 'O Jesus Christ, give me a blanket in order that I may believe',[6] quoted as evidence. The early trader Joel Samuel Polack, noting that the 'attempts to instil a real belief in the Christian Religion into the minds of the benighted natives has hitherto decidedly failed', cynically put this down to the fact that Maori often accepted the European religion only 'from the crafty feeling of bettering their present condition', and were only too quick to renounce such belief when a contrary way promised benefit.[7]

Indeed, missionaries themselves often ruefully commented that this appeared to be a problem. The Rev. A.N. Brown, visiting Northland in 1837, noted that Maori there were hardened to Christianity, opposing all that was said to them:

> One native remarked that they got nothing from the Missionaries — that all their good things came from the Traders. Another said it was false to call our Books the Word of God for they did not come down from Heaven — that we wrote what we wished and sent it to Paihia to be printed. A third remarked that they would all 'believe' if they were paid for it &c.[8]

Such comments are based on a one-sided view only — on the Maori side the issue was seen somewhat differently. To Maori, the culture from which the missionaries, traders and settlers came was obviously blessed with great material wealth, and this was seen as evidence of the great power of the God of that culture. The gods were meant to protect and provide for their people. As the Europeans possessed enormous ships, powerful weapons, and a vast variety and quantity of amazing goods, then this must testify to the superiority of the God of the missionaries over those of the Maori. So the growing interest in transferring allegiance to this greater power, or at least adding it to their other deities, was a more legitimate move than is often appreciated. That the missionaries, as representatives or priests of the new Atuanui, would then supply the people with the articles which came along with that power, was an obvious conclusion. In this case, then, the prayer 'give me a blanket in order that I may believe' is not merely a trade-off, but an invitation to the deity to prove its power and so earn allegiance. This was entirely in line with the Maori concept of the atua.

The first missionaries were laymen, untrained and unequipped for their immense task. It was the view of Samuel Marsden, then in charge of the Australasian mission field, that the New Zealanders should first be civilised and then introduced to the Christian gospel.[9] So the first men sent to settle into the new land were skilled tradesmen and not missionaries. Of the first three, William Hall was a carpenter, John King (though a shoemaker by trade) had been trained in flax-dressing and twine-spinning, and Thomas Kendall was employed for the purpose of being a schoolmaster to the Maori, and himself learning their language.[10] This latter was substituted by Marsden for his other choice of tradesman, a smith.

This policy had the effect of relating the Christian message to material goods in the minds of Maori — especially as the early lay settlers were encouraged to barter goods with local people in order to aid their own survival, to get to know the people of the land, and to promote the 'civilisation' of the country.

These laymen were expected to establish themselves in a foreign and undeveloped country with little continuing moral support, and also to establish good relations with Maori through the teaching of skills, literacy and the gospel. In addition they were to set a high Christian example. It is no wonder that their early results were not always all that might have been hoped for.

Ordained missionaries followed, eventually meeting with more success. But in the early period, despite sincere motivation, these very often proved to be biased, lacking in understanding, and intolerant of the traditional beliefs of Maori. Consequently the message was implied, and indeed often given directly to the people, that their beliefs were mere superstitions, their opinions absurd, their doctrines heathenish, and their natures depraved. It was William Colenso's belief that before the arrival of Europeans, Maori had no religion, neither from the point of view of virtues based on religious concepts, nor any system of divine faith and worship. Their gods, maintained Colenso, were merely imaginary beings, not worshipped, but more often abused or derided.[11] Bishop Pompallier of the Catholic Mission referred to Maori as 'infidel New Zealanders who were warriors and cannibals'.[12] The Rev. Robert Maunsell, in his journal, referred to his 'disgust' and 'abhorrence' of the practices of the Maori, and judged their waiata as 'filthy and debasing'.[13] Henry Williams recorded in 1828 that they were 'governed by the Prince of Darkness in all their movements', and told one person that his people were 'wrong in all their ways'.[14]

In such cases the missionaries were guilty of taking their own narrow view of religion and imposing it on a culture vastly different from their own. As a result, they did not see what was present in Maori life. That Maori did indeed have a well-developed religious outlook cannot be doubted. Spiritual beliefs formed the basis of the culture and were implicit in every aspect of daily life. All behaviour was ordered according to the demands of the spiritual world, and based on the laws of tapu which underlay all areas of existence. Ceremonies addressed to the atua preceded and accompanied every stage of life and every significant undertaking. The difference between the two systems, then, was that while Europeans had formulated their views into a formal system which separated the areas of life into 'religious' and 'secular', the Maori belief system had not been so formalised, and no such dichotomy existed between the sacred and the profane. Consequently, Maori considered such matters to be a natural part of daily existence.

Such misunderstanding of the rich basis to their life was bound to leave more than a residue of dissatisfaction in the mind of Maori, even as they later accepted Christian baptism. In addition, having been told so repeatedly, they soon became persuaded that their beliefs were indeed without foundation or value. The Rev. William Wade, attempting to learn traditional beliefs from an old chief, was told '. . . of what use is it to talk about these things, you know very well they are nothing but lies'.[15]

The feeling of superiority in the Europeans can be seen in the words of Thomas Kendall, who wrote in 1820, a mere five and a half years after the arrival of the missionaries:

The Native Spirit has been roused, by the long intercourse of the Natives with Europeans; but none of them having yet been converted to Christianity, the Native Heart with its blind attachment to its barbarous customs remains unchanged, and inclines its possessor to pursue them with additional vigour . . . [16]

That the missionaries might have expected Maori to turn their back on centuries of tradition and adopt thoroughly foreign customs and ways of belief in such a short time, appears now to be very naive. Little accommodation was made by the Europeans, except perhaps in matters affecting their own survival, such as diet. On the whole, they sought to convert Maori from an external standpoint, rather than becoming one with them and so exerting some influence from within.

Cultural differences between Maori and missionary were major. Missionaries were sometimes faced with a clash of loyalties between the interests of their nation and those of their new charges. On one hand they were to introduce the people to 'civilisation' as they knew it, and on the other hand needed to involve themselves in Maori life in order to familiarise themselves with indigenous beliefs. In most instances missionaries detached themselves from the Maori by living apart, in an English-style house, surrounded by a fence. On their trips through their area they would pitch a tent and sleep apart from their Maori companions. In this way they no doubt hoped to provide an example of ideal, even 'right', society. European settlers and the occasional missionary who lived in the villages with the local people were criticised by missionaries for their lapse in social and moral standards. On the whole, missionaries attempted to impose particular English theology and social customs on a people whose beliefs were entirely alien to such thought, rather than immersing themselves in the culture of the new country and allowing a Maori Christian theology, and consequent social order, to develop in line with indigenous ways.

The culture gap was, naturally, a two-way thing. As missionaries could not appreciate the indigenous culture, so Maori had even less conception of the abstract beliefs of Europeans. A preacher learnt this one Sunday when he was explaining the story of Lazarus to a group of people. His account of the raising of the dead man was met with disbelief on the grounds of experience and simple logic. The preacher was asked if he himself had seen anyone raised from the dead and when he was forced to reply that he had not, the group laughed heartily at the credulity of Europeans in believing such tales.[17]

Added to this handicap was a further problem to be reconciled by Maori. The early contact period was not confined solely to Maori contact with missionaries. On the contrary, the earliest and most frequent influence was often from traders and whalers, and a little later the settlers.[18] By the 1830s Kororareka in the Bay of Islands was described by the missionaries as 'Hell', with hundreds of sailors and whalers to be seen on a Sunday brawling in the streets and fighting over Maori women.[19] In the decades to come, missionaries in other parts of the country also severely criticised the behaviour of such people, often blaming them for causing lack of interest in the message of the mission. The Rev. A.N. Brown, at Cloudy Bay in 1837, asked a group of whalers if the sabbath was observed among the one hundred or more Europeans at that place and Queen Charlotte Sound. One of the men observed that the mission 'would stand a better chance of succeeding with the natives than with us, for I think they are the best of the two'.[20]

Early traders and whalers often perpetrated acts of cruelty, injustice and violence on Maori. Escaped convicts also reached these shores and stayed, using the people for their own ends. Samuel Marsden, in a letter to the Church Missionary Society (CMS) in 1814, wrote of 'wanton cruelties, robberies, and murders of the natives'.[21] Five years later, provoked by hearing of a case of sailors abducting two young women and later leaving them in another area to be killed and eaten by an enemy tribe (this incident motivating an episode of revenge), Marsden wrote that he reflected with pain, grief and shame upon the crimes of his countrymen 'who, by their wanton atrocities, spread war, misery, and death even amongst the poor heathen nations who have never done them the smallest injury'.[22]

Other missionaries complained of such cruelty also,[23] and one church historian, telling of instances in which Maori were treacherously treated with no fault on their side, noted that the cases were 'alas! only typical of a number.'[24] Traders also frequently cheated the people, paying ridiculously low prices for goods bought, passing off inferior quality merchandise, and practising such tricks as mixing sand with sugar or including stones in bags of foodstuffs to increase their weight.[25]

On occasions traders and other travellers are known to have misrepresented the missionaries to their own advantage. Henry Williams records that he once met a man, Mr Merning, who told the clergyman of his arrival in Taranaki. They had been greeted by men carrying muskets, so had called out that they were missionaries, at which they were given a hearty welcome. Williams commented that Merning was 'an infidel and his companion a Jew, both enemies to our cause, but in this instance it was convenient for them to hail for Missionaries.'[26]

A Missionary Society document in 1817 concluded that because of such incidents, not only were the lives of missionaries and settlers in danger, but that efforts to civilise and bring Christianity to the New Zealanders were greatly hampered. Consequently, the report stated, any advantage to England which might have accrued was now destroyed.[27]

Despite all this, Maori sometimes preferred traders to missionaries. The missionaries generally had no goods for sale or trade, and barter was of prime interest to Maori. Whereas the missionaries chose to live apart from the indigenous people and did not marry into their race, traders lived in the villages and became absorbed into families and tribes. So it happened that the trader often obtained a high standing in an area while the missionary remained an outsider, of no rank and therefore not a fit associate for anyone of chiefly class.

Settlers followed, and many of these were far from sympathetic to Christianity, with some resenting the missionaries for their attempts to obtain fair dealings on behalf of Maori — a policy which was detrimental to the interests of dealers and settlers. The Maori, despite tribal differences, had a fairly common system of religious belief, and a universal acceptance of it, so to their view Europeans might also be expected to adhere to a common set of beliefs. As contrasts between the habits of the traders and missionaries were observed, some loss of confidence in the new message was bound to occur in the minds of Maori. So while on the one hand they were meant to be learning by the Christian example of one set of Europeans, contradictory lessons were being picked up from a further set.

The Early Picture

Missionary journals and reports are full of complaints about the contrary lessons being learned by Maori from their contact with other Europeans. Henry Williams, for instance, despaired that while the people of his area kept the sabbath, they were often faced with the sight of European shipowners and workers publicly showing 'their entire disregard to the sacred day of the Most High'.[28] On one occasion when Maori refused to assist with the loading of a ship as it was the Ra Tapu, Williams noted, 'Thus we find Heathens preaching to a Christian, calling his attention to the command of Heaven . . .' The reply of the 'Christian' to the 'Heathen', however, was they were not missionaries and did not regard such things.[29] Thomas Chapman remarked in 1855 that the 'wickedness of very many of the "civilized" is excessive . . .'[30] Charles Baker, visiting the settlement of Wairoa (Northland), found the natives 'bitterly opposed' to all he said, and blamed this on Europeans who were 'scoffers at religion' and who had given Maori the idea that while the Bible was true, missionaries gave a wrong interpretation of it and so had corrupted the word of God.[31]

For Maori of the period, relating the very different values of Europeans was a perplexing problem, and it was one which was to weigh heavily against the Christian faith for many years to come. The Rev. J.W. Stack summed up the situation:

If the lives of Maori Christians are not at this day so pure as they should be, let us bear in mind that the sin lies in a great measure at our own door. The convert who, with a simple-child-like faith, accepted at his teacher's hands the plain precepts of the Gospel, and acted up rigidly to the letter of the law, was at first shocked to observe European Christians trampling underfoot the precepts of their own creed, and tempting the convert to sell themselves for sin for reward, scoffing at the Bible and the restraints of religion, and by their abandoned conduct setting an example that could not fail to be infectious when once the doubt was instilled into the convert's mind that this teacher was not infallible, that all men did not think with him that a life of sin was a life of death.[32]

To make matters even worse, the example of some of the mission workers was not all that was desired either. In 1820 Samuel Marsden spoke of the 'dreadful evils that have crept in amongst the missionaries' — so much wickedness, contention and unfaithfulness that he was astonished the mission had not been completely annihilated. Some of the workers had been weak and led astray, some were wicked and had fallen from steadfastness and wounded the cause, others had been idle and unfaithful, or worldly minded.³³ Slander, over-indulgence in drink, use of improper language, and trading for profit were all problems which concerned Marsden on future occasions too. The Rev. John Butler noted in 1821 that all the single men attached to the mission had 'committed fornication among the heathen!!'³⁴

But such lapses should be kept in reasonable perspective as regards the spread of the Christian message, for these 'sins' were not regarded so seriously by Maori. Slander and improper language were problems only within the English-speaking community — for very few Maori understood the newcomers' language at this time. They had no intoxicating liquor of their own and had not yet acquired a taste for it — therefore they had no previous judgement against it on a moral basis, though no doubt stern warnings had been given in their contact with missionaries. Premarital sexual relations were usually permissible in Maori society, and so this most seriously regarded of all the 'sins' would not have caused too much adverse comment, though again the missionaries could be seen to be not practising what they preached.

A further great stumbling block was provided by the opposition of the various denominations of Christianity. The Wesleyans, arriving in 1822, some years after the missionaries of the Church of England, were well received by the earlier arrivals and helped a great deal by them in their initial years. But with the passing of time, relations between the missions deteriorated. There had been an agreement between the two that the CMS would preach their doctrine along the east coast of the island, and the Wesleyans in the western areas, but disputes occurred over the definite boundaries to be observed. As disagreements caused problems between the missions, the people were not slow to see the conflict between them. In 1838 the arrival of the first Catholic priests meant immediate hostility between Protestant and Catholic.

Bishop Pompallier recorded that when he arrived at Hokianga, Protestant missionaries went among the Maori saying that the Catholics intended to seize the country, and kill or burn the people. In addition, Pompallier claimed, Protestants stated that Catholic doctrines were full of errors and wickedness, and it was necessary to rid the country of them as soon as possible.³⁵ The fact that Pompallier and the first mission fathers were French was also used against them by Protestant missionaries. Maori were reminded that following the murder of Marion du Fresne and sixteen of his men in 1772, revenge was exacted by the remaining sailors by the slaughter of about 250 of their people. Missionaries also put fear into

Maori by suggesting that conversion to Catholicism might result in colonisation by the French, with dreadful tales of the consequences being given.

As the years passed, relations between the groups did not improve, and CMS and Wesleyan missionaries lost no opportunities to make their abhorrence of Catholics known. The Rev. A.N. Brown once recorded meeting a party of 'Roman Catholics and Heathen', referring to them as 'pretty much synonymous in New Zealand.'[36] The Protestant missionaries present at the celebrations attending the signing of the Treaty of Waitangi were outraged to find Bishop Pompallier accorded honour among the officials, and so refused to join in to the fullest extent.[37] The Rev. Thomas Chapman in 1842 accused the 'young Jesuits' of 'seeking to ingratiate themselves by, in every respect becoming a native, — sleeping, eating and fawning with them.' He added that they were 'enemies of the cross of Christ', and 'untiring servants of the "Beast"!'[38] Church orders to the Catholic fathers were that they should not hold themselves apart from Maori, and not look down on them. In addition, they were ordered not to attempt to buy souls with goods.[39]

On the other side, according to missionary allegations, Catholics sought to undermine the world of the Protestant churches by circulating pictures of 'a chronological tree which represented the Protestant bodies as lopped-off branches fit only to be cast into the fire'. A copy of this picture given to the Hokianga chief Te Taonui was seen by missionary William Woon who reported to the WMS secretaries that Martin Luther, John Calvin and John Wesley were depicted as rotten branches cut off. As the Protestant missionaries were married, their church was said to be full of adultery. Woon, in a contribution to the Wesleyan Methodist magazine in 1846, wrote that 'Papists' at Wanganui were telling Maori 'that Martin Luther was expelled from their Church for committing adultery with Catherine Parr!!!'[40] Pamphlets were published and distributed by both sides, each denouncing the other.

Because of doctrinal differences and the competitive pursuit of areas of conversion, the early decades of Christian contact were marked by bitter attacks between the churches. The arguments were very noticeable to Maori who were often involved directly in them as one missionary fought another in the villages. On one extraordinary occasion in 1849, William Williams and the Rev. Father J. Lampiler conducted a fierce verbal battle at Tauranga, on the matter of their respective creeds. The priest challenged Williams to a trial of fire, proposing that two oxen be provided, with each missionary, in the manner of Elijah, calling upon God to send fire to consume the sacrifice which was more acceptable. The great multitude that gathered to witness the match eagerly collected firewood but Williams refused the challenge on the ground that Elijah acted on the authority of God, and he did not possess that authority.[41] After waiting some ten hours, the watchers eventually disbanded, no doubt greatly disappointed at the lack of such a dramatic show of divine power.

The result of these disputes was very often that Maori did not align themselves with any of the denominations, or even lost faith in all of them. Certainly the importance of the Christian message was seriously undermined. Archdeacon A.N. Brown, calling on the great chief Te Heuheu Iwikau of Ngati Tuwharetoa in 1849, received the honest comment:

When you are at Taupo I am a Churchman. When the Wesleyan missionary is here, I belong to his church. When the R.C. Priest calls, I am a Papist, and when no European is here, I am a Heathen.[42]

Another man, much later, summed up:

Every incoming trader, every new sect, spoke at first softly, then louder and louder, until the air trembled with strident and bitter revilings — one creed shouting this, another besmirching and bellowing that! So what could we do? If we forsook the faith of our fathers, which creed should we select and adopt? For they all spoke of 'Truths', yet condemned the Truths of the other! And the end was that we sat on our heels and doubted the preaching of either![43]

But there were also factors which aided the promotion of the gospel in the early period.

At the time in which Christianity was becoming a major influence on Maori, particularly in the 1830s in Northland and Waikato, there was a large number of slaves — the result of the intertribal wars of the 1820s. The missions were also concentrated in those areas and the teachings of Christianity appealed to these enslaved people for two main reasons. As slaves they had no standing within their new tribes, and they found a new status and identity in membership of the Christian religion. In addition, missionaries deplored the practice of slavery and defended the rights of the captives, so under their influence the treatment of slaves was much improved. The new religion, then, was often of special appeal to this class. When Christianity became accepted by the local chiefs, slaves were freed — a further factor recommending the mission teachings. Many of them returned to their original homes, taking the teachings with them.

The Early Picture

But prime among the factors which promoted the teaching of the gospel was the remarkable enthusiasm and aptitude of Maori for literacy. From the early years a great share of the energy of each mission was put into the schooling of the people, and from 1827 when the first scriptures were printed in their own language, their eagerness to learn to read was amazing. Adults of all ages, as well as children, arrived at mission stations for lessons. Henry Williams, to meet the demand, taught large outdoor classes by forming words with cut-out wooden letters hung on a huge board.

Missionaries were often astounded that the art of reading had preceded their initial visits to more remote areas, through the efforts of newly literate pupils who had passed on their knowledge to their home tribes. When the Rev. William Williams moved to Poverty Bay in 1840 to set up a new mission station, he found that many of the people could already read and write — a result of his returning several freed slaves from Northland to their original home some years before. So it came about that within a few years Maori were often more literate than many Europeans in New Zealand. The Rev. James Watkins of Waikouaiti found that when he was marrying Maori women to European men, the brides could most often write their names in the marriage register very clearly, while their new husbands could mark themselves only with an 'X'. Often Maori witnesses to the ceremony would authenticate the groom's mark by expertly writing their own name.[44]

This spread of literacy was to have a far-reaching effect on the missions. In every area missionaries found they could not satisfy the demand for scriptures, with people walking very long distances in order to obtain a volume. Robert Maunsell said in 1839 that he could sell numbers if he had them. Referring to the supply of 50 he had received, he remarked, 'but what are they among so many? Five hundred would not be enough.'[45] Others complained similarly. The Rev. William Wade of the Wesleyan mission reported after a trip through the North Island in 1838 that the cry was the same in almost every place he stayed — 'Books, books, "E mate ana matou i te pukapuka kore!" We are ill (or dead) for want of books.'[46]

The spread of the new message through oral means also meant that Christian communities arose in remote areas before missionaries travelled to those places. Again many missionaries, and other travellers, reported that they came upon villages in which services were held regularly, and often with community prayers recited morning and night. Such an incident occurred to the Rev. Johannes Riemenschneider, who in 1846 while visiting a new area greeted a young man, Te Whiti-o-Rongomai, later to become leader of the Parihaka Movement, with the words, 'I come in peace, bringing God's word.' The reply of Te Whiti — 'We know that word and greet you, in God's peace' — was to surprise the missionary, but not nearly so much as when he found that his host could recite whole passages of scripture from memory.[47] Henry Williams, arriving at Papakutu Pa near the mouth of the Otaki River in 1839, found the chief, Te Kuru, knew the words of many hymns but not the tunes and so had composed tunes of his own to fit them. After singing one of these to the clergyman, the chief commenced to recite the Morning Service. Williams reported that he was sure the man would have recited it to the end if he had not stopped him. So delighted was the missionary that he gave the chief a primer and two prayer books, only to find the man could not read. In his case he had committed all the words of the hymns and the service to memory.[48]

It is clear that the Maori's great interest in literacy was not at first because this was seen as a means of understanding the new religion. In fact, the opposite would be even more true. The arts of reading and writing were seen by Maori to be almost magical. One man told of how his people put the missionaries to the test, for the purpose of seeing if indeed something written by one could be understood by another, and when this was shown to be true they concluded that the atua pakeha was more powerful than the atua maori.[49] When they grasped the notion that messages could be conveyed through the cryptic markings, the appeal to learn the art was immense. Many learned at mission stations then taught their own people. In the beginning it was a novelty, a game, and a great fashion to be able to read and write. Before long it was noticed by tribes who had not yet mastered the art, that those closer to mission stations who were receiving regular attention from European teachers were benefiting markedly. In Hokianga in the early 1830s, chiefs from a distant area requested teachers for their people, also saying they had noted that such other tribes were better off than they were, being at peace, and were working and thriving rather than fighting and wasting away.[50]

It was a deliberate policy of the missions before 1840 to restrict all instruction in reading and writing to the Maori language. This ensured that the people had access to scriptural material only, and so kept them away from more secular or non-Christian written influences for as long as possible.[51] Partly for this reason, and partly because of the magical appearance of literacy, the very books themselves were often regarded as possessing great power. Mission books were therefore often in great demand even by those who could not read, for their protective properties. At times any book or document at all was highly revered — be it scripture obtained

The Early Picture

from missionary or ship's cargo list bought from a sailor. In the 1830s it was widely believed that books protected their owners in times of war, and even aided them to soundly beat their enemies. The bullets or clubs of owners of books would be divinely guided to their marks, while their own bodies would be untouchable, by the same power. These books also professedly had the power of bringing the dead back to life when placed on the chest of the dead person.[52] On occasions when individuals or groups later reverted from their Christian beliefs, it was frequently found that their scriptures were burnt or buried for the purpose of avoiding or counteracting any evil influence they might also possess.[53]

To Maori the new art of literacy was a further proof of the divine source of the missionaries' teachings. So the cry 'give me a blanket . . .' became, rather, 'give me a book in order that I might believe' — meaning, give me the knowledge. Even as they learned the skill of reading the lesson of the great power of the European God was given to them, and as they read the scriptures of the new religion it was firmly reinforced in their minds.

Notes

1. For fuller consideration of missionary intentions, see John Owens, 'The Unexpected Impact: Missionary Society in Early 19th Century New Zealand', in Christopher Nichol and James Veitch (eds), *Religion in New Zealand*, pp. 17–18.
2. John Butler, Journal, 18 November 1920. R.J. Barton (ed.), *Earliest New Zealand (Journals and Correspondence of Rev. John Butler)*, p. 49.
3. Butler, letter to the Rev. J. Pratt, 8 November 1819. Barton (ed.), *Earliest New Zealand*, p. 49.
4. For a more lengthy consideration of Maori-European relations in this early period, see Harrison M. Wright, *New Zealand, 1769–1840: Early Years of Western Contact*, chapters 6 and 7.
5. Judith Binney, *The Legacy of Guilt: A Life of Thomas Kendall*, p. 80, gives 1828 as the 'turning point in the North', this being when Maori recognised some authority held by the mission. It was also the year Hongi died, and by this time there had been much progress with the missionaries' use of the Maori language and publication of the scriptures in the native tongue.
6. Reported by William Yate, dated between 1828 and 1834, *An Account of New Zealand*, pp. 222–23. But note that Yate's book was later severely criticised by other missionaries as giving a very erroneous view of the New Zealand missions. In addition, the line given needs to be considered in the context of the rest of the passage.
7. J.S. Polack, *Manners and Customs of the New Zealanders*, vol. 2, p. 235.
8. A.N. Brown, Journal, 30 July 1837.
9. Note that this view has been much disputed since. For instance, see the Rev. J.F.H. Wohlers, 'On the Conversion and Civilisation of the Maoris in the South of New

Zealand', *TPNZI*, vol. 14, p. 128, where Wohlers argues that people need a higher idea in their mind first.
10. For an excellent study of Thomas Kendall, see Binney, *Legacy of Guilt*.
11. William Colenso, 'On the Maori Races of New Zealand', *TPNZI*, vol. 1, 1868, pp. 385–86.
12. Jean-Baptiste François Pompallier, *Early History of the Catholic Church in Oceania*, p. 36.
13. Robert Maunsell, Journal, 26 September 1836. See also entry for 30 July 1839. Henry E.R.L. Wily and Herbert Maunsell (eds), *Robert Maunsell LL.D. A New Zealand Pioneer. His Life and Times*.
14. Henry Williams, Journal, 30 January, 16 February 1826. Lawrence M. Rogers (ed.), *The Early Journals of Henry Williams 1826–40*, pp. 100, 103.
15. William Wade, *A Journey in the Northern Island of New Zealand*, p. 86.
16. *Missionary Records*, July 1820, p. 308. Cited by Wright, *Early Years of Western Contact*, p. 119.
17. William Morley, *The History of Methodism in New Zealand*, p. 46. See also C.J. Wilson (ed.), *Missionary Life and Work in New Zealand 1833–1862*, p. 61.
18. For more details of the history of early European arrivals in New Zealand, see J.M.R. Owens 'New Zealand Before Annexation', in *The Oxford History of New Zealand*, chapter 2, particularly pp. 30–33.
19. See Owens (ibid.), p. 48 for details of the Kororareka Association which through 'lynch-law' transformed the town by 1840.
20. Brown, Journal, 16 June 1837.
21. Samuel Marsden to CMS, published in *Missionary Records*, November 1817.
22. Marsden, Journal, 15 September 1819. John Rawson Elder (ed.), *The Letters and Journals of Samuel Marsden 1765–1838*, pp. 172–73.
23. See for instance, William Williams, *Christianity Among the New Zealanders*, pp. 4–10.
24. Morley, *History of Methodism*, p. 146.
25. Ibid., p. 176.
26. Henry Williams, Journal, 11 November 1839. Lawrence M. Rogers (ed.), *The Early Journals*, p. 450.
27. Memorial of the Committee of the Church of England Missionary Society, 1817. Robert McNab (ed.), *Historical Records of New Zealand*, vol. 1, pp. 417–21.
28. Henry Williams, Journal, 24 March 1833. Rogers (ed.), *Early Journals*, p. 300.
29. Henry Williams, Journal, 4 February 1833. Rogers (ed.), *Early Journals*, p. 289.
30. Thomas Chapman, Journal, vol. 2, p. 587.
31. Charles Baker, Journal, 3 November 1833.
32. J.W. Stack, *Notes on Maori Christianity*, p. 6.
33. Samuel Marsden, Third New Zealand Journal, 1 September 1820. Elder (ed.), *Letters and Journals*, p. 362.
34. Butler, Journal, 22 January 1821. Barton (ed.), *Earliest New Zealand*, p. 113.
35. Pompallier, *History of Catholic Church*, p. 36. See also p. 44.
36. A.N. Brown, Journal, 7 April 1844. See also entry for 15 February 1842 for an account of a confrontation between Brown and a Catholic priest.
37. See a short account of this in A.G. Bagnall and G.C. Peterson, *William Colenso*, p. 91.
38. Thomas Chapman, Letter to CMS, 19 February 1842.
39. Peter McKeefry (ed.), *Fishers of Men*, pp. 4, 11, 19–20.
40. William Woon to WMS, 30 June, 19 August 1841, 10 April 1844, 30 September 1846. See also James Buller to WMS, 19 July 1847.

The Early Picture

41. William Williams, *Christianity Among the New Zealanders*, pp. 335–39.
42. Brown, Journal, 13 November 1849.
43. William Baucke, *Where the White Man Treads*, pp. 84–85.
44. T.A. Pybus, *Maori and Missionary*, p. 16.
45. Wily and Maunsell, *Robert Maunsell*, p. 52.
46. Wade, *A Journey in the Northern Island*, p. 125.
47. B. Mitcalfe, *Nine New Zealanders*, p. 52.
48. Henry Williams, Journal, 23 November 1839. Rogers (ed.), *The Early Journals*, p. 456.
49. Elsdon Best, *Tuhoe: Children of the Mist*, vol. 1, pp. 563, 1030–31.
50. Morley, *History of Methodism*, p. 47.
51. Some missionaries, though, favoured the teaching of English. John Butler argued in 1819 that the Maori would then quickly become 'an English nation', and would then have the scriptures and other useful written material. Butler, Letter to J. Pratt, 6 November 1819. Barton, *Earliest New Zealand*, p. 46. See also F. von Hochstetter, *New Zealand, Its Physical Geography, Geology and Natural History*, p. 216.
52. M.A. Rugby Pratt, *The Pioneering Days of Southern Maoriland*, pp. 82–83. See also W.H. Oliver and Jane M. Thomson, *Challenge and Response*, p. 30.
53. For a full account of Maori response to literacy, see C.J. Parr, 'A Missionary Library, Printed Attempts to Instruct the Maori, 1815–1845', *JPS* vol. 70, no. 4, pp. 429–50.

2. Politics and Problems

With the arrival of more and more settlers in the mid-part of the nineteenth century came the demand for land on which Europeans could live. By the time settlers were arriving in numbers, from 1840 onwards, the Maori had already undergone great cultural changes as a result of some 26 years of missionary influence. Their own traditions based on tribal law under the chief system, and institutions such as tapu, had been weakened. Yet the European way was no substitute for the very different situation of Maori. Consequently neither could give full support and guidance, and yet both could be manipulated to the disadvantage of Maori, or to the advantage of anyone assuming authority.

The Church Missionary Society officially opposed the colonisation and settlement of New Zealand on the grounds that this would be detrimental to its people in this crucial period of social development. The Lay Secretary of the Society, addressing the English House of Lords Committee on New Zealand in 1838, gave among the reasons for mission opposition, that experience showed colonisation would result in 'the greatest wrongs and most severe injuries' being inflicted on the indigenous people.[1] While the 'religious improvement and civilisation of the natives' was 'in favourable progress', this would be at least interrupted if not defeated.[2]

But the opposition of the Missionary Society was overruled by the motive of advantage to the British. Settlers were moving to New Zealand anyway, so it was desirable for their sake that some form of administration be formulated for their protection, and for that of Maori. The British were also aware that should they fail to colonise the new land, another country would do so. The French appeared to be the greatest threat, but Americans also worried the missionaries. While growing rumours about their intentions were no doubt based more on fear than fact, this provided further motivation for the eventual decision.

Those with an interest in settlement argued against the missions that the work of the missionaries would be enhanced by settlers. Edward Jerningham Wakefield, nephew of Colonel William Wakefield of the New Zealand Company, maintained that 'a body of respectable settlers as co-operators and supporters' would act as an example to Maori.[3] He supported his position by claiming that the ones who were engaged in employment with whalers showed 'improvement' in that they dressed in European clothes, 'spoke a good deal of English', and were acquiring knowledge and skills such as carpentry, whaling and European methods of boat-handling. These examples illustrate Wakefield's opinion that the Maori should be Europeanised by being taught the English language and customs. At the same time, however, he was also forced to mention some negative aspects of contact — 'the habits of drinking . . . boastful and insolent behaviour . . . callousness . . . and an overbearing, grasping, and bullying demeanour of chiefs'.[4]

Even as settlers arrived others, apart from missionaries, began to foresee growing problems, and controversy arose over the relative advantages and disadvantages for the indigenous New Zealanders. One concerned individual ('author of various writings on political and scientific subjects'), in 1847 published a pamphlet in which he foretold the destruction of the Maori through 'loss of influence' and consequent 'aversion' between the races.[5]

The Rev. Octavius Hadfield wrote in 1847 that the methods of colonisation employed by the British government were very empirical. He complained that there was no investigation of either the laws, the usages, or the customs of Maori, and no attempt was made to suit any laws to their specific conditions. He concluded, 'how they can expect to succeed is to me marvellous'.[6]

The stated goals of the New Zealand Company regarding the purchase of land in the colony were undeniably high, though perhaps practically naive. Although Colonel William Wakefield was instructed to ensure that all sellers of land be fully informed of the significance and consequence of sale, the land purchase system was soon open to much abuse by unscrupulous dealers. Governor Gore-Browne, in 1859, referred in a dispatch to the hunger for land in the North Island, saying that

Europeans were determined to possess it — rightly if possible, but if not, then by any means at all.[7]

Tactics which were definitely questionable, though not strictly illegal, were employed to force Maori to sell land. For instance, after the setting up of the Native Land Court in 1863, the people were advised to apply to the courts for title to their land, and money was advanced to pay the necessary surveying and legal fees involved — with the result that owners were forced to mortgage their land in order to pay for crown title. Land courts were held in the towns, and large groups of owners would be required to spend long periods in town waiting for their cases to be heard. Storekeepers would allow them to run up huge amounts of credit, then eventually force the sale of the land for repayment. As well as suffering financially through such practices, the substandard conditions endured by those in such situations meant that disease became prevalent and many died as an indirect consequence of such sales.

It must also be remembered, however, that as well as fault on the part of some Europeans, examples of this were also to be found among Maori. Within their ranks also existed landowners who were happy to sell for a few material goods, and others who unscrupulously 'sold' land to which they had no real title.

A growing distrust of Europeans by Maori was the natural result of these questionable methods of land acquisition. This distrust was reinforced by knowledge of examples of the situations of other races under colonial rule by European nations. One such instance was witnessed by the chief Pirikawau during a trip to the Cape Colony in 1854. Writing back to New Zealand he attested to the ill-treatment of South African Negroes by whites, pointing out that they were slaves with no standing, and warning that the same could happen to Maori.[8]

As problems created by social tension between the two cultures escalated, Maori tended to relate them all to the alienation of land. This was for more than the obvious reason that land was required in order to accommodate more settlers, and more settlers brought greater tensions between the two races, and therefore more problems. There was also a more spiritual factor involved. Rather than having merely a utilitarian view of the land, Maori possessed a strong emotional attachment to the earth, and seeing it taken from the people's control, resented even more the cultural and spiritual implications this held. The land was the substance of Papatuanuku, the Earth Mother, and was revered and held in trust by the tangata whenua. When the people inhabiting the land increasingly belonged to another culture and possessed a different attitude to the earth,

Maori felt they were losing their very identity and reason for being, and began to fear for their very survival.

As early as 1853 distrust of the motives of Europeans was causing so much fear, and the problems caused by the loss of land had reached such proportions, that the first anti-land-sale meeting was held. From this the Maori King Movement was set up, with land purchases the prime motivating factor. The reasoning behind the movement was that should the tribes of New Zealand unite under one king, they would have the strength and organisation to demand equality, freedom and justice. This attempt to deal with Europeans by using their own methods illustrates the feelings of Maori at the time. They could see themselves being forced into the position of landless underdogs — a race without identity or rights. Such a position would be equivalent to slavery for such a formerly proud people.

It was a problem which had also been seen by farsighted Maori many years before. The chief Te Waharoa, as early as 1835, had expressed his fears to the Rev. A.N. Brown:

The land will remain forever to produce food, and after you have cut down the old trees to build houses, the saplings will continue growing, and in after years will become larger trees; while the payment I ask for will soon come to an end. The blankets will wear out, the axes will be broken after cutting down a few trees, and the iron pots will be cracked by the heat of the fire.[9]

The social consequences of sale were disastrous for Maori. Not only did they lose the land with which they identified themselves, but the unity of the tribes was undermined by individual dealing through the Native Land Court. Maori was set against Maori through disagreements over whether or not to sell, and chiefs who were reluctant to part with tribal land had their authority questioned by those of lower rank who were agreeable to sale. On occasions, it has been claimed, some Europeans even supplied weapons to those willing to sell, in order to fight against their own people who stood in opposition.[10]

The situation was to deteriorate even further with the land confiscation policy of the 1860s. As the people protested against the escalation of sale and instances of improper dealings, this punitive policy alienated even greater areas of land from Maori ownership, justified by charges of anti-government activities. Many more examples of injustice were perpetrated under the guise of this policy, including the confiscation of lands of tribes which had no part in the original 'offences'. The Rev. William Williams wrote in 1868:

> *God's hand has been against us. As a community and as a government we have been puffed up, first with an idea that we were in the right, and secondly that we were able to put down the natives by our own strength. We have been trying now for a very long time to stem the torrent, but we are carried away from day to day further from the object we have wished to attain . . . we are now brought very low.*[11]

Some months later Williams was to write again about the confiscation of land, saying that whereas once he thought it was just, he had since looked further into the subject and now believed it to be unjust.[12] Williams went so far as to recommend that the whole of the confiscated land be returned. He was also to conclude that the settlement of the land, coming at the very time when the gospel was beginning to gain a hold on the people, and bringing with it 'all the manifold temptations and changes of circumstances introduced by a new race of men', together with the mismanagement of European administration, had a most prejudicial effect on the progress of Christianity.[13]

The result of the land troubles and wars was that Maori were left with a deep distrust, and even hatred of Europeans. The chief Te Wherowhero is reported to have said around 1860:

> *Uenuku, the man-eater, used to be my god; but when the clergymen came to this land, I was told to put away my god, for the Pakeha God was the true one, Jehovah, the preserver of man, the Creator of heaven and earth. When I accepted your God, I thought all wrongs were to be made the subject of investigation, great wrongs as well as little ones. When it came to this affair, I alone was left to worship his God, whilst he, the Governor, went off to pick up my cast away God, Uenuku, the cannibal. And now the Governor, the supporter of Jehovah, has skipped forward and carried off Uenuku the cannibal to Taranaki as his god for the destruction of man.*[14]

The missionaries were also included in this, with their sincerity often doubted. When colonisation came about despite their wishes to the contrary, missionaries had been instrumental in drafting the Treaty of Waitangi, explaining its content to the people, and persuading them to sign it, believing as they did that it was for the protection of Maori interests. In fact several missionaries actually carried the Treaty from tribe to tribe to have it signed by them, as happened in the Bay of Plenty and East

Coast areas where the reverends A.N. Brown, J. Stack and William Williams acted in this way for Governor Hobson.[15] Inevitably this was later to be misunderstood by those they were trying to protect, and a common saying of Maori at the time was to the effect that the missionaries pointed towards heaven, and while the Maori were looking upward the settlers took their land. This idea was to be expressed in many forms. King Mahuta, in a Legislative Council debate in 1903 stated it this way:

When the Pakeha first came to this Island, the first thing he taught the Maori was Christianity. They made parsons and priests of several members of the Maori race, and they taught these persons to . . . look up and pray; and while they were looking up the pakehas took away our land.[16]

An old song of the Nga Puhi people translates as follows:

It was in the year '14 that Christianity landed at Oihi and reached the Maori people. It was there that Marsden stood up, and his message was this: God is in heaven, look therefore to the sky. But the Maori people turned and gazed below to the land, the soil of Aotearoa. They beheld it decoyed away with the iron spade, the iron axe, the flaming red blanket and the iron jew's harp. Thy goods, O Governor! Alas, the land has gone, adrift on the great ocean of Kiwa.[17]

William Leonard Williams said that the people believed that missionaries had been sent to the Maori to put them off guard, 'inducing him to accept Christianity, and then, when the time was ripe, bringing in an armed force to oust the simpleton from his land'.[18] A speaker in Wanganui varied the same idea by saying 'The missionaries were sent to break in the Maoris as men break a wild horse; to rub them quietly down the face to keep them quiet, while the land was being taken from them'.[19]

Missionaries were often held accountable for other problems caused by colonisation. The Rev. Thomas Chapman reported in 1847 that several times he had been confronted over the matter of a road being built through the country by the government. When he pointed out the usefulness of the highway the people agreed that it was indeed very useful — for the Governor to send soldiers and great guns through the island. The complainants cited the example of the Romans in their occupation of Britain — they also cut a road through the country in order to conquer it.[20]

At least one missionary had another charge levelled against him. The Rev. James Watkins, Wesleyan missionary and the first to settle in the

South Island (1840), tells how in this year he talked to a man who had returned from the Bay of Islands, and claimed to have a puka kakari, or war book. Such books were believed to be potent charms — their carriers were invulnerable to either bullets or clubs in battle. In addition, any warrior possessing one would be invincible as his own bullets would not only hit their mark, but would travel from enemy to enemy until ten had fallen from a single shot! The local people believed that Mr Watkins had a supply of such books but was keeping them from the Maori — a charge that the missionary tried hard to refute.[21]

Other factors also helped foster a growing feeling of social dissatisfaction. One of the earliest to be felt was the challenging of traditional Maori society with its classified structure. The increasing awareness of the technological superiority of Europeans quickly undermined the less tangible mana of the rangatira class, and once this source of power and influence was downgraded, the tribes tended to disintegrate — both physically, as more members left for the towns, and spiritually, as the lack of effective leadership further affected the formerly proud Maori sense of identity. Traditionally, all members of the tribe knew where they belonged within the social unit, and each possessed mana equivalent to that position. Without this sense they could not function socially or spiritually, and the new system provided little to replace it. Chiefs stood to lose their mana by the adoption of Christianity, and the conversion of their people had the same effect even if the chief did retain the traditional beliefs. Under the new scheme the slave became as good as the master, and their standing as equals under Christianity meant that the chief was again reduced in the eyes of the people.

Missionary condemnation of other traditional institutions — warfare, polygamy and tapu — also quickly undermined the status of chiefs and tohunga. As warfare decreased because of missionary intervention and the unacceptable destruction enabled by new weapons, warriors could no longer easily gain status through military victories. To the chief, having more than one wife was socially desirable for economic, political and hereditary considerations, and so once more his standing was diminished with the Christian teaching against polygamy. Chiefs and tohunga (very often the functions went together) suffered as the religious equivalents among the newcomers — teachers, preachers and catechists — were only too quick to point out the failings of tohunga. With these traditional institutions condemned by Christian missionaries, chiefs found they had no more mana, and the discipline and pride of the Maori decreased accordingly.

The Early Picture

The Taupo chief Te Heuheu told Edward Jerningham Wakefield in 1841 that he had refused to become a Christian 'as he saw in the converting of his people an inevitable levelling of ranks, and the end of his regal sway'.[22] It was perhaps, in most cases, a rather idealistic view of this phenomenon which was later given by the Rev. J.W. Stack:

> ... in embracing Christianity the rangatira class ... did what the rich young man spoken of in the Gospels would not do — they gave up all to follow Christ. They gave up their tapu and mana, by which their influence and dignity were maintained, and voluntarily handed over their power to the Church and reduced themselves to the rank of the poorest by setting at liberty their slaves ... The chief, to prove his sincere acceptance of the Lord Jesus as his master, dismissed the tillers of his fields, the hunters and fishers of his preserves, the servants of his household, and degraded himself to the rank of one of his own slaves, by defiling his sacred person with the abomination of the cooking fire. Men who had ruled powerful communities and distinguished themselves in times of peace and war, and whose influence extended far beyond their own tribes, humbled themselves as little children before their own slaves, and often submitted to be taught by them the first principles of the Christian faith.[23]

With the passing of the decades, the early fears of the Missionary Society were to be more than realised. Settlement, bringing with it the problems of social tension inevitable to the mixing of two totally different cultures, and government by a quite alien system at the expense of traditional rule, could not fail to break down the very fabric of Maori culture. That the message of the gospel was to suffer was an obvious consequence.

Whether the Mission Society's ideal of 'civilisation' and 'Christianisation' before colonisation would have had much better results if put into practice, must remain debatable, for that would depend entirely upon unknown factors — the calibre, understanding and tolerance of the mission teachers, the degree of those attributes attained by Maori before open non-mission contact, and the amount of time allowed to effect the changes and have them incorporated into a new social system.

Notes

1. On the subject of the impact of civilisation in the Pacific generally, see K.R. Howe, 'The Fate of the Savage in Pacific Historiography', *NZJH*, vol. 2, no. 2, pp. 137–54.
2. Minutes of Evidence before Select Committee on the Islands of New Zealand, House of Lords, 1838, pp. 243–46. Cited in W. David McIntyre and W.J. Gardner (eds), *Speeches and Documents on New Zealand History*, pp. 4–7. See also the pamphlet *Documents exhibiting the views of the Committee of the Church Missionary Society on the N.Z. Question*, published by CMS in 1839; and pamphlet *Further statement of the Committee of the Church Missionary Society relative to the New Zealand Mission*, 1840.
3. Edward Jerningham Wakefield, *Adventure in New Zealand*, vol. 1, p. 104.
4. Ibid., pp. 335–36.
5. 'Aristoboulos', *The Universal Destruction of Aboriginal Races by Colonizing Nations and Eventually of the New Zealanders. The Cause of This Evil and its Sure Preventive*.
6. Octavius Hadfield to Venn, 18 May 1847. Quoted in Keith Sinclair, *The Origins of the Maori Wars*, p. 107.
7. Quoted in Keith Sinclair, *A History of New Zealand*, p. 123. The original source of the quotation not given.
8. This example given by John Te H. Grace, *Tuwharetoa*, p. 443.
9. A.N. Brown, Journal, 1835. See John Caselberg (ed.), *Maori Is My Name*, p. 29.
10. Maharaia Winiata, *The Changing Role of the Leader in Maori Society*, p. 49.
11. William Williams to CMS, 30 November 1868.
12. William Williams to CMS, 26 July 1869.
13. William Williams, *Christianity Among the New Zealanders*, p. v.
14. Octavius Hadfield, *The Second Year of One of England's Little Wars*, pp. 75–76. Or see Caselberg (ed.), *Maori Is My Name*, pp. 83–84.
15. T.L. Buick, *The Treaty of Waitangi*, p. 207.
16. *NZPD* 1903, vol. 142, p. 1141. Cited in Michael King, *Te Puea*, p. 173.
17. Cited by Apirana T. Ngata and I.L.G. Sutherland, 'Religious Influences', in Sutherland (ed.), *The Maori People Today: A General Survey*, pp. 346–47.
18. Frederic Wanklyn Williams, *Through Ninety Years*, pp. 254–55. See also Bishop W.L. Williams, *East Coast Historical Records*, p. 34; A.N. Brown, Journal, 22 April 1845, 21 November 1846; Baucke, *Where the White Man Treads*, p. 84.
19. T.G. Hammond, *In the Beginning*, p. 72. On this subject see *AJHR* 1862, E-9, 28; Henry Williams (Jnr), Letter, 19 August 1899.
20. Thomas Chapman, Letter to CMS, 1847, accompanying Journal of 1846, Chapman Letters, p. 325.
21. M.A. Rugby Pratt, *Pioneering Days*, p. 82.
22. Wakefield, *Adventure in New Zealand*, vol. 2, p. 117.
23. J.W. Stack, *Notes on Maori Christianity*, p. 6.

3. Disease and Decline

The size of the population of New Zealand at the time of the visits of Captain Cook from 1769 is debatable. Cook himself estimated that Maori numbered about 100,000. Later opinions, considering Cook's very restricted knowledge of the country and taking into account the populous inland areas such as Waikato, Rotorua and northern areas around Hokianga and Kaipara that the explorer missed, tend to multiply that figure several times. A popular estimate with many writers is between 200,000 and 250,000,[1] but this has been disputed, with as few as 110,000 suggested by others.[2] Whatever the truth of pre-Pakeha population, it is known that by 1858 Maori numbers had dropped to under 60,000 and continued to decline for the remainder of the century, reaching a low of 42,113 as found in the 1896 census. Certainly writers at the time attested to the falling population. James Busby, the British resident before 1840, seeing the extent to which disease was prevalent among Maori, predicted the country would be 'destitute of a single aboriginal inhabitant' in the near future.[3] Judge Maning, writing in 1887, said since his arrival in New Zealand, in the area of his observation Maori had decreased by 'rather more than one-third'.[4]

Census figures for Maori population between 1858 and 1901 are as follows:[5]

      1858: 56,049   1874: 47,330   1878: 45,542
      1881: 46,141   1886: 43,927   1891: 44,177
      1896: 42,113   1901: 45,549

The great decline in the Maori population was due to several factors.

Firstly, the tribal wars of the 1820s accounted for thousands of deaths. The part that European weapons played in this bloody period of history has been debated. Muskets had been traded by whalers before this time, and the mission itself cannot be freed from blame in this respect also. Thomas Kendall, one of the first three mission workers in the country, was among those who supplied weapons to Maori — no doubt seeing this as a way to gain the friendship of the people in an attempt to get information to assist his work with the language. In addition, early mission workers were at least partially dependent upon Maori for their food, for which they traded goods. As the people wanted the weapons more and more, this was the payment they demanded. Samuel Marsden wrote a letter to Kendall in which he remonstrated strongly with him over his trade in muskets, calling it 'a great sin in the sight of God, and sordid to the Christian mind'.[6]

The great chief Hongi Hika, returning from his trip to England with Kendall, stopped in Sydney to sell gifts from King George IV and others, buying muskets and ammunition with the proceeds. Back in New Zealand, equipped with an army with some 300 muskets, he set out on a campaign of carnage that was to last ten years. This caused a demand for guns throughout all the tribes as each people found they must either defend themselves on the same basis, or be annihilated. George Clarke, CMS missionary (later Chief Protector of the Aborigines), wrote of this great demand, saying that Maori would make great sacrifices for a musket — working hard for months in order to obtain one, or indeed even willing to part with slaves or 'prostitute his children to a diseased sailor'.[7]

The musket itself has, on occasion, been defended as not really responsible for the wars of the 1820s, as intertribal wars had always taken place and this time of unrest might have occurred even if new weapons had not arrived; the limited numbers available meant that not all members of a taua were equipped with them; and they were not very reliable weapons. The potency of the musket, however, was not merely in its direct killing power. When warriors were seen to be killed from a distance, apparently by means of a loud report only, this was at first thought to be evidence of supernatural intervention, and any foes who fought with the assistance of the atua were known to be invincible. Many battles, therefore, were over almost before they began — but with disastrous results for the side without the atua pu. Even when knowledge of muskets became better known, the awe attached to them had a great demoralising effect on those who did not possess them, while engendering great confidence in those who did. Numbers were not so important — even a few muskets

The Early Picture

carried by a taua ensured success against the people without them, or with fewer.

Consequently, battles raged throughout the northern half of the North Island, the most populous part of the country, with tribes pitted against each other in an effort to settle old scores, or solely to defend their very lives. The weapons trade soon became the prime consideration, as tribes with them were assured survival and increase, and those without were doomed to be wiped out, or at least severely depleted. While muskets could be obtained from traders by bartering goods, mainly timber, flax and vegetables, they could sometimes also be bought from other tribes, by swapping for slaves. This latter method also increased the intertribal battles as slaves were sought for the purpose of such exchanges. Archdeacon Walsh wrote that it was estimated at least one quarter of the total number of Maori perished in these wars, and probably a further quarter in the raids of Te Waharoa, Te Wherowhero and Te Rauparaha.[8] Judge Maning referred to the musket as 'the first grand cause of the decrease of the natives since the arrival of the Europeans'.[9]

Missionary involvement in the supply of muskets was to mean that in the long run the mission generally was very much the loser. While some missionaries engaged in the trade, many more refused to do so. This policy of individual conscience had even more effect on the missions, for with some tribes possessing power over neighbours, the missionaries were often hard-pressed to keep the peace. On occasions, should they refuse to arm their own people, they were condemning them to almost certain annihilation. So the musket, as with other material goods, could be used by either missionary or Maori as an inducement to conversion. The willingness or refusal of the representative of the church to supply weapons, therefore, often had a direct bearing on the acceptance or the rejection of the Christian message.

There were further consequences of the wars of the 1820s, which contributed to the decline of the Maori race. Although on many occasions entire tribes were wiped out, in other cases it was the prime members of a people, the warriors, who were killed, with the remainder either left with insufficient means to recover their full strength or taken prisoner where as slaves they were often ill-treated with the same result. As the tribes which did survive in depleted form were deficient in young males, the remaining women were often pressed into service as 'ship-girls' as a means of obtaining necessary goods — muskets and ammunition being prime among these. Archdeacon Walsh tells of chiefs rounding up young widows and girls and taking them in parties to the Bay of Islands where they were employed for this purpose.[10]

Disease was undoubtedly a very large factor in the decline of the population. Infectious diseases such as measles, dysentery, tuberculosis, typhoid fever and whooping cough spread among them since earliest contact with Europeans. Maori accounts tell how a serious epidemic swept through the country soon after the visits of Captain Cook,[11] and many more such diseases raged through the villages following subsequent visits by foreign ships. Venereal diseases no doubt contributed by lowering the resistance of the people to other new sicknesses. To a race who possessed no natural immunity to such ailments, and had no knowledge of how to treat the sufferers, the results were disastrous. Mission reports are full of instances of epidemics sweeping through an area and resulting in a high proportion of deaths — 20 or 30 percent and above being common. In one incident, it is said that only two individuals out of a village of 300 escaped a measles epidemic.[12] An Otago man testified that in his youth the mate pakeha were his people's worst enemy. On one occasion when a ship from Sydney brought an epidemic of measles, most Maori in the area died, with whole families being wiped out.[13]

The traditional institution of the hui aggravated the problem of epidemics. Members of different hapu and tribes travelled to neighbouring areas for special social occasions, including deaths. At such times they would be housed communally, often in cramped conditions which were ideal for the wholesale spread of infectious diseases. The visitors would then return home to spread the illnesses still further.

Patients were also treated in ways which greatly aggravated the disease. Many instances are reported of measles sufferers being immersed in cold streams in an effort to counteract the fever and reduce the rash — this often being more responsible for deaths than was the disease itself. Lady Martin told how, also in the case of an epidemic of measles and dysentery, all those who came to the hospital she had set up recovered, but in the surrounding country the mortality was 'frightful'.[14] Others were treated with traditional remedies, such as medicines prepared from wood or bark, but these proved to be ineffective against the new diseases.[15] The Rev. Charles Baker was only one of many missionaries who noted this treatment in his diary frequently in the 1850s, often having to report the deaths of the sufferers.

Changes in the social conditions of Maori were to a large degree responsible for the spread of diseases. To facilitate trade for wanted goods (most particularly muskets), the people left their former high-sited and therefore well-drained habitations and resided for long periods in less healthy places. Flax by the ton was needed by traders, so workers lived near low-lying swampy areas in order to supply it. The result was the prevalence of respiratory problems which also lowered the resistance of the people to the introduced illnesses. Maning, writing of this problem, tells of one group of 40 people living in such circumstances, who were all dead eight years later.[16] In the north of the North Island, the wetlands were worked for Kauri gum, with the same consequences. A Magistrate reporting in 1880 on the very bad health of those engaged in this activity warned, 'if they still persist in living in their present condition, there can be only one future for them — extinction as a people — and that at no very distant period.'[17] While workers lived in this way and devoted their energies to the work in hand, their diet was often neglected also. The combination of bad living conditions, overwork and insufficient food was a lethal one in numberless cases.

The situation of Maori involved in dealings with the Native Land Court was very similar. In the words of one of the country's members of Parliament in the 1880s:

I believe we could not find a more ingenious method of destroying the whole of the Maori race than by these Courts. The Natives come from the villages in the interior, and have to hang about for months in our centres of population . . . . They are brought into contact with the lowest classes of society, and are exposed to temptation, and the result is that a great number contract diseases and die . . . . Some little time ago I was taking a ride through the interior, and I was perfectly astonished at hearing that a subject of conversation at each hapu I visited was the number of natives dying in consequence of attendance at the Native Land Court at Wanganui.[18]

Similar results were noted in other areas also. On the other hand, in the same period those tribes and communities which continued to live away from European centres were still healthy and still thriving — for instance the people of the isolated Urewera country.

Despite the common belief that introduced animals, particularly the pig, improved the diet of Maori, the opposite was often true in the early period.[19] Rather than providing a source of food, animals were more often responsible for destroying crops and stores of foodstuffs. The introduced rat destroyed much food, and killed the herbivorous kiore, which was a former food source. Cats and dogs were sometimes eaten, but these drastically reduced the native bird-life — particularly the ground birds, which before the arrival of animals had no natural enemies. Cows, horses and sheep arrived early, but survived only in small numbers with many becoming wild and uncatchable. Overall, the introduction of animals was detrimental to the diet of Maori, rather than advantageous. Vegetables, though, were another matter. Corn and potatoes were grown extensively by the end of the eighteenth century, with wheat following in the early nineteenth century. Other vegetables — pumpkins, carrots and green vegetables — were introduced by early missionaries and settlers.

But the same problems as already mentioned ensured that even when these alternative foods were freely accessible to Maori, it was not always to their advantage. The growing popularity of the potato soon saw a corresponding neglect of such traditional foods as the aruhe or fern-root. When this coincided with the desperate need to trade food for European goods, weapons and ammunition again being frequently desired, Maori would often sell the whole of a potato crop and have very little left to live on. Lady Martin attests to this factor as the cause of regular epidemics of dysentery. The best of the summer crops were sold to the English, and often the people were compelled to eat the seed potatoes on which their next year's supply of food depended. A liking for fermented corn, combined with the generally inadequate diet, resulted in bad abscesses and skin diseases.[20]

In pre-Pakeha times Maori had no knowledge of alcoholic drink, and when this was first introduced found it most distasteful and named it waipiro, stinking water. With the passing years, however, they acquired a taste for strong drink, and drunkenness became a real problem among men and women alike. Unscrupulous traders commonly supplied adulterated brews of poisonous quality, and the effects of this were also to be long-lasting as children often suffered neglect as a result.

Other changes in social conditions also affected the health of the race to its cost. The older style of raupo house was generally well-sited for shelter and drainage; it was well insulated from draughts, and easily kept warm by means of a fire. When Maori began to emulate European styles of housing the change was often not for the better because frequently a weatherboard house would remain unlined or otherwise unfinished, and so would not be so effective in keeping out the cold. In addition, the new house would often not be so carefully sited — proximity to working grounds now being the most important consideration.

The adoption of European clothing also contributed to health problems. Firstly woollen blankets replaced the former flax garments for wrapping around the body, then European clothing became favoured and worn. While these were much warmer, problems could also arise from their use. Maori, generally, would possess only one blanket or set of clothes, and when this became wet would continue to wear it, perhaps sitting in front of a fire to steam dry. The result to individual health could be detrimental.

The new afflictions were thought by Maori to be supernatural in origin. In traditional belief, the atua brought ill-health as the result of a breach of tapu, or as a consequence of makutu. The conclusion drawn, therefore, was that the ill-health which was overcoming the people by the thousands was the result of neglect of the former beliefs and practices in favour of the new. An old man speaking to William Baucke spoke of this matter:

> ... in the olden time our tapu ramified the whole social system. The head, the hair, spots where apparitions appeared, places where the tohungas proclaimed as sacred we have forgotten and disregarded. Who nowadays thinks of the sacredness of the head? See when the kettle boils, the young man jumps up, whips the cap off his head and uses it for a kettle-holder. Who nowadays but looks on with indifference when the barber of the village, if he be near the fire, shakes the loose hair off his cloth into it, and the joke and the laughter goes on as if no sacred operation had just been concluded. Food is consumed on places which, in bygone days, it dared not even be carried over. Therefore, what can you expect but that the spirits should avenge the insult by retaliating on the sacrilegious offenders with the life of those most dear to them?[21]

Maori believed that the mauri, or life principle, of any thing, living or non-living, was the dwelling-place of the protecting deities. Should this be polluted in any way, then the deity withdrew and its protection was no longer present. In such a state it was open to all bad influences. This was the spiritual state of the Maori after some decades of continuing contact with the alternative system of the Europeans. With the removal of the tapu nature of the mauri, Maori, individually and collectively, no longer had the protection of the atua. Consequently, recourse to the old remedies and practices would not have any effect, and Maori were completely without hope.[22]

On the basis of this, the response to illness was very often fatalistic. Should the ailment be thought to be the result of this withdrawal of protection, or even the result of divine retribution, cure was often not looked for, as such power was not able to be overcome. Death, in such cases, was inevitable, with the patient quickly accepting the situation with resignation. Europeans during this period often spoke of Maori patients or sufferers as not possessing the necessary will to live.²³

When a cure was sought, a tohunga might be called in, but the power of these figures was most often inadequate to effect any cure against European diseases. The atua pakeha was therefore acknowledged to be stronger than the atua maori, and European medicine the only remedy against mate pakeha. It is to the shame of missionaries that they sometimes took the opportunity to encourage this belief in the superiority of the European God. The Rev. James Hamlin, noting in his annual report for 1854 that measles, whooping cough, diarrhoea and dysentery had carried off many in the area, wrote:

> *The Lord in his afflictive dispensations thus warns the careless of his danger and says to him, 'He that being often reproved hardeneth his neck shall suddenly be cut off and that without remedy.'* ²⁴

This meant, too, that disease was frequently blamed directly on the European God, or even on the prayers of the missionaries. The Rev. A.N. Brown had people tell him on the occasion of the sudden death 'in a fit' of a young lad, that they didn't remember any such incident previously, and so attributed it to the 'God of the Missionaries'.²⁵ The Rev. Richard Taylor found that those in his area attributed their great mortality rate to the Christian faith, saying that previous to their embracing it they died only of old age or in war.²⁶ Seeing the people die while Europeans lived through these sicknesses, Maori were bound to come to the conclusion that the great atua pakeha protected his own people while smiting all others. Once more it was a perception that was to have an adverse effect on the Christian mission over the following years.

As well as the physical side of changes in social conditions, there were spiritual effects which were at least as important to Maori. As many of the former habits gave way to European methods and practices, so the traditional ritual element associated with them broke down. The new crops tended to be grown without the former rites, trees were felled for trade without customary karakia, and the approach to all manner of work became more secular as earlier beliefs gave way to an economy based on trade rather than subsistence. As a consequence the skills and ritual functions of tohunga and rangatira were used less and so the traditional religion went into decline, decreasing the essential vitality of the race even further. A Maori witness at a Native Land Court meeting once stated in his evidence, 'The atua of whom I speak is dead.' When told that gods do not die, he replied, 'You are mistaken; gods do die unless there are tohungas to keep them alive.'²⁷

Such problems also put the people in a spiritual dilemma. The new illnesses were mate pakeha, and the appropriate agency for help was therefore the atua pakeha. But recourse here, which was usually sought too late, and only after traditional methods had failed, most often appeared to be useless as the people still died. Even worse, it seemed that the God of the Europeans was against the indigenous people and desired their destruction. Or was it rather that the atua maori were heaping punishment on their own people because they had largely abandoned their former beliefs and practices? With such a dilemma confronting them, it seemed Maori could not win — whichever way they turned it would be to their detriment. The problem lay in a celestial power-struggle between the gods of Maori and Europeans. After 1858, when the census taken in that year showed the European population was now greater than that of the Maori,[28] there seemed no doubt that it was the new Atuanui who had the clear advantage.

Several other reasons may also have contributed to the great decline of the Maori population. One rather grisly factor was the fashion in England during the early contact period of possessing a preserved Maori head. As it was learned there was a ready trade in these articles, and good sums were offered for such specimens, this proved a further incentive for warfare. Those most desired were heads which were well tattooed — of chiefs or others of high station such as warriors — and these were usually obtainable only as result of a battle. Samuel Marsden, who in the earlier years denied that such a trade existed, was forced to admit in 1831 it was indeed true. In a letter to the CMS he complained of fourteen heads of chiefs being on board a European boat.[29] On Marsden's intervention, the importation of such heads into New South Wales was prohibited by the Governor of that state, and a proclamation to that effect was printed in the *Sydney Herald*, 25 April 1831.[30] This order reads in part:

> *... there is strong reason to believe that such disgusting traffic tends greatly to increase the sacrifice of human life among savages ...*

One writer has suggested that the continuing Maori depopulation through the century was due to the decline in the fitness of the race through less hard work, and to the end of the intertribal wars, which acted as a sort of agency for 'natural selection' by removing the weaker members. Even more responsible, he also argues, was the inbreeding which was practised in an effort to keep ownership of land within the family or close clan.[31]

What was most apparent was that every one of the given reasons for the numerical decline of the Maori race was due to the influence of

Europeans. Maori, recognising this as the nineteenth century progressed, often expressed their increasing lack of spirit in such sayings as, 'As the Pakeha rat drove out the Maori rat, as the introduced grasses drove out the Maori fern, so will the Maori die out before the white man';[32] or, 'As clover killed the fern, and the European dog the Maori dog; as the Maori rat was destroyed by the Pakeha rat, so our people also will be gradually supplanted and exterminated by the Europeans'.[33]

Notes

1. K.R. Howe, *Race Relations in Australia and New Zealand*, p. 44; Gordon Lewthwaite, 'The Population of Aotearoa', *The New Zealand Geographer VI* (April 1950), p. 49; M.P.K. Sorrenson, 'Land Purchase Methods and Their Effect on the Maori Population', *JPS* vol. 65, no. 2, p. 183.
2. Joan Metge, *The Maoris of New Zealand*, p. 4. See also J.M.R. Owens, 'New Zealand Before Annexation', in W.H. Oliver with B.R. Williams (eds), *The Oxford History of New Zealand*, p. 49. In addition, see D. Ian Pool, *The Maori Population of New Zealand 1769–1971*; and the four articles published by Hocken Library, *The Maori Population*. It is not the purpose of this work to come to a conclusion on this matter.
3. Peter Adams, *The Fatal Necessity: British Intervention in New Zealand 1830–1847*, p. 88. Busby's comment was typical of a number.
4. F.E. Maning, 'A Pakeha Maori', *Old New Zealand; A Tale of the Good Old Times*, p. 206.
5. Figures supplied by the Government Statistician. Note that no Maori censuses were taken in the years 1851, 1861, 1867 or 1871.
6. Marsden to Kendall, 26 April 1820. John Rawson Elder (ed.), *Letters and Journals*, pp. 333–34.
7. George Clarke, MS, 'Letters and Journals, 1822–49'. Cited by D.U. Urlich, 'The Introduction and Diffusion of Firearms in New Zealand 1800–1840', *JPS* vol. 79, no. 4, p. 400.
8. Archdeacon Walsh, 'The Passing of the Maori', *TPNZI*, vol. 40 (1907), p. 158. See also Sinclair, *Origins of the Maori Wars*, p. 15; Owens, 'New Zealand Before Annexation', p. 45.
9. Maning, *Old New Zealand*, p. 206.
10. Walsh, 'The Passing of the Maori', p. 159.
11. Elsdon Best suggests this may have been spread by an ill-fated boatful of people led by a Scotsman in 1782, who had come with the purpose of civilising the Maori but were all killed. See Best, *The Maori*, vol. 2, p. 37.
12. Walsh, 'The Passing of the Maori', p. 163.
13. Spoken by Tuhawaiki to George Clarke and Colonel Wakefield. George Clarke, *Notes on Early Life in New Zealand*, pp. 62–63. Cited in Caselberg (ed.), *Maori Is My Name*, p. 26.
14. Lady M.A. Martin, *Our Maoris*, p. 86.
15. See William Baucke, *Where the White Man Treads*, pp. 207–11 for an example.
16. Maning, *Old New Zealand*, p. 210.

The Early Picture

17. *AJHR*, 1880, G-4, 2–3. See also, Walsh, 'The Passing of the Maori', pp. 170–71.
18. Bruce, in *NZPD* vol. 52, 1885, 515. Cited by Sorrenson, 'Land Purchase Methods', p. 191.
19. On the whole subject of Maori health, see Wright, *New Zealand 1769–1840*, chapter 4.
20. Martin, *Our Maoris*, p. 83. See also, Maning, *Old New Zealand*, p. 212.
21. Baucke, *Where the White Man Treads*, p. 123.
22. Elsdon Best, *Christian and Maori Mythology: Notes on the Clash of Cultures*, pp. 3–4.
23. For examples see Walsh, 'The Passing of the Maori', p. 164; Maning, *Old New Zealand*, p. 125.
24. James Hamlin, Annual Report to CMS, year ended 31 December 1854.
25. A.N. Brown, Journal, 30 June 1835.
26. Richard Taylor, Journal, 22 November 1851.
27. Johannes Andersen, 'Maori Religion', *JPS* vol. 49, no. 196, p. 522.
28. Europeans numbered 59,413 against Maori figures of 56,049. Government Statistics.
29. Marsden, 18 April 1831. See Elder (ed.), *Letters and Journals*, p. 498. See also p. 496.
30. Elder (ed.), *Letters and Journals*, pp. 499–500.
31. Baucke, *Where the White Man Treads*, pp. 124ff.
32. Raymond Firth, *Economics of the New Zealand Maori*, p. 456.
33. F. von Hochstetter, *New Zealand, Its Physical Geography, Geology and Natural History*, p. 222.

4. Principle and Practice

The acceptance of Christianity from the 1830s was by no means an irrevocable step for Maori. As discrepancies were noted between the principles and the practices of the Europeans as a race, so the faith of converts was affected. The people were well aware of the effect the newcomers had on the indigenous culture, and naturally resentment arose.

In the traditional system of belief and society, religion and law were one. The institution of tapu was the basis of civil order, its spiritual aspect being seen in the ritual practices. With the coming of Europeans, the same appeared to be true, for the laws of that society were laid out in the scriptures. The missionaries and the early governors were often seen together, and in this way too the religious and secular laws were not observed to be separate.[1] Wiremu Tamihana Te Waharoa, writing to the Governor and his advisers in June 1861, referred to the Taranaki war stating that the government commencement of hostility was hasty and ill considered. He pleaded:

> ... it is for you to do things deliberately, as you have an example to go by. The Word of God is your compass to guide you — the laws of God. That compass is the Ten Commandments.[2]

Because of this, European influence as a whole tended to be associated with the missions, with missionaries regarded as the ethical and spiritual leaders of the new society. Inseparable, then, from the growing counter-cultural movement which took place from the mid-nineteenth century onwards, was a loss of faith in the Christian mission.

Apart from the more general reasons already mentioned, there were several more specific concerns which encouraged the loss of credibility of the missionaries and their religion.

During the government campaigns in the Waikato area in the 1860s, Maori noted that missionaries would accompany government forces, and naturally assumed this showed their support of the government position. Bishop Selwyn and the Rev. Dr Maunsell, for instance, acted as chaplains to the government forces in the 1864 engagements in the Waikato area, and Archdeacon Brown did the same for the troops at the battles near Tauranga in the same year. To Maori, this action was synonymous with that of the tohunga karakia who would accompany a taua for the express purpose of reciting chants which would ensure the victory of their people and the defeat of the enemy. That missionaries possessed such power was not doubted. As early as 1832 clergy had been blamed for such acts, Henry Williams reporting then that warriors engaged in a skirmish complained that their guns would not shoot straight, for even though often at close range, the bullets flew off the victims. This they attributed to the influence of missionaries.[3]

In the case of Selwyn's presence at Rangiaowhia (Rangiaohia), the lesson was especially bitter. In an infamous incident government forces burnt Maori women and children in their houses — an act that was to have incalcu-lable consequences for the mission from that time onwards. The fact that the Bishop was present with the troops was never to be understood by the Maori, and is the direct cause of at least one incident of bloody revenge, in the killing of the Rev. Mr Volkner at Opotiki by Kereopa whose two daughters had been burnt alive.[4]

When government troops also set fire to Maori churches, it was the last vestige of Maori belief in Europeans' sincerity regarding their own religion which was burnt to ashes. The fact that buildings dedicated to the service of God were wilfully destroyed was bad enough, but that bibles and prayer books containing the sacred Word were inside and were also therefore violated, was nothing less than an act of extreme sacrilege which could have been perpetrated only by a people of the utmost hypocrisy and religious inconstancy.[5]

Maori also realised that when their own race, as converts to Christianity, fought government troops, it was a case of Christians fighting Christians, with both sides calling on God for assistance. When Maori were defeated, God was seen to be on the side of the Europeans. This further strengthened the lesson which was also to be found in the case of the diseases which visited the Maori race and left Europeans. It was no wonder, then, that Maori were to lose even more faith in the God of Christianity. The Rev. J.W. Stack, speaking of the period of war in Waikato, recognised that the inconsistencies of Europeans had 'ruined' all the mission work among the Maori:

> *How can Christians, they said, be guilty of such unchristian conduct towards those who are their brethren in Christ? No wonder the majority of the Maoris lost belief in the Divine origin of the Christian religion, which they strongly suspected was a political intervention to beguile the unwary, and render them more easily subjugated.*[6]

To Maori, a further inconsistency occurred in the practice of government troops fighting on Sundays. There is more than one occasion on record of Maori breaking off battle on the sabbath, only to be annihilated while peacefully congregated at Sunday service, the British soldiers being only too ready to take advantage of the situation. One man testified:

> *At Ruapekapeka*[7] *they desecrated the Sabbath, which we, in our ignorance, supposed would pass without fighting. We left our pa to avoid the shot and shells while morning prayers were read by one of the teachers.*[8]

At Paparata in 1863, the Forest Rifles, a civilian unit, also attacked on a Sunday when their Maori adversaries were at divine service.[9] On another occasion a group of Maori warriors, having rejected the Christian message, decided to attack the opposing troops, the Forest Rangers, in similar circumstances, thinking they would avail themselves of the same advantage. Unfortunately, they again credited the 'Christians' with much worthier principles than they actually possessed — a former member of the European unit testifying that 'nothing short of compulsion would cause any member thereof to attend any form of service'. The result was again disastrous for the Maori.[10]

Such lessons on the principles and practices of Christians were learnt early by Maori. Archdeacon Brown took a service at Paihia using the text James 4:1, 'From whence come wars'. The chief Hone Heke, who was present with his people, approached the Archdeacon following the service and advised him to go and preach the same service to the soldiers.[11] The chief Renata Tamakihikurangi, addressing settlers in Hawke's Bay in 1860, made it clear that Maori had no wish to fight Europeans. The English people were always vaunting themselves against Maori, believing themselves to be noble whereas they were a wretched race, and it seemed that they desired to destroy the Maori. The Europeans, he stated, said they were good and fair-skinned people themselves, while God had made the Maori 'bad and black', yet that thought was not to the credit of the Europeans, and such judgement should be left to God.[12]

On the other hand, when Maori adopted spiritual principles and laws, they were often to keep them to the letter — this being part of their tradition. Such an example can be seen in the lead given to the Tauranga people by Henare Taratoa during the battle at Gate Pa. Taratoa's rules of warfare, based firmly on Christian precepts, were carried out strictly, with wounded enemies being carefully tended by members of the Maori side, even at considerable risk to themselves.[13] William Williams in 1832 described one tribe who, having become Christians, kept the sabbath in a manner which would have shamed many country parishes in England. At the time, they were building a larger chapel as the old one was then too small.[14]

A further feeling among Maori was that, while missionaries had always been active in their efforts to prevent warfare between tribes, they were not so quick to see that this was also done between Maori and government. The Rev. Charles Baker, after talking to the people of Ohuki near Tauranga, in 1861, recorded their view that the missionaries had been remiss in not urging the Governor to make peace. When Baker replied that the Church had interceded through its representatives but the Governor felt it his duty to administer correction, the reply of the people was that killing is not correction.[15] To Maori this obviously strengthened the feeling that missionaries were agents for the government, with the function of keeping the minds of the people occupied while their land was being plundered.

Misunderstandings of Christian teachings were inevitable, due to the great gulfs between the two cultures, and these also helped to undermine the gospel of the missionaries. One early misunderstanding centred on the Bible's assurance of salvation from sickness and death for believers.[16] The Rev. J.A. Stack noted that Maori often took this literally, to mean that believers would not die a temporal death.[17] However, when converts and mission workers were seen to sicken and die, it seemed that the scriptures were in error. James Hamlin also came across this misunderstanding and reported that Maori were astonished that their mission teachers died — a fact that was interpreted to the advantage of the local tohunga, for obviously the tohunga's power was greater than that of the teachers. This had an effect on the mission, as people stopped attending services — their faith having been based on the assurance of freedom from sickness.[18]

Henry Williams, and no doubt other missionaries, experienced difficulties when he preached to Maori that all would rise again on the day of judgement. Several times he records addressing them on this topic — at first mentioning their great surprise, and another time noting that they 'laughed exceedingly at the idea of the resurrection of the body.'[19]

Similarly, the Rev. A.N. Brown told how listeners found it difficult to understand the passages of scriptures that referred to 'salt of the earth', 'If so be that being clothed we shall not be found naked', 'strong meat', and 'keys of the kingdom of Heaven'.[20] Henry Williams noted in 1834 that at one meeting with Maori Christians he had to correct 'several ideas of an extravagant nature'. He commented 'thus error creeps in on every side'.[21]

Naturally, Maori could interpret the scriptures only from their own basis of understanding, and this also led to further misinterpretations. An example of this was a sermon given by a Maori preacher who took as his text the verse, 'O, foolish Galatians, who hath bewitched you, that ye should not obey the truth . . .'[22] — he interpreted this as supporting the factual basis of makutu.[23] The Church taught against this view, and while this appeared to missionaries to be a matter of Maori interpreting scripture to their advantage, to Maori the same claim might be made against missionaries who it seemed gave teachings contrary to the Word of God.

On several occasions new converts adhered so seriously to the word that they conducted themselves in a manner far beyond the letter of the new religious law. Edward Jerningham Wakefield once visited Pipiriki, 80 kilometres north of Wanganui, to find that the village was ordered with the most strict discipline, under the eye of their chief Te Kai, who now filled the role of a 'stern religious pastor'. The place was well-kept and clean, with work done 'as though by clockwork', but each weekday was conducted with the solemnity of a Sunday. There was almost total silence, with no chatter, greetings or laughter, 'not even a smile', from adult and child alike. The chief knew the greater part of the New Testament by heart, and quoted from it to support almost all he asserted. He had interpreted a verse which states that a man who looks at a woman lustfully has committed adultery in his heart,[24] and added the conclusion that as a thief laughs as he steals then laughter is the way to sin. While the Pipiriki people were the 'best-behaved natives' Wakefield had seen, he also noted that the children seemed prematurely grown into little old men and women, and there were long faces everywhere. As for Te Kai, Wakefield felt that apart from his exaggeration of religion into absurdities, he was otherwise a model for many a white missionary, and in fact many English clergymen wanted the same worthiness of character.[25] A chief also once told the Rev. A.N. Brown that 'his people had for a very long time past observed the Sabbath by "sitting still" on that day.'[26]

Translation difficulties were often at fault for misunderstandings of scriptures. The Rev. Hanson Turton recorded in 1845 that the people of Waokena had misinterpreted a verse which reads, 'But I keep under my body, and bring it into subjection'.[27] This had been translated in the early translation as 'E kuru ana ahau i taku tinana' (I beat my body with my fists). This was being carried out literally by the Waokena Christians, with dreadful results to their own bodies.[28] This was amended in later translations, by the use of the verb pehi — to repress.

The biggest problem that occurred regarding Christians teachings was in the area of death and judgement. In traditional Maori belief there was no corresponding notion of a weighing of one's deeds with an appropriate fate to follow — rather, every soul regardless of status or previous action travelled to an afterworld at death. Consequently Maori had no fear of death, for they had no fear of future punishment for sins committed in life.[29] The missionaries, on the other hand, constantly preached the eternal consequences of sin, endeavouring to teach this lesson to the unprepared 'heathen' whose soul was in certain danger. Henry Williams often addressed the people on the place of fire and brimstone as a place for the wicked, and on the subject of the wrath to come. A.N. Brown also believed implicitly in the eternal damnation of unbelievers, and often recorded in his journal remarks to that effect when any person who had not expressed belief died.[30] On one occasion he told some warriors off to a battle: 'Go then — go to Hell and wail for ever and ever'.[31] It must be wondered if he gave the same words to government troops when he accompanied them, and preached to them.

This doctrine was, understandably, not well received by Maori, and from the beginning of their introduction to the gospel it provided a stumbling block to acceptance. The traditional belief was infinitely more acceptable, and for a long period Maori rejected the notion that they should fear death — a response which missionaries found difficult to accept. Brown tells of warning another party of warriors 'of the punishment which would await their diabolical wickedness in another world', only to be told by the chief Te Waharoa, 'If you are angry with me for what we have been doing, I will kill and eat you and all the Missionaries.'[32]

This related to a further doctrinal point which was incomprehensible to Maori. While the former custom of eating slain enemies had been abhorred and fiercely denounced by missionaries as barbaric and heathenish, in the Christian rite of Holy Communion they were taught that it was a blessed act to eat the body and drink the blood of the slain Christ. This inconsistency was even more incomprehensible to Maori because in their tradition to eat the body of another was to show contempt by such an act of indignity, yet this was the way Europeans treated their God.

Another matter which was not understandable because of differences in the customs of Maori and Europeans was that of the sale of the scriptures. Missionaries sometimes gave away copies of the new translations to those who wanted them but more often they asked for some form of payment, reasoning that these would be more valued if the people made some donation towards them, and also perhaps trying to avoid the accusation that they were themselves buying their converts with books. Maori were agreeable to purchase as their enthusiasm for reading was so great, and at times offered very high prices for a single copy. The Wesleyan missionary John Hobbs reported in 1833 that a pig weighing between 50 and 100 pounds had been offered for a copy of a booklet of scriptures published in the Maori language.[33] The Rev. H.H. Turton wrote in 1841 that a party of Maori had brought more than 270 large baskets of potatoes, some pigs, and £2/12/6 as 'payment for the Gospel'. The missionary then remarked, 'how true then are the words of the French Priests in this island that we sell the Gospel . . .'[34]

Even while they bought the scriptures, the fact that something supposed to be as sacred as the very Word of God could be bought with things as noa, or non-sacred, as food or money, was bound to leave contrary thoughts in the minds of Maori. In addition, by the mid-1840s some missionaries were reporting growing resistance to buying, as the people were told by the Catholic Fathers that the missionaries pocketed the money. In the long run, then, it was the missions that paid the price when the scriptures were sold.

Disputes between different churches also had a detrimental effect on the Christian missions overall. In some areas villages and even families were divided, with some members belonging to one denomination and their relatives to another. Edward Shortland wrote that at Moeraki in Otago in 1844, the people, though mostly Christian, were divided into two parties — the 'children of Wesley' and 'the Church of Pahia' [Paihia, so CMS]. This caused constant disputes on the subject of religion, and division and bad feeling was introduced into almost every family. The village had two chapels and there was much rivalry between the two.[35]

The CMS and WMS missionaries disagreed over their respective rights to teach the gospel in the Taranaki area, and it was here that the most serious examples of separation can be found. Wesleyan missionary H.H. Turton wrote a series of open letters to Bishop Selwyn, published in the *Daily Southern Cross* in 1844, in response to a public protest by the Bishop against the WMS. In these Turton accused Selwyn of provoking division where there had been none before, saying the Bishop had told his people not to worship with the Wesleyans but to keep themselves separate, that teachers of one denomination should not instruct members of another, but that all distinctions of the Church should be observed rigorously. The result, observed Turton, was that the scriptures were literally fulfilled, that 'a man's foes shall be they of his own household', for here could be seen 'the awful sight of father and son, mother and daughter, tuakana and teina [older and younger siblings] hating each other with a mortal hatred.' This had resulted in one people living in different villages, and in other cases in separate divisions of the same pa. Turton gave the example of one village in which feeling had risen so high between near kinsmen that they had erected a fence across the village so one party might not be able even to look upon the other. The people would not eat together and persecution was beginning on both sides.[36] Three years later the situation had apparently not improved as the residents of Waokena, mainly members of the Church Missionary Society, refused to allow the few Wesleyans to build a chapel or hold services. The Wesleyans left the village and built another close by, but the Church people followed them and held opposition services.[37]

While disputes were not uncommon before the coming of the new message, tribes and families now sometimes continued feuds by arguing over trifling points of doctrine, with missionary being cited against missionary, the outcome often being determined by the relative mana of the clergyman quoted.[38]

The principles of the missionaries were also seen to be at odds with their practices over a further aspect of land sales. In addition to the accusation that missionaries diverted the attention of Maori to heaven while the land was taken from under their feet, it was also noted that a number of the missionaries themselves were large landholders from the early years. Following the tribal wars of the 1820s, in the welcome peace of the 1830s many Maori had willingly parted with their land, but within a few years they had woken up to the fact that so much had gone for ever, leaving them with nothing lasting in return. At Waitangi, prior to the signing of the Treaty, the chief Te Kemara was to cry:

> O Governor! My land is gone, gone, all gone. The inheritance of my ancestors, fathers, relatives, all gone, stolen, gone with the missionaries. Yes, they have it all, all, all . . .[39]

Some CMS missionaries owned vast areas. The Rev. Richard Taylor claimed to have bought a staggering 50,000 acres,[40] the catechist W. Fairburn had acquired 20,000 acres, the Rev. Henry Williams 22,000. Other missionaries and mission workers owned many thousands of acres each — Charles Baker, George Clarke, Richard Davis, James Hamlin, James Kemp, John King, Richard Matthews, W.G. Puckey and James Shepherd among them. Much criticism of the missions resulted, and all such cases were reviewed by the Land Claims Commission between 1840 and 1843. In most cases the amount awarded by the commission was much reduced from that claimed.[41]

It should be noted that other CMS missionaries and functionaries did not engage in the acquisition of land — notably Robert Maunsell, Thomas Chapman, William Colenso, Octavius Hadfield, James Stack and William Wade. Wesleyan missionaries, apart from one or two minor exceptions, refrained from buying land as this was against their own standing regulations.[42] The idea of large land purchases was also contrary to the policy of the Catholic Church, and by 1840 this mission had bought only about 250 acres in four lots for mission stations, the largest of these being about 150 acres. In addition, however, a few other small lots had been given to the church by Maori.[43]

But if some were seen to act according to their regulations, there were also times when others were observed to be rather biased. Wesleyan missionary John Whiteley, writing to the Native Minister Christopher Richmond in 1857, advised him to buy all Maori land that he could, even if subject to dispute, and to pay 'as low a price as possible, for these claims — the lower the better for themselves'.[44] On the other hand, Wesleyan missionaries were often disliked by settlers because they advised Maori not to sell their land, or to insist on a good price when they did so.[45] The Catholic Church also advised Maori to hold on to their land.[46]

Overall, the 'landsharking' of a few was again to reduce the missions generally in the eyes of Maori, and early European settlers too. E.J. Wakefield, a strong critic of the missions, claimed that missionaries were motivated to buy in the 1830s because they foresaw an influx of settlers, and made use of their knowledge of the language and customs of the Maori to obtain more secure title to land than could be obtained by others.[47] Certainly the prices paid in some of the early transactions were far from realistic. Samuel Marsden acquired about 200 acres for a mere twelve axes, and Thomas Kendall and William Hall bought 50 acres of excellent land for only five axes.[48]

So it was that missionary involvement in the land issue, both in buying and in advising the Maori against sale, was to work against them. Even when they had the interests of Maori at heart, this caused problems within tribes and also made Europeans align themselves against the missions. Consequently the effectiveness of the church suffered, through loss of unity and lack of confidence in the institution and its representatives.

The attitudes of missionaries to Maori were often difficult to relate to Christian principles of brotherhood and non-judgement. Missionaries complained that Maori were dirty and smelt.[49] Henry Williams once recorded in his journal that he disliked the habit of shaking hands that Maori had adopted from Europeans, as this brought him into 'contact with the filthy creatures of every place'.[50] E.J. Wakefield stated that missionaries never treated their Maori mission teachers as equals, and in fact these teachers were generally their house servants at the same time, blacking the missionaries' shoes, cleaning windows, making beds, grooming horses and cooking their dinner. None of their pupils dined with them at the same table, or could converse with them equally.[51] Charles Baker, rebuking people for working on a sabbath, and others for refusing to do a job for him, recorded that it was painful to have to deal so summarily with Maori, but it was 'necessary to have a screw upon them'.[52]

This attitude was even more prevalent among the lay settlers, many of whom regarded Maori as savages, dirty in all things, lazy, and inferior mentally, morally and socially. Generally, the more educated the settler, the less prejudiced and more sympathetic they appeared to be; but the majority were working-class opportunists and capitalists who emigrated with only one view in mind — to improve their own economic status.[53] On the other hand, E.J. Wakefield described Te Puni, the chief of Petone, who was a great friend of his uncle Colonel William Wakefield, in the following way:

Epuni [sic] *himself was a gentleman in every sense of the word, and would have been recognised as such in any society. I never saw him do an action, make use of a gesture, or betray a feeling, inconsistent with the most refined good manners . . . . There was an influence in his very look and speech, which must have disarmed the most ungenerous despiser of savages.*[54]

The wide gulf between the cultures was a problem at the bottom of every difference of opinion between Maori and European.

Missionaries frequently referred to New Zealanders by such terms as 'deluded Soldiers of Satan', or 'prisoners of Satan', and even when they had accepted the Christian faith they were still often dubbed 'heathens' —

as opposed to Europeans who were known as 'Christians' despite their beliefs or practices. Henry Williams tells how in 1828 a Maori spoke to a group of his people, telling them that the tempter came first to Adam and Eve as a black man, this being the reason why there are now black people in the world. Such teachings, if not given to them by the missionaries, were apparently not denied by them — Williams records he was 'much astonished at the man's knowledge'. These attitudes reinforced the lesson to Maori that they were inferior members of the human race, and even related to the work of the arch-deceiver of mankind.[55]

A man speaking of the relative beliefs of Maori and missionary remarked that his people were hurt when missionaries condemned the traditional beliefs:

When they said: 'This is the truth; our book says so. Thou shalt not steal, etc.,' was it wrong to smile behind the hand and reply: 'Prevent it. You put a padlock on your door; it is merely a sign, which I can smash off with one blow. I, on the contrary, place a tapu upon mine, which can only be tampered with on pain of a horrible death. Your goods are safe so long as the coveter is barred by personal friendship, or the fear of a suffering in a hereafter which no one has yet seen. The effect of my tapu is instantly seen, and feared, whether I am present or away on a journey. Yet you condemn my tapu as a superstition. Now, which is the more reliable?[56]

The teachings of missionaries were often over-strict. Such 'sins' as working on the sabbath were condemned and the transgressors commanded to stop. The Rev. A.N. Brown remonstrated with one group for playing cards (this on a weekday, and not on a Sunday), a sin they had learned among other 'works of darkness', from 'Europeans at Auckland'. Brown went on to note:

This transitional state of the Natives from comparative barbarism to miscalled civilisation, is most dangerous to their spiritual state. It proves that they were too young in Grace for the full tide of colonisation to rush in upon them, and raises the question whether their civilized barbarism was not preferable to their present barbarized civilisation.[57]

The over-zealousness of the missionaries in the control of their converts' behaviour often permeated the area of secular activities as well as the religious, as when a Wesleyan missionary forbade his flock's attendance at a canoe race held as an anniversary celebration![58]

The Early Picture

Overall, missionaries often failed to have sufficient faith in their converts. Maori teachers were given much work but little responsibility; and even later in the century when Maori members were admitted to the institutions of the Church, their value was not appreciated fully. The Rev. T.S. Grace, writing his annual letter in 1877, criticised this devaluation, rightly seeing it as working against the interests of the Church. He stated that while the European membership of the Anglican Diocese was two or three thousand, the Maori membership was 17,000, and though one half of the clergymen were Maori, Europeans held the purse strings and official proceedings were conducted in English, so keeping the Maori members submissive.[59]

The expectation of Europeans, that Maori would become fully Christianised in such a short period of time, was quite naive. To Maori it was not a case of completely casting aside old beliefs and totally replacing them with new. It was, rather, a matter of combining the two systems in an easy syncretism. Lieutenant-Colonel W.E. Gudgeon told how a Maori catechist had once said to him that though he was a sincere Christian he knew one god could not attend to everything, and therefore at times he would also call upon some atua maori who understood his position better than any European god could possibly do.[60] Another man told William Baucke that although he belonged to the Wesleyan sect he didn't believe all that church taught, but he kept a part reserved for his ancestral faith. To illustrate the dilemma of Maori he related an allegory to the effect that different missionaries came to his people, each saying they had the exclusive path to heaven while those of the others led to hell. These men all had long, lean, sorrowful faces. Then came a man with a round jovial and smiling face, and asked what the Maori was doing with men with long faces. When told, the new man proclaimed there's no such place as hell, come and drink, dance and be jolly, and the two would love each other, be brothers and be happy. So the Maori went and journeyed with him. Therefore, concluded the teller, not knowing who is right, Maori follow their own inclinations, merely pretending to follow particular sects. Europeans, he added, preach one thing and act another; they taught Maori not to fight yet do so themselves, they tell Maori women to be chaste yet admit their own increasing illegitimacy.[61]

The Rev. T.S. Grace, in 1877, ably summed up the position of Maori at that time. In regard to the great change that had come over the connection of the mission and Maori he wrote:

> *In early years they received Christianity — and I may say Colonisation — at our hands without doubting, and, to a great*

Principle and Practice

> *extent, on credit. Colonisation, war, confiscation and English vices have followed each other in quick succession, while the expectations anticipated from representations made when they signed the 'Treaty of Waitangi' have not been realised. Now they turn round and question their first advisors, and look at the whole of our connection with them as a scheme by which to get their lands, and, as they can point to the large blocks of land acquired by the early Missionaries — whom they say began the business — they appear to think they have good reason for coming to this conclusion. These things, together with the course some of our brethren took in the war, have completely changed our position with these people.*
>
> *But now a change has come to the Maoris. Formerly they consulted us in all matters connected with their teaching and worship, and invariably abided by our directions. Now they assume the entire management of their own affairs and seem to consider they have a perfect right to do so.*[62]

The situation as it developed is seen to be even more regrettable when related to words which had been written prior to 1840 and published in information for the use of colonists:

> *The New Zealander possesses a character which, at no distant period, may become an example of the rapidity with which the barbarian may be wholly refined, when brought into contact with a nation which neither insults nor oppresses him, and which exhibits to him the influence of a benevolent religion, in connection with the forces of practical knowledge.*[63]

This, then, was the situation between Maori and missionary in nineteenth-century New Zealand. As European rule had not fulfilled its promises, Maori looked for something which would.

Part of the tragedy of those who reject colonial rule as not suited to their temperament or situation, is that having experienced the innovations of the new technology, they are no longer able to return to their former way of life. In the case of the New Zealanders, placed as they were between two systems, the movement had to be towards a new Maori culture. As with the new technology, it was now not possible for them to reject totally the religion which they had accepted. So it was towards a new Maori theology that the new path led.

The Early Picture

Notes

1. See examples in Apirana T. Ngata and I.L.G. Sutherland, 'Religious Influences', p. 345; Johannes Andersen, 'Maori Religion', p. 514.
2. *AJHR*, 1861, E-1, B, 16–17.
3. Henry Williams, Journal, 22 July 1832; Rogers, *Early Journals*, p. 251.
4. See Ngata and Sutherland, 'Religious Influences', p. 348; W.L. Williams, *East Coast Records*, p. 82; John Te H. Grace, *Tuwharetoa*, pp. 419, 421.
5. See the words of T.G. Hammond, *In the Beginning*, pp. 71–72 and 101–102, on this matter.
6. J.W. Stack, *More Maoriland Adventures*, p. 183.
7. This battle was on 11 January 1846. See Tom Gibson, *The Maori Wars*, pp. 62ff, for a brief account of this.
8. From an account attributed to Hone Heke, by interpreter James Merret. Cited in Caselberg (ed.), *Maori Is My Name*, pp. 68–69.
9. For details see Richard Taylor, *The Past and Present of New Zealand; with its Prospects for the Future*, pp. 139–40. See reference to this subject, H.W. Williams, 'The Reaction of the Maori to the Impact of Civilisation', *JPS* vol. 44, no. 176, p. 241; and Morley, *History of Methodism*, p. 173.
10. W.E. Gudgeon, 'The Tohunga Maori', *JPS* vol. 16, no. 62, p. 83. Also Gudgeon, 'Maori Superstition', *JPS* vol. 14, no. 56, p. 175.
11. R. Burrows, Diary, 9 March 1845. R. Burrows, *Extracts from a Diary kept by the Rev. R. Burrows During Heke's War in the North, in 1845*, p. 10.
12. Octavius Hadfield, *One of England's Little Wars*, pp. 78–79.
13. For details, see H.T. Purchas, *A History of the English Church in New Zealand*, pp. 185–86.
14. William Williams, *Christianity Among the New Zealanders*, p. 147.
15. Charles Baker, Journal, 27 October 1861.
16. For examples, see 1 Corinthians 11:30–32; James 5:15; Luke 20:35–36.
17. J.A. Stack, Journal, 4 October 1829.
18. James Hamlin, report to CMS, 31 March 1855.
19. Henry Williams, Journal, 5 August 1827, 12 June 1831. Rogers (ed.), *Early Journals*, pp. 64, 181.
20. A.N. Brown, Journal, 17 November 1846.
21. Henry Williams, Journal, 5 September 1834. Rogers (ed.), *Early Journals*, p. 389.
22. Galatians 3:1.
23. William Morley, *History of Methodism*, p. 58.
24. Matthew 5:28.
25. Wakefield, *Adventure in New Zealand*, vol. 2, pp. 83–86.
26. Brown, Journal, 1 October 1835.
27. 1 Corinthians 9:2.
28. H. Turton, Journal, 1 November 1845. Cited by C.J. Parr, 'Before the Pai Marire', *JPS* vol. 76, no. 1, p. 42. See also R. Taylor, Journal, 18 December 1845.
29. On this subject see Johannes Andersen, 'Maori Religion', pp. 540–43; Elsdon Best, *The Maori*, vol. 2, pp. 31ff; Gudgeon, 'Maori Superstition', p. 169.
30. Brown, Journal, 4 September 1835.
31. Brown, Journal, 27 March 1839.
32. Brown, Journal, 2 April 1836.
33. John Hobbs, Letter, 24 January 1833.
34. Turton to WMS, 26 May 1841.

35. Edward Shortland, *The Southern Districts of New Zealand*, p. 136.
36. Turton to Bishop Selwyn, in the *Daily Southern Cross*, 15, 22, 29 June 1844.
37. William Woon to WMS, 19 April 1847.
38. Wakefield, *Adventure in New Zealand*, vol. 2, p. 357.
39. Te Kemara, 5 February 1840. T. Lindsay Buick, *The Treaty of Waitangi*, p. 127.
40. This particular case was rationalised by saying that it was purchased in order to save a tribal war over disputed land.
41. More details can be gained from Arthur S. Thomson, *The Story of New Zealand: Past and Present: Savage and Civilized*, vol. 2, p. 155. See also pp. 154, 156–58.
42. See M.A. Rugby Pratt, *The Pioneering Days of Southern Maoriland*, pp. 196–97; Hammond, *In the Beginning*, p. 84; H.H. Turton to WMS, 23 June 1844.
43. Lillian Keys, *The Life and Times of Bishop Pompallier*, pp. 289–90.
44. Richmond MSS 111, 17 August 1857. Cited by Keith Sinclair, *Origins of the Maori Wars*, p. 107. Note that Whiteley was murdered in 1869 by Pai Marire adherents, led by a man who had been a convert of Whiteley's.
45. Alexander Marjoribanks, *Travels in New Zealand*, p. 104.
46. Lillian Keys, *Bishop Pompallier*, p. 311.
47. Wakefield, *Adventure in New Zealand*, vol. 2, pp. 447–48. See also comments of Marjoribanks, *Travels in New Zealand*, p. 103; and H.T. Purchas, *The English Church*, note pp. 140–41.
48. *Missionary Register, 1816*, 327; *1817*, 520. See Raymond Firth, *Economics*, p. 443.
49. See J.F.H. Wohlers, 'On the Conversion of the Maoris in the South of New Zealand', *TPNZI*, vol.14, pp. 123–34.
50. Henry Williams, Journal, 6 December 1839. Rogers (ed.), *Early Journals*, p. 461.
51. Wakefield, *Adventures in New Zealand*, vol. 2, p. 455.
52. Charles Baker, Journal, 29 September 1856.
53. See Keith Sinclair's chapter 'The Settlers' View', *Origins of the Maori Wars*, for a good account of this subject.
54. Wakefield, *Adventures in New Zealand*, vol. 2, pp. 29–30.
55. Henry Williams, Journal, 27 January 1828. Rogers (ed.), *Early Journals*, p. 99.
56. William Baucke, *Where the White Man Treads*, pp. 83–84.
57. Brown, Journal, 3 April 1848.
58. Wakefield, *Adventures in New Zealand*, vol. 1, pp. 335–36.
59. T.S. Grace, Letter, 18 November 1877. Brittan and Grace (eds), *A Pioneer Missionary Among the Maoris, 1850–1879*, p. 287.
60. Gudgeon, 'Maori Superstition', p. 168.
61. Baucke, *Where the White Man Treads*, pp. 217–18; see also pp. 83–84 for another such illustration. And see *Daily Southern Cross*, 'Mr J.C. Firth's Conference with Tamati Ngapora and the King Natives at Orahiri', p. 4.
62. T.S. Grace, Annual letter, 18 November 1877. Brittan and Grace, *A Pioneer Missionary*, p. 286.
63. John Ward, *Information Relative to New Zealand, Compiled for the Use of Colonists*, p. 61.

Part Two

The Maori Response

5. Jesus or Jehovah?

In a clash of two different cultures, one that might be considered technologically advanced and the other more primitive, a definite initial impact occurs, with consequent change almost totally on the side of the less developed culture. But the nature of the change is not as straightforward as a simple adoption of the new culture, for the system of one society cannot be entirely imposed upon another group whose very different set of traditions have been worked out over a long period of development to suit their particular situation. The change in that case must be more gradual, and one of adaptation rather than wholesale adoption. In New Zealand this can be seen very clearly in the area of religion.

From as early as the 1830s response to European culture, and therefore the Christian religion, manifested itself in the formation of many new religious movements. These involved a number of various aspects, but overall they were an effort to syncretise the new teachings brought by the missionaries with the beliefs and situation of the Maori.

Many of these included in their systems much of the religion of the early Hebrews, for as the situation of the indigenous people altered throughout the century under the influence of the colonists, so Maori found a ready-made model for their situation within the framework of the new religious teachings. There must be some irony in the situation in that Maori, in responding to the culture of those who had brought the new religion, should choose to identify with another people instead — the knowledge of whom had been given by those they were sometimes rejecting.

The Maori Response

By the time of the signing of the Treaty of Waitangi in 1840, Maori began to see themselves in a position similar to that of the Israelites of so many centuries before — under the power of foreign rule in their own land. In 1845 the Rev. R. Burrows recorded that Hone Heke was addressing his people, comparing themselves to the persecuted children of Israel.[1] The chief Te Aroha, in a speech to Charles Davis in 1869, referred to the landlessness of his race, saying, 'We are like wandering Israelites without a Home'. Reihana Te Aroha was also to refer to that period as 'the abomination of desolation spoken of by Daniel the prophet'.[2]

From early in the contact period, Maori had the idea that their race was descended from that of the Israelites, and as they began to recognise more situational parallels between the two peoples, so that belief was reinforced. In 1841 a member of the Otumoetai hapu (Tauranga) showed familiarity with the idea of descent from Ishmael;[3] and Richard Taylor recorded in 1846 that Maori were taking up the idea of being the 'lost tribe' of Israel.[4] Some went so far as to adopt practices of the former people. H. Hanson Turton, a former Wesleyan missionary, visiting a village in the Thames area in 1861 in his position as Resident Magistrate for the Auckland district, found the people following Mosaic law to the extent that offences such as 'cursing, adultery, and witchcraft were to be punished by stoning and so on throughout.' When Turton talked to them about it, the reply was that if God had commanded it, it must be right, and that if it was right then, it could not be wrong now.[5]

This notion of Hebraic descent was not initially of the Maori's own making, but was given to them both directly and indirectly over a period of time. The first and direct source of the idea was the early missionaries themselves. In the very early period of Maori–missionary contact, the theory was advanced among several of the prominent church authorities that the Hebrew and Maori languages had much in common. Thomas Kendall and Professor Samuel Lee of Cambridge (England) had both seen similarities between the two tongues, and Robert Maunsell also noted 'the similarities between the fundamental principles of the Hebrew language and those of Maori'.[6]

Samuel Marsden, supporting his view by a few cultural parallels between the ancient Israelites and the Maori, stated, 'I am inclined to think that they have sprung from some dispersed Jews, at some period or other, from their religious superstitions and customs, and have by some means got into the island from Asia.'[7] Thomas Kendall, despite the fact that he had little knowledge of theology, and was not familiar with the structure of any language other than English,[8] followed the theory of the time that there was a definite connection between the Maori and the early civilisations of the ancient world. The main basis of the theory was the biblical story of the great flood, which had the post-diluvian world populated by the sons of Noah. Kendall became more and more convinced that the New Zealanders were descendants of the Egyptians, from the family of Ham, and in an effort to add weight to his own theory of links between Maori religion and that of the ancient Egyptians, even went so far as to purchase several carvings which he sent to European experts with his interpretations.[9] Bishop Pompallier pointed out a number of parallels between the biblical account of Adam and Eve, and the tradition of Maui and Kina, and concluded that the ancestors of the Maori were not totally ignorant of the divine traditions mentioned in Genesis.[10]

This response of the missionaries was not an isolated case, for mission workers in other foreign fields noted similarities between the indigenous peoples and other cultures. Articles on such matters were frequently published in the *Missionary Register*.[11] On the basis of the biblical teaching that the earth was populated from two primal parents it followed that all people had to be able to trace their origin from one place. To the missionaries, therefore, the matter of Maori having descent from the ancient peoples could not be doubted, and in fact they wanted it to be true. The only question, then, was from which branch had they come?

Others based their views on similarities of languages. Octavius Hadfield, after some study, concluded there could be no doubt of the common root of the Maori language and Greek and Sanskrit. In notes (1847) concerning the roots 'pu' and 'whaka' he concludes: 'The correspondence of these words is not only interesting in a psychological point of view, but almost amounting to a proof, that the meaning of the original roots from which they have been respectively developed must have been identical.'[12]

Many others in the years to come also pursued these notions, and the theory of the New Zealanders having some link with the people of Israel was commonly believed at the time. Therefore it was familiar to Maori, and as it was supported by their interest in their genealogy, it was accepted, and passed on among them from tribe to tribe. The fact that their people were the subject of a book of divine origin naturally held great appeal, and this belief was to be reflected in the rise of a variety of religious movements in the decades to come.

The Rev. Richard Taylor recorded in 1846 that a Maori called John Williams came to him one day and said he had discovered from which tribe his people were descended. From reading the blessing that Jacob bestowed upon the twelve tribes of Israel, he had come to the conclusion that they were descended from Benjamin because they had exactly fulfilled what Jacob said of them: 'Benjamin shall ravin as a wolf: in the morning he shall devour the prey, and at night he shall divide the spoil.'[13] As the Maori translation of this verse reads 'Ka kainga e ia te tupapaku i te ata', which means literally that he shall eat the dead body in the morning, so Williams concluded that Benjamin's tribe became man-eaters. Therefore Maori were obviously the descendants of Benjamin.[14] It is evident from this case that the notion of Maori descent from the Israelites was well known to the people. This was not an instance of John Williams coming to that conclusion for himself, but merely of deciding on a particular tribe to which they belonged. Also based on the belief in Hebraic descent, Maori themselves were to identify the atua Hema with Shem, the son of Noah.[15] W.E. Gudgeon tells of once meeting a man who 'like many of his race was an authority on the Bible', and who asserted that 'there was not one single incident in the world's history as related in that book that was not also to be found recorded in Maori tradition'.[16]

While the theory of the Maori as descendants of the ancient Hebrews may have interested that race from the point of view of their original ancestry, this would not have been enough on its own to account for their growing conviction on the matter. It was not on an intellectual level that the appeal was based, but on the recognition of the parallels which existed between the situations of the two peoples, and knowledge of the history of the Hebrews had to be present in order for Maori to see these similarities.

The Old Testament was at last freely available to Maori in their language, in full, after 1858 when Maunsell's translation was finally completed. Bishop Selwyn opposed its publication in pamphlet form as it was translated, as its reading without the aid of missionary interpretation would lead to misunderstanding of the scriptures.[17] Too few of the missionaries had become sufficiently fluent in the new language quickly enough and well enough to impart spiritual doctrines, and there was a consequent lack of trained Maori teachers who possessed the necessary understanding of the vital cultural background to be able to explain the new teachings to their people. But despite the misgivings of Selwyn, odd books of the older scriptures had been available much earlier.

The first three chapters of Genesis (Kenehihi) and the twentieth chapter of Exodus (Ekoro'ha) had been printed in Sydney in August 1827. Together with the first chapter of John (Ioani), 30 verses of the fifth chapter of Matthew (Mataio), the Lord's Prayer, and seven hymns, this constituted the first translation of the scriptures into Maori. Four hundred copies were printed. In 1830 William Yate also included a translation of

Genesis 1–3, and the Ten Commandments, together with various chapters of Matthew, John, 1 Corinthians, plus prayers, catechisms and hymns in the booklet of scriptures he had printed. The third translation of scriptures into Maori, in 1833, included the first eight chapters of Genesis; and in 1848 the Psalms of David were included in the Anglican Prayer Book. It is interesting to note from these details that in the first few years the translation of the Old Testament scriptures appears to have been considered as important as that of the New Testament. From this time on, though, priority was given to the New Testament and the first complete edition of this, the Rev. William Williams' translation, was published in 1837, 5000 copies being printed. Meanwhile, however, Maunsell's translation of Te Kawenata Tawhito (the Old Testament), from Hebrew, was continuing. As each of three parts was completed (in 1848, 1855 and 1856) copies were sent out to selected members of the clergy and lay people for correction, with the final instalment published in 1858.[18] The full Bible, containing both Old and New Testaments, though, was not available until 1868.

However, parts of the scriptures of the Old Testament were often available to Maori before these publication times. As various chapters and books were completed, copies would be sent to capable people for comment and correction, and these would doubtless be shared with at least selected Maori members of a missionary's congregation, if not more generally, for the purpose of soliciting their reactions to the language. The journal of Charles Baker, for instance, gives clear evidence that he used these scriptures in his services before official publication.

In addition, other short excerpts from various books were published at odd times; for instance, in about 1840 William Colenso printed his imperfect translation of part of Ezekiel 37 containing the vision of the prophet among the bones, and another of the first seven chapters of Daniel plus the book of Jonah. Robert Maunsell recorded in July 1839 that he had translated 'Moses' song and some of the chapters of Isaiah that refer prominently to the sufferings and glory of our adorable Lord', and that he had his 'lads' copy them out and circulate them, with much success. Others were now coming, he added, with pens and papers to make their own copies.[19]

As well as the scriptures themselves, there were other sources from which Maori obtained knowledge of the Hebrews' history and teachings before these were fully translated.

The journals of some missionaries give occasional indications as to what was being preached in the early years, and it is evident from these that stories of the ancient Hebrews were frequently passed on to mission congregations. Naturally those parts of scriptures translated were used often. William Woon, of the Wesleyan mission, addressed 400 people in November 1834 from the first chapter of Genesis, and used this to teach the origin of the sabbath.[20] The same missionary records preaching from other Hebrew scriptures on occasions also — such as in December 1837 when he preached from Moses' invitation to Hobab, and noted that those present listened with deep attention.[21]

The Rev. Charles Baker, as shown by his journal, also made much use of these scriptures in his sermons and services. From 1846 onwards there are many references to his use of the books of Genesis, Exodus, Psalms, Isaiah and others. On 22 July 1846, for instance, he noted that he told the children's class the history of Joseph — a story that is basic to the understanding of the history of the Jews' captivity in Egypt and the exodus from that country. Robert Maunsell, speaking in 1839 of his men's and boys' classes which had a total of 50, plus visitors, told how after the reading and catechisms were over, he would assemble all the participants in the chapel and ask them questions. He gives the example, 'Thus should the question be asked "Who was Daniel?" the answer would be, "The prophet who was saved in the lions' den", to which I would add a short history of Daniel, when and for what reason he was cast into a lions' den.'[22]

Less formal methods of spreading such knowledge were also used. Again the journals tell how story-telling sessions occurred during more informal visits between Maori and missionary, and mission workers would take any opportunity to draw parallels with scripture on any relevant occasion. The times of travels, sometimes over long distances and for extended periods of weeks or months, as well as for shorter journeys, were often occasions for such story-telling. The Rev. William White once used such an opportunity to relate the story of Joseph to a Maori who the missionary said had previously proved himself of somewhat deceitful character, with the result that the listener underwent a complete change of personality and eventually became a highly trusted local preacher and teacher.[23]

At the time of baptism into the church, missionaries very often gave their converts, or the converts themselves chose, a new 'Christian' name, but it is notable that very often these were taken, rather, from the Hebraic scriptures. Such names as Abraham, Isaac, Jacob, Noah, David, Samuel, Saul, Nicodemus, Job and many more were fairly common; and it seems inevitable that the histories of their namesakes would have been explained to the people receiving them. In this way too, knowledge of the Old Testament history would have been spread from the earliest times of Christian baptism.

It was also the habit of missionaries to use Hebraic references in their speech, and God was often referred to as the 'God of Israel'. The Rev. A.N. Brown, in his journal in 1835, wrote, 'How cheering the thought that the Lord of Hosts is with us — the God of Jacob is our refuge.' The same missionary, referring to the improvement in health of a chief, remarked: 'In Ngakuku's case the great Physician seems manifesting himself as to the Israel of old. "I am the Lord that healeth thee".'[24] So the image of God which was given to the people was often that of Jehovah of the Old Testament, rather than the Father of the Christian scriptures. A hymn composed by missionary Nathaniel Turner, and sung in Methodist mission services around the 1840s, concerned 'a determination to travel to the heavenly Canaan, and a description of the joys which awaited them there.'[25] William Whiteley referred to one of his early converts, Simon Peter, as 'an Israelite indeed in whom there is no guile',[26] and Charles Baker referred to a woman called Maraina as having been a 'Mother in Israel' to her people.[27]

With every scriptural reference given by members of the missions, knowledge was spread, for the Maori people's great love of story, together with their traditionally trained faculty for remembering such tales and repeating them, would ensure that they spread quickly and quite accurately within a short period. William Baucke tells how, as a race, Maori were very keen and highly skilled and accomplished storytellers who could take some small fact or incident and weave a whole story around it, embellishing the original with a whole background of interest.[28] Baucke tells how he once told a travelling companion the fables of the fox and the grapes, and the fox and the crow, then noted:

> *... when he retold these stories, they did not seem to be the same; they were epics; they were poems, enriched with appropriate local colouring, wherein the play of fancy sparkled and scintillated. They were no longer allegories; they were living, passionate realities, feeling pain and pathos, whose inner soul was dissected with keen skill and intricate reasonings — this motive laid bare, that desire elucidated, another plain fact surrounded with impenetrable hedgings of hidden meaning; here a suggestion of realism, there animal instincts made human. They were comparative, indicative, ethical, moral, dramatic — each section rounded off, each detail interwoven with the next, supremely, attractively, complete.*

Maori could often repeat almost verbatim, long conversations with other people, interspersed with explanatory notes on the manner and reactions of the parties involved. With such attributes of oral fluency and memory, as well as a tradition of storytelling, it is no wonder that the biblical accounts of the Israelites, with their troubled history, caught the full imagination of the Maori, and when they saw themselves in a similar plight, were able to make this known in a most eloquent fashion.

After the mid-1840s, missionaries began to teach reading and writing of the English language as well as Maori,[29] and following this time those Maori who could read English had access to the full scriptures. By the late 1840s there are more references to the teaching of English — Mr Warren of Hokianga had twelve lads making encouraging progress, some of them already reading in the English Testament; in the 1850s Mrs Beatrice Maunsell had 'a special classroom where from thirty to forty young women were daily taught in English'.[30] But as early as 1820 Samuel Marsden had been teaching the English language to 'some very fine youths' at his seminary for New Zealanders at Parramatta, Australia, where he had 25 sons of Maori chiefs living.[31] Although these numbers would be relatively small for some years, the additional knowledge gained was no doubt passed on quickly and widely.

It is quite possible that contact with Jews themselves might also have contributed to the interest of Maori in the Hebrews. Jewish pioneers to New Zealand, particularly acting as traders and businessmen, are known to have been in this country from at least the late 1820s.[32] It appears that most of these established good relations with Maori with whom they traded. Joseph Barrow Montefiore, trading around the west coast area of the North Island, noted that Maori possessed a great love of bargaining. They therefore welcomed traders not only for the goods they brought, but for the sake of making a bargain, and these traders were often respected more than the missionaries because of it.[33] For this reason, and also because traders did not condemn the other's religious beliefs, Maori were often more open with them, and Joel Polack, the Jewish trader, was able to observe their customs and learn of the legends. Consequently Polack acquired respect for the people, and back in England published two books on his experiences.[34] A settler writing in the middle of the century about the 'religion, vices, and morals of the Colonies' states that at this time there was 'a fair sprinkling of Jews' in the country.[35]

Even though it is not the custom of Jews to proselytise, and it is unlikely that any active effort would have been made to convert Maori to Judaism, it is certainly probable that Maori learned more about the stories contained in the older scriptures from such people. Even the knowledge that the religion of the Hebrews was still practised by a group of respected settlers must have had some positive influence on Maori — particularly when they now saw themselves as in the same position as the other people had been so long before.

There was, therefore, a full background of knowledge available to Maori regarding the history, habits and religion of the ancient Israelites. The scriptures, presented to Maori as the revealed and infallible Word of God, would have been sufficient on their own to provide the knowledge, but the importance of these was emphasised by copious references to them by missionary and settler, and their authenticity was supported by the presence of members of the Jewish race and religion in their midst.

It is not the purpose of this work to examine in full the theory of the descent of the Maori race from that of the Israelites, nor to make any statement about its basis in fact or otherwise. What is important in this case is that the theory was widely believed in nineteenth-century New Zealand.

It should also be noted that New Zealand Maori have been compared not only to the inhabitants of the Egypt-Canaan-Mesopotamia area, but to other races also. On the basis of language similarities and cultural parallels, they have been likened to a variety of other peoples — particularly those of Indo-Aryan background. Indeed, Herries Beattie made a collection of comparisons between the Maori and other races, in which he noted points in common, linguistic and cultural, between the New Zealanders and a great number of others. These included several South American peoples, namely: the Indians of Guiana, Ecuador, and Gran Chaco, Lake Titicaca, and the Incas; North American Indians and Inuit; the native peoples of Africa, New Caledonia and Australia; Europeans including the Welsh, Swedish, Irish, Scots and English; East Indians of Philippines, Celebes and Malaysia; South-East Asians of Cambodia, several Indonesian islands, Laos, Burma, Mauritius; East Asians of Mongolia, Japan and Tibet; Arabians and the indigenous peoples of the Indian continent; Melanesians of the Solomon Islands and New Guinea; and of course the Tahitians and other Polynesian peoples.[36] It is interesting that Beattie does not mention the ancient Israelites, though he may have seen his collection as in addition to those works published by others on that subject.

From early in the contact period, then, Maori believed that their origins were in the same people of whom they read in the scriptures. From the mid-nineteenth century plenty of parallels had been found by the suffering race to support the belief. They saw themselves as captives in their own land, subject to Europeans as the Israelites had been to a number of other peoples throughout their history. As the earlier overlords had plundered Israel, so had the substance of Aotearoa been taken over by a

The Maori Response

foreign race. The people saw similarities in many passages of the Hebrew scriptures, and so their religious response was built upon that foundation.

Several factors may have encouraged the acceptance of the older scriptures even further. Owing to the later translation of the Old Testament, it was not fully in the hands of Maori until twenty years after the New Testament. While this was an obvious priority from the point of view of the Christian missions, the fact that the missionaries kept referring to these other scriptures and yet apparently keeping them from the people, was to be seen rather differently by Maori. It appeared that the Old Testament contained esoteric or restricted knowledge — a concept familiar to Maori as that was the way of the whare wananga. This inference led to the conclusion that Europeans considered themselves of a much higher spiritual station than the New Zealanders. Once those scriptures were in their hands, it could be inferred that the missionaries didn't want Maori to have them because they would learn of the Israelite–Maori parallel and so would desert the Christian faith. Every missionary or settler who spoke against the descent of the New Zealanders from the Hebrews would be thought to be denying the fact for the same purpose.

The content of the Old Testament also had more points of familiarity with tradition than did the New. It put much emphasis on the genealogy of the Israelites — similar to the interest in whakapapa by the Maori. Many parts, particularly the verses of the book of Psalms, could be related to traditional waiata, karakia or oratory. The many accounts of epic journeys, and of tribal societies, held much appeal because of points of commonality between the two races.

Doctrinally too, the Hebrew religion suited the traditions and situation of the Maori, and so had more appeal than Christianity.

The depressed economic situation of Maori, and their declining sense of racial pride, meant that rather than finding solace in the doctrine of a peaceable saviour, satisfaction of grievances could be gained better through a more powerful leader who would take matters into divine hands. Yahweh, the God of Israel, was such a leader, who would actively lead his people into battle against their oppressors. This was an image of a leader with which the people could readily identify because of its parallel in the traditional culture. The atua were actively concerned in everyday human matters — accidents, poor crops, sickness, all manner of misfortune, could be attributed to a god avenging some breach of tapu. So too was Yahweh concerned in the everyday affairs of his people. Ironically, it may again have been the missionaries who gave this idea to Maori in their preaching of the omnipotence of God. Samuel Marsden himself had set the example when he said that tapu would not heal wounds, preserve the people from danger, restore them to health when sick, nor save them from death — but God could do all these things for them.[37]

On the other hand, the image of Christ had no great appeal, for no aspect of his related to what was desirable in Maori tradition. A man who was not a successful warrior, and in fact not a warrior at all, and who had been killed (for Maori found it difficult to believe in a physical resurrection) was not a figure who could command great respect on traditional grounds. So the Christ of Christianity was seen in a very much lesser position than was the God of the Hebrews. The Rev. A.N. Brown in 1835 referred negatively to those who 'for so long a period made a profession of Christianity' but whose 'hearts never embraced a crucified saviour'.[38]

In the early 1830s at a village in the Bay of Plenty district, a European talking to a tohunga on the matter said the priest dismissed the Christian God as 'too quiet, too lazy, and so no good for the Maori.' He didn't kill people so his mana was small. On the other hand, the atua maori had great power and could kill easily. The tohunga, when told of the power of the Devil, said that this then was the real European God and advised the man to pray to the Devil.[39]

At the very basis of their religious thoughts Maori had to find themselves more in line with the older teachings. The prophets of Israel, far from teaching a belief in one God as did Christianity, acknowledged the presence of many. Yahweh was not presented as the only existing deity — he was merely the only one to be followed by the Israelites, to the exclusion of those of other peoples. Likewise, the Maori in each area possessed their own tribal gods, which were seen as more powerful than those of other people. When the Rev. Richard Taylor preached on 5 January 1845 that there was one God, Te Heuheu of Taupo answered that there are many gods because one man couldn't make everything — all houses, canoes, and all other things.[40] The chief's further remark that the European God was a child as he had only just come to the land, while their own gods had been there from the beginning, is another very interesting comment. It could suggest that deities who had seniority were more powerful — probably the result of gaining strength through experience, victories and long-term support by the people. Here, then, is a further reason why Maori could come to the conclusion that the God of the Old Testament was a more effective figure than that of the later teachings.

The image of Yahweh, rather than the 'Father' figure of the Christian scriptures, is relatable to Io of the Maori pantheon. The Io theory is one which has been long debated, with some saying this was a traditional concept, but others maintaining its existence only from European influence.[41] Whether the supremacy of Io was an ancient belief and knowledge of him was only now declassified and able to be imparted to those non-initiates outside the select group which made up the whare wananga, or whether the concept was indeed inspired by missionary teachings, is not an issue here. The point to be considered in this case is that from the disclosure of the knowledge of Io in the 1860s, Maori themselves saw the cosmology as headed by that supreme figure. From this time on, the mass of Maori people had knowledge of the existence of a Supreme God called Io, and believed that he was part of their traditional system. This remote but all-powerful God was seen to relate to the image of the God of Israel rather than that of Christianity. As tradition was opposed to the Christian idea of a Father God and an earthly manifestation as in the person of Jesus, from the closing decades of the nineteenth century this provided a further separation between Maori and missionary.

Examinations of the terminology of the translated scriptures brings forward more interesting factors. In the books of the Old Testament the word 'God' is translated as 'Atua':

He mea hanga na te Atua i te timatanga te rangi me te whenua.[42]
In the beginning God created the heaven and the earth.

The Maori, naturally possessing only their own particular background of understanding, related this to their conception of the traditional atua — having no notion of the rather different image which the Europeans had for their God. Elsdon Best noted that the generally accepted or understood meaning of the word atua to the bulk of the people was that of a malignant power. It was not, therefore, a good choice by the missionaries who were wanting to convey a rather different image of the Christian 'Father'.[43]

On the other hand, the view of the God of the Hebraic scriptures was much more familiar. The early missionaries found that Maori often saw the God of the Old Testament in the same light as the traditional warrior atua Maru. The Rev. Richard Taylor recorded that the people used to pray to Maru to avert earthquakes from them.[44]

Both the words 'Lord' and 'Jehovah' were translated as 'Ihowa', and this apparent reference to Io was repeated over and over in scripture to reinforce the connection. In the first chapters of Genesis the scriptures refer to 'the Lord God', translated as 'Ihowa te Atua' — to Maori readers an even more obvious reference to a traditional-style atua. That Ihowa was indeed the name of God, there was no doubt, for He himself stated it:

> *I oku putunga ia ki a Aperahama, ki a Ihaka, ki a Hakopa, ko te Atua Kaha-rawa toku ingoa; kihai hoki ratou i mohio ki ahau, ko IHOWA toku ingoa.*
>
> And I appeared unto Abraham, unto Isaac, and unto Jacob, by the name of God Almighty, but by my name JEHOVAH was I not known to them.[45]

On this topic Elsdon Best refers to Renan's statement in his *History of the People of Israel* that the holy name of Yahweh became contracted into Iahou or Io, and theorises that the name of Jehovah has been carried westward, and that of Io eastward, from a common centre. He adds that 'one old Maori tradition gives the name of two primal gods, Io and Ha. Oriental scholars tell us that Ea, or Ia, or Aa, was identified with Ya, Yau, or Au, the Jah of the Hebrew.'[46] Again this is not the place to pursue this topic, but it must be remembered that this was a subject about which there was much speculation throughout the nineteenth century, and it is therefore relevant when considering the beliefs of the time.

To the general Maori populace after the dissemination of the knowledge of Io, if not to initiates of the whare wananga earlier, there is little doubt that the Atua Jehovah and Io would be considered the same.

On the other hand, in the New Testament when Jesus is referred to as 'Lord', the term 'Ariki' is used. So while it seemed that the missionaries themselves, as translators of the texts, were further supporting the Maori–Hebrew link, at the same time it appeared they were devaluing the position of Jesus to that of a high chief. Maori knew only too well that their race was not part of the tribe led by that chief, for it had been made quite clear to them from the beginning of contact. But that now appeared to be a lesser consideration, for a much greater power, Ihowa himself, was their leader.

Supporting the Ihowa–Io connection even further, there is a parallel in the concepts of Yahweh and Io in that the sacred names of both were strictly regarded as esoteric knowledge. Not only the name but even the knowledge of Io was restricted to members of the whare wananga, while the name of Yahweh was regarded as too sacred to pass the lips of anyone — a concept with its origin in the Hebrews' third commandment.

An even further consideration may have supported Maori allegiance to the God of the Old Testament rather than to that of the gospels. While Christian references to the 'Father' are definitely monotheistic, the earlier scriptures do include references to Yahweh as 'the God of gods'.[47] Translated into Maori as 'te Atua o nga atua', the conclusion is clear that while the great God of the Europeans might be proved to be more powerful than the atua, he was, however, not alone. The fact that this reference in scripture supported the traditional view, against the statements of the missionaries, may well have further reinforced a common belief that the representatives of the church gave a wrong interpretation of the Bible. In this case, their own book was able to show how the missions had been wrong in denying the existence of the atua maori.

In its mystical dimension the Hebrew religion was also closer to Maori tradition, in that communication from God to people was often through direct physical intervention rather than more subtle examples of mysticism as in the New Testament. While traditionally the will of the atua could be divined through certain practices, this usually became clear by the result of a battle, or some other action, as also happened in Old Testament stories. On the other hand, the 'miracles' of Jesus were not always believed by Maori because of that people's practical approach to life.

To Maori with their traditions of cosmology, the view of Christ had to differ greatly from that of the missionaries. Traditional mythology included many stories of deities such as the demi-god Maui, and personifications of natural phenomena such as Hine-Titama, but these figures were on a different plane from the ideal of Io. Such divinities were culture heroes and it is likely that this is the way many Maori saw Jesus Christ. With both human and divine parentage, Jesus was a demi-god — as appeared to be confirmed by the scriptures' use of the term 'Ariki' which emphasised his human rather than divine nature. The Christian notion of his genetic descent from, or his spiritual oneness with, the Supreme God had no precedent in the Maori system. The Io of Maori tradition was far beyond the notion of producing a son — the procreation of people being the act of the departmental deity Tane. That the God of Christianity had done so, could only further reduce his image in favour of Yahweh.

In all ways the mythology of the Hebraic religion was more compatible with Maori tradition than was that of Christianity. The New Zealanders welcomed stories of a warrior leader such as Yahweh, and the protection which he extended to his people; and the accounts of the ancient prophets were reconcilable to the traditional social system which included similar instances of prophetic seers. Christian mythology, however, with tales of virgin births and resurrection from the dead, was not easily absorbed. Overall, then, the image of Christ, as understood by Maori, was of a much lesser deity who paled in comparison with the active and powerful Atua of the Hebrews.

The Old Testament doctrinal emphasis on the Judaic teachings of justice, righteous war and fear of God were more familiar to Maori than were Christianity's love, grace and salvation. The missionary John King wrote in the early period of the missions that despite his efforts to teach them the faith he found it 'difficult to make any impression on their minds of the evil of sin, or of the love of God in Christ Jesus'.[48]

Notes

1. R. Burrows, Journal, 27 April 1845. *Extracts*, p. 32.
2. The *Daily Southern Cross*, 'Firth's Conference', pp. 6, 11.
3. A.N. Brown, Journal, 26 December 1841.
4. Richard Taylor, Journal, 21 November 1846.
5. *AJHR* 1882, E-5A, 5.
6. Robert Maunsell, *Grammar of the New Zealand Language*, p. viii.
7. Samuel Marsden, Second New Zealand Journal, 9 November 1819. Elder (ed.), *Letters and Journals*, pp. 219–21.
8. Judith Binney, *Legacy of Guilt*, p. 24.
9. Ibid., pp. 133ff.
10. Jean-Baptiste François Pompallier, *Early History*, pp. 48–49.
11. See, for instance, 'Parallels between the Gods of the Indian and European Heathens', *Missionary Register*, 1819, pp. 92ff.
12. See Grey manuscripts.
13. Genesis 49:27.
14. Taylor, Journal, 21 November 1846.
15. W.E. Gudgeon, 'Maori Religion', *JPS* vol. 14, no. 55, p. 118.
16. Ibid., pp. 116ff.
17. Frances Porter (ed.), *The Turanga Journals*, pp. 317–18.
18. T.M. Hocken, *Bibliography of New Zealand Literature*; C.R.H. Taylor, *A Bibliography of Publications on the New Zealand Maori*.
19. Henry Wily and Herbert Maunsell, *Robert Maunsell*, p. 55.
20. William Woon, Journal, 24 November 1834. Reprinted in a letter to Wesleyan Mission Society, 1 December 1834.
21. Woon, Journal, 12 December 1837. See Woon's letter to Beecham, 23 January 1838.
22. Wily and Maunsell, *Robert Maunsell*, p. 56.
23. Morley, *History of Methodism*, p. 57
24. Brown, Journal, 10–13 August, 30 June 1835.
25. William Morley, *History of Methodism*, p. 85.
26. W. Whiteley, Letter to the Rev. J. Beecham, 4 October 1835.
27. Charles Baker, Journal, 17 February 1844.
28. See Baucke's short chapter on 'The Maori as Storyteller', *Where the White Man Treads*, pp. 153–57.
29. See C.J. Parr, 'Missionary Library', pp. 444, 446; Parr, 'Maori Literacy 1843–1867', *JPS* vol. 72, no. 3, p. 214; H.W. Williams, 'Reaction of the Maori', p. 233.
30. Morley, *History of Methodism*, p. 120; Wily and Maunsell, *Robert Maunsell*, p.118
31. Marsden, Letter to the Rev. J. Pratt, 7 February 1820. Barton, *Earliest New Zealand*,

p. 34. Also, Report to Committee of CMS to Annual Meeting, held 21 May 1821, Robert McNab (ed.), *Historical Records of New Zealand, Vol. 1*, p. 533.
32. For details of some early pioneers, see Lazarus Morris Goldman, *The History of the Jews in New Zealand*, pp. 27ff.
33. Goldman, *History of the Jews*, pp. 28, 34.
34. In addition to *Manners and Customs*, Polack published *New Zealand, Being a Narrative of Travels and Adventures during a Residence in that Country between the years 1831 and 1837*.
35. 'Hopeful', *Taken In: Being a Sketch of New Zealand Life*, p. 136.
36. Herries Beattie, MS M.1. 582/E9, Notebook 65, 'Racial Comparisons and the Maori'.
37. Marsden, Third New Zealand Journal, 1 August 1820. Elder (ed.), *Letters and Journals*, p. 274.
38. Brown, Journal, 21 August 1835.
39. G.M. Henderson, *Taina*, pp. 27–28.
40. Donald McLean, Journal, 5 January 1845.
41. On this subject see J. Prytz Johansen, *Studies in Maori Rites and Myths*, pp. 36ff. Also, Johannes Andersen, 'Maori Religion', pp. 546ff.
42. Genesis 1:1.
43. Elsdon Best, *Tuhoe*, p. 1023.
44. Taylor, Journal, 8 March 1844.
45. Exodus 6:3.
46. Best, *The Maori, Vol. 1*, p. 90.
47. For example, Psalm 136:2.
48. William Williams, *Christianity Among the New Zealanders*, p. 22.

6. Indigenous and Imported

As well as the doctrinal similarities that existed between the Hebrew and Maori systems, there were even more points of contact on the social and cultural level of the two peoples, and these were to provide further support for the theory of Maori descent from the ancient Israelites.

The concept of tapu, which was basic to the entire life of Maori, can be related to the Hebrew notion of the sacred as seen in many practices. In New Zealand the sacred had two aspects — negative in terms of prohibitions, and positive in terms of protection. The prohibitions, though, were based on some positive purpose, such as the safeguarding of sacred areas, and so the institution of tapu was a protection to the people — be it practical as in the preservation of food sources, or to ensure spiritual protection in the appeasement of atua. The same aspects can be seen in the laws imposed upon the Hebrews, in rules which were designed to protect the people during their 40 years of wandering and afterwards, and in strict prohibitions on such areas as the tabernacle. The daily life of Maori was ordered according to the wishes of the atua in just the same way as that of the Hebrews followed the commands of Yahweh. Revelation, from dreams, divination and omens, was to Maori just as much proof of deities concerned with earthly activities as was a set of stone tablets inscribed with the law. In each case, moreover, these laws were overseen not by humans but by their divine source, and reward or punishment came also from that direction. So the kumara crop was heavy in the way that manna fell from heaven in the wilderness, and foes were defeated in both cases when sacred laws had been adhered to. But each of the powers also punished disobedience, and not only could help be withdrawn when not earned by proper allegiance, but the atua or Yahweh could even work against their people should the commands be forgotten or ignored.[1] In both cases the judgement and its consequences were inevitable and immediate — deeds were not accountable at death or some future period, but the results were clear from what earthly fortune followed.

Both the Maori and Hebrew systems included rules relating to ceremonial impurity. Although the reasoning and purpose relating to the two cultures' prohibitions regarding women's ritual participation at times of menstruation and childbirth were very different, there were practices of separation and appropriate rites in each case.[2] In the case of death, similar ideas of impurity surrounded the dead body, and the place where it had lain.[3] Again certain rituals were carried out in order to restore cleanliness. Judge Maning, who gives a good account of an occasion on which he became unclean by touching a skull and the result of this incident, notes, 'This tapu was, in fact, the uncleanness of the old Jewish laws, and lasted about the same time, and was removed in almost the same way.'[4] Just as the Hebrew scriptures state that those who are unclean because of contact with an unclean object shall be cut off from their people,[5] so too Maori who had been rendered tapu because of a similar violation of the sacred were kept strictly apart from others until the cleansing be effected and the tapu lifted. Just as the penalty for major infringements of Judaic law was death, so the inexorable power of tapu brought about the death of anyone who violated that law.

The matter of religious imagery provides a further parallel. While the Judaic religion is aniconic, the Old Testament could be seen to show some allowance in the symbolic depiction of the presence of God, as in the brazen serpent of the Mosaic period. The Maori also did not usually depict the major atua with images — the figures adorning carved houses being those of ancestors and culture-heroes. The niu, small divinatory sticks with carved heads as used by the tohunga in rituals, were aids to divination and not images for worship. While Christianity claims no image worship either, Maori (as have members of other religious systems) found the crucifixes, images of Jesus, Mary and the saints, and religious pictures suggested a rather different view, and the Judaic position in this case would have been more familiar and acceptable to them.

As the Hebrews had their prophet-leaders who were intermediaries between Yahweh and the people, and who were also their political leaders, so a parallel can be found within Maori culture. Prophecy was an accepted part of Maori life, being practised by tohunga and indeed by anyone who might possess the power of foresight. Tohunga acted as intermediaries between atua and people in their reading of divine will. The more political function of the leader was performed by the rangatira or ariki but very often these figures combined the roles of priest and political leader. Therefore the roles of the Hebraic prophet-figure had their counterpart in the functionaries of Maori society. When religious movements arose in response to the need of the people, the charismatic figures and prophets who arose to lead them had their models in both systems — being relatable to the former tohunga and also to the Judaic prophets.

Old Testament stories tell of how dreams were often interpreted as containing messages or omens — Jacob, Joseph, Solomon and Daniel being among those who received some sort of premonition by this method. Dreams were also taken as portentous in Maori society. Father Servant told of how these were related in minutest detail, discussed at length, and repeated in villages all around, with interpretation being sought from those skilled in the art, and action taken according to the message contained within it.[6] This was a parallel which was certainly noted by Maori, for Tuta Nihoniho referred to the guidance which could come from dreams in his 'advice to young soldiers when going into action' in the Pai Marire-Government battles between 1865 and 1871 — 'Like unto the dream of the Syrian heard by Gideon and his officer, which dream was a true one, as also was its interpretation. The dreams of the Maori are much the same.' As the Hebrews were warned that false prophets might pretend to revelation in dreams,[7] so too Nihoniho warned that some dreams could speak falsely, and so he advised reliance upon those whose dreams have proved reliable in the past, and on those who are accustomed to such experiences, for they can rightly be styled 'seers'.[8]

The concept of utu as practised by Maori was similar to the allowance made for revenge in Judaic law.[9] Early missionaries, bewailing the custom of Maori to take vengeance for every deed or insult inflicted upon them, saw the similarity to the scriptures. Henry Williams recorded in 1833 upon meeting an old chief who was determined to obtain satisfaction for people who had been killed, 'It does not enter into their theory of making peace unless they receive an eye for an eye, a tooth for a tooth . . .'[10]

Similarities in the division of time existed between the two systems also. The traditional Maori calendar began each month with the new moon, as did that of the Israelites, and each day began and ended at sunset, as did the Jewish day. After the arrival of the Christian missionaries and with the establishment of the colony, the Gregorian calendar, which paid no attention to the phases of the moon was adopted generally, as was the idea of the day beginning at midnight. When Maori in their new religious movements reverted to the lunar calendar and again marked days from sunset to sunset, they were returning to the traditional scheme, and coincidentally following the custom of the Israelites.

Practices concerned with rites of passage show several parallels between the two peoples. In neither society was there any real initiation into the community at birth, for this was automatic, though in New Zealand babies were often dedicated to an appropriate atua. In Maori society males were usually circumcised, so this custom is common to both cultures. The marriage customs of Maori relate to those of the early Judaic period in that these were not solemnised by any particular ritual, but were marked from the time that a couple began living together by mutual and family consent[11] — though in the case of a marriage at chiefly level there might be some ceremony directed towards an alliance of two tribes united in this way. In these cases the arrangement of betrothal from birth was sometimes practised. The Maori rite of whakapa, which was undertaken by a man before his death for the purpose of bestowing his ancestral mana on his inheriting son, has its parallel in the ritual of blessing practised in similar circumstances by the Hebrews.[12]

Death customs again include several points in common. As mentioned previously, in each case there was a state of uncleanliness associated with it. Joel Samuel Polack, the Jewish trader who traded with Maori around the North Island in the early part of the nineteenth century, noted a number of parallels between Maori and Hebrew, including many regarding death. According to Polack sacrifices were made by both peoples at the death of a chief, and the anniversaries of deaths were observed. Burials were preferably sited at the same place as ancestors and relatives of the deceased were buried, and when the tribe moved from one place to another, bones were sometimes exhumed and taken to the new place of residence for reburial. Scriptural stories read by Maori told of how Jacob was taken to Canaan for burial so he could rest in the same place as his ancestors,[13] and the bones of Joseph were taken by Moses when the Israelites left Egypt.[14] Polack noted that Maori occasionally embalmed their dead, and compared this to the Egyptian custom (though not the method), referring to the death of Jacob in Egypt, and his embalmment.[15]

Regarding the use of appropriate symbols (carving in the case of the Maori, and sculptures for the Hebrews) on the tombs of especially revered persons, Polack gave illustrations of several elaborate tombs of Maori chiefs and referred to the tomb of Joshua as an example of the Hebrew practice. That the last utterance of a dying person might be prophetic, was also common to the two cultures, this being seen in the Hebrew case in Jacob's gathering of his sons to his deathbed so he might tell them what would come about in the 'last days'.[16] There was extreme reverence paid to the deceased, and great care taken in the funerary procedures in both cultures. Extravagant mourning for the dead was another common feature,[17] and Polack contrasted this with the 'hard-hearted' Europeans who are 'less obstreperous in their distress'. In addition, Maori belief in the sacred nature of the personal belongings of the deceased was compared to the Hebrew custom of destroying the main articles of furniture and other belongings of the dead person.[18] Samuel Marsden also compared the New Zealanders' protection of the bones of their dead to that of the Israelites, and made further reference to the removal of the bones of Joseph.[19]

Marsden noted the similarities between Maori and Hebrews regarding some customs of war:

When they go to war the priest always accompanies them, and when they draw near to the enemy he addresses them in similar language to that which the Jewish High Priest addressed to the Jews of old, as recorded in the 20th chapter of Deuteronomy, verses 2, 3 and 4. 'And it shall be when ye are nigh into battle, that the Priest shall approach and speak unto the people and shall say to them, Hear, O Israel: ye approach this day unto battle against your enemies: let not your hearts faint; fear not, and do not tremble, neither be ye terrified because of them. For the Lord your God is He that goeth with you, to fight for you against your enemies, to save you.' When a chief falls in battle they cut off his head and preserve it as a trophy of victory, as David cut off the head of Goliath and took it to Jerusalem. The conquering chief at New Zealand carries the heads of the chiefs he kills into his own village, where they are exhibited to public view. The conqueror also burns the bodies of the chiefs he kills in battle, and the dead body when the head is cut off can only be handled by the chiefs. No common person is permitted to touch it, but it is placed on the fires by the chiefs. We find a similar custom mentioned in the 31st Chapter of the First Book of Samuel, verses 11 and 12, respecting the bodies of Saul and his sons when they were killed by the Philistines: 'And when the inhabitants of Jabesh-gilead heard of that which the Philistines had done to Saul, all the valiant men arose, and went all night, and took the body of Saul and the bodies of his sons from the wall of Bethshan and came to Jabesh, and burnt them there.'

The Maori Response

Marsden also compared the act of cutting off the heads of enemy chiefs and collecting them together as 'similar to what was done to Ahab's sons when Jehu rebelled against him.'[20]

The New Zealanders made offerings to the atua on appropriate occasions, such as the offering of the first fruits of a harvest or the first catch of a hunting expedition. Sacrifices, for instance that of a dog in connection with the building of a canoe,[21] were also offered. Such practices are relatable to the Festival of First Fruits practised by the Israelites,[22] and to the sacrifices offered to Yahweh by them also.

An additional rite which has similarities between the two cultures was noted by Elsdon Best, who tells of the slaying of a man whose blood was then sprinkled on the door timbers of a food store in order to enhance a rite ensuring the continuing fertility of the kumara. This he saw as an older form of the Jewish custom of slaying a lamb and sprinkling the door posts and lintels with its blood.[23]

Both of the races in question attached a deep and emotional significance to the land. As previously discussed, it was this issue more than any other factor which motivated Maori to rebel against European domination. The New Zealanders' emotional response to the land must be recognised as a religious response, for the land is the substance of Papatuanuku — the female primal parent. So too was the land of religious significance to the Israelites, though for a different reason. As the land of Canaan was that promised to them by Yahweh, and eventually delivered into their hands, so it was theirs by divine right and will. In both cases, then, the alienation of land was not merely a political issue but a religious one.

The Maori practice of marking tribal boundaries, or delineating an area under a prohibition, was seen by one missionary to have a biblical parallel. Pou rahui, prohibition markers, were set up to identify such areas, or to mark covenants between different hapu. The Rev. J.A. Wilson, who saw two such posts on a path near Rotorua marking a peace covenant, noted the similar covenant made between Jacob and Laban.[24]

The social organisation of each of the cultures can be compared in that they both consisted of the race generally subdivided into tribes, subtribes and extended family units.

As regards the religious functionaries of each society, here too a parallel can be drawn. Though Levite priests and tohunga may seem far from comparable, both were regarded as apart from the everyday concerns of life, and had a right to be supported by the community. The Rev. T.G. Hammond, on a visit to the village of Parihaka in 1910, was told by an old man who had been a great Bible student that in traditional Maori society there was a certain order of men who were termed 'Hamakapua' (in other dialects Amo-kapua or Ahurewa) and they were the Levites of the scriptures.[25]

In both cultures the priesthood was generally a hereditary institution, though in the New Zealand case other high-born people of proven capacity may be trained in priestly arts, and women of distinction could also undertake the functions of tohunga.

The matter of slavery provides several more instances of customs in common. In the Hebrew system slaves were acquired by a number of methods — by capture, purchase, abduction, birth, or self-sale to escape poverty or pay for debts. The first three of these cases relate to the Maori custom — those captured in war or abducted from an enemy tribe at any opportunity often being kept as slaves. These could be exchanged or sold at the will of the owner. The other instances are not applicable to the Maori situation for in New Zealand there was no hereditary slave class — children of slaves being born free members of the tribe in which they were living. The absence of a money-based economy and a society based on individual ownership meant that financial or property debt was not a great problem. The Hebraic system was more complicated and bound by a number of rules pertaining to each case, and differentiated between slaves of Hebrew or foreign races. The Maori system was much simpler — there being no outside races to be considered, and the lack of a hereditary slave class and practice of temporary slavery brought about by debt, meant that no rules were necessary to cover such instances. In each case the manner of treatment of slaves varied considerably — from being well treated as one of the family and people, to being treated very badly. In New Zealand slaves could be disposed of at the will of their owner, and sometimes were sacrificed on a ritual occasion. While the Hebrews were not to kill a slave purposely, and human sacrifices were not required on such occasions, they were certainly known to them, and Polack noted that this was a custom of the nations around Palestine.[26] In both cultures there was provision for slaves to become a part of the tribe or family, and marry into the general people.

Polygamy was practised by both Maori and Hebrews — this being normally restricted to chiefs in the Maori culture, with these usually having between two and four wives. The first wife was dominant with any additional wives under her, though in the Maori situation should a subsequent wife have higher rank she might take precedence. A further class of slave-wives in New Zealand equates with the concubines and handmaids of the Israelites. Polack, noting the local custom of a man marrying sisters, compared this to the case of Jacob's marriage to first Leah and then Rachel.[27] It was also the custom in both cultures that upon the death of a man his brother should take the deceased man's widow as his wife.

Divorce was allowable in both societies, and the reasons for separation were similar. A further parallel exists in the matter of adultery, for in the case of the Maori a man could kill his wife and her lover for this offence, and the Hebraic law provides the death penalty for both the man and the woman involved.[28]

Succession in a Maori family was according to the law of primogeniture, as it was also in Hebrew society. In both cases there also occurred the practice of teaching a child of rank of its heritage. As the Hebrews were enjoined to teach the commandments to their children, so too were Maori carefully instructed in their genealogy and in the esoteric knowledge of the race through the institution of the whare wananga.[29]

For a Maori, particularly of chiefly rank, to die childless was a very regrettable thing, and if necessary childless couples would adopt children. For the Israelites too there was a strong desire to be survived by one's children, for it was in their remembrance and the continuation of one's line that one achieved immortality. Both peoples regarded their ancestors with reverence, and desired to be remembered by their descendants in their turn; and in each culture to kill the sons of a man was to deprive him of his hope of continuance in this way. Barrenness was therefore a curse to both peoples, it being seen as some sort of divine retribution or judgement passed upon them for some misdeed.

Various names were given or taken by Maori to denote anything significant in a person's lifetime — from physical characteristics or talents, to incidents attached to their life. Polack pointed out a parallel here too with the Israelites whose names were often changed or given because of some similar characteristic, offering as examples, among others, Rachel being named for her profession of shepherdess, Esau from his hairiness, and the changing of Jacob to Israel.[30]

Because of the tapu that surrounded a person, and which was particularly concentrated on the head, any hair cut from a person, and especially so in the case of a chief, was sacred. Therefore it had to be carefully disposed of in the sacred area set aside for tapu objects. As the Israelites were commanded that they should not cut the hair of their head or beard in a particular fashion, so hair also assumed sacred significance in that society.[31]

The Maori custom of tattooing urged Joel Polack to comment that it 'incontestably proves the Asiatic origin of the people'. The cutting of the flesh or printing of marks upon the body was forbidden to the people of

Yahweh,[32] but Polack pointed out this was a habit of the Hebrews who punctured themselves in imitation of the nations around Palestine until prohibited by Mosaic law.[33]

Another interesting parallel, which was no doubt noted by Maori in their reading of the Hebraic scriptures, occurs in the significance of the number twelve in the mythology of each system. As they read of the twelve sons of Jacob and hence twelve tribes of Israel, the twelve fountains of Elim, even of the twelve men of the tribe of Benjamin and twelve of David who were killed in the battle between Joab and Abner,[34] they were bound to recall the twelve names of Tane and of Io, the twelve levels of sky (Io dwelling in the twelfth), and other lesser references. While this is subject to the same possible reservation as the Io theory, when added to so many other parallels in the social and cultural aspects of the two societies, in the minds of the New Zealanders it might have provided a further point of contact after the 1860s.

It should be made quite clear that the similarities considered here are not necessarily confined to the Maori and Hebrew cultures, but most were common to many other civilisations also. Polack, as well as noting the likenesses with Israel, also pointed out analogies in a number of other civilisations including those of the Greeks, Romans, Egyptians, Indians, Chinese, Arabians, Persians, and many others. It should also be understood that there were areas in which the two cultures in question were dissimilar — for instance, in Maori belief in an afterlife, a doctrine that is not explicit in the Hebrew scriptures. Furthermore, it could be claimed that the parallels which do exist are those which are typical of almost any primal society.

The point which is relevant here is that Maori were not looking for instances of contact between their own and any nation other than that of the Israelites. They had been told that they were descended from that ancient people, and the scriptures of that nation had been presented to them as the Word of God. Naturally, then, as they read, either consciously or subconsciously they looked for factors which would tend to prove or disprove the notion. As it was, the verdict was to come down overwhelmingly on the side of a definite relationship between the two. So John Gorst was to write in 1864 that most Maori were 'exceedingly fond of reading the books of the Old Testament, in which they find described a state of civilisation not unlike their own.'[35]

At the same time as Maori acceptance of their connection with the Hebrew race, came a subsequent and corresponding feeling of separation from Europeans generally. This was evident from the beginning, but when seen alongside the parallels which existed between Maori and Israelites, the lesson was even more striking.

In European society, the law was in the hands of the government rather than God. Both the Hebrew and the Maori systems were a form of theocracy, and while Maori thought this should be true also of the Christian nation which had settled among them, it had become abundantly clear that this was not so. God's justice, in the new scheme, would take place at some unknown time in the future, or in another existence, and this was a notion which was unfamiliar and unwelcome to Maori. Regarding earthly justice, then, the European system had no appeal. There was no allowance for revenge — rather than utu exacted on the basis of life for life, the Christian gospel was to turn the other cheek and permit offences against one to go unavenged.

It seemed to Maori that Europeans lacked contact with their God, for such agencies of communication as divination and dreams were condemned by them. So too were the practices of the Maori religious functionary, the tohunga. While in the Hebrew system Maori found the traditional figures could relate to the many prophets of Israel, the Christian missionaries were jealous of the station of Jesus and denounced all other religious leaders as 'false prophets' come to mislead the people.

So it might also be supposed that the Christians were actually going against the Word of God as they did not keep to all the injunctions given in the scriptures. Yahweh had commanded that the month should begin with the new moon, and that the sabbath be kept on the seventh day, yet both of these had been altered in the new system.

The beliefs and customs of the Christians regarding death were quite opposed to those of the Maori — the former being conservative and restrained emotionally, and the latter being extravagant and uninhibited. In addition, Europeans were not concerned with either uncleanliness associated with death, or of its tapu nature, and therefore often violated Maori beliefs and customs.

To Maori, Christians no doubt seemed somewhat less than thankful to their God, for while his name was praised and invoked, the fruit of the land was not regularly dedicated or returned in thanksgiving, and nor were specific sacrifices offered. Likewise, they had a rather utilitarian view of the land and did not treat it with the reverence which Maori reserved for an ancestor. Christian missionaries and mission workers were regarded as paid functionaries of their society, and since this view was opposed to Maori ideal, the New Zealanders rejected this aspect of the Christian Church.

Polygamy was detested by the Christian missionaries who not only forbade any followers to take a further wife but demanded that an intending convert give up all but one of his spouses. In the case of the chief Te Awaitaia in the mid-1830s, the Wesleyan mission required that he give up eight of his nine wives, whereupon he was married to the one according to church ritual, and admitted to baptism.[36] In many other cases, however, the men refused to comply with such demands and were refused entry into the church.

Divorce was not regarded kindly by missionaries either. Converts who had been married in a Christian ceremony were to find that it was to be far more difficult to put aside their wife or husband because of the new teachings, and this was another point upon which Maori and Christian customs differed.

Slavery was a further issue on which the two cultures were opposed. This was a traditional part of the Maori social set-up, but was regarded as a grave sin by the missionaries, who from the earliest time demanded the release of all slaves. Such a move meant that the status and the economic position of owners of slaves was much reduced, so naturally these demands were met with some resentment. Allied to the matter of slavery was that of relative rank. With the acceptance of Christianity any person of high standing lost their former mana, for in the new system all were equal. This is a teaching which stopped many of the chiefs of the earlier years particularly from embracing the message of the gospel. Henry Williams found how the two matters were entwined when he gave the teaching of judgement to all, irrespective of rank, to the northern people in 1833. He noted that the chief Tareha was 'in a great rage' over it, and denounced the doctrine as fit for 'Slaves and Europeans, but not for a free and noble people like the Nga Puhi'.[37]

The whole question of family and succession in the Christian system seemed unsatisfactory to Maori, as it no longer assumed much significance. As the emphasis now was on personal salvation, and a continuing life after death was promised for believers, the concept of the continuance of the family line by one's descendants was of no great concern. Consequently, the ancestors too were devalued.

The matter of tapu not only had no place in Christianity but had been strongly denounced by the missionaries. Such practices, therefore, as the careful disposal of sacred substances and materials, and the sacred nature of certain spots, was regarded as superstitions and so condemned. Overall Europeans, as represented by missionaries, were of very sober demeanour, not given to levity or laughter — a characteristic of little appeal to Maori.

The Maori Response

Christianity as seen by Maori was that displayed by those members of European society in nineteenth-century New Zealand, and the two cultures were widely separated by geography, history and technological development. While missionaries had been happy to give the Maori the idea of descent from the other people, at the same time they made it quite clear that the gap between Maori and European was indeed great.

When seen in the light of the scriptures, the religious significance of this separation between the Maori and European cultures was major. In the New Testament it was shown that Christians and Jews were opposed, and in fact references to Jews in the later scriptures were to the effect that they were set apart from the Christians for their unbelief. Those termed 'Jews' were those who had rejected both Jesus and his teachings, and had even persecuted and killed him.[38] To give to Maori the idea that they were descended from this race, and in addition to give 'proof' of this in the Word of God, was therefore almost equivalent to instructing them that it was their duty to reject the message of Christianity and become, rather, as that people of old.

It was not a conclusion which has been isolated to the people of New Zealand. In Italy, for example, one peasant upon reading a Bible given to him by Protestant missionaries was not only convinced that Judaism was the true persuasion but converted many of his fellow villagers to that view also. This group became Jews and later emigrated to Israel. Other Christian groups too have at different times changed their allegiance to Judaism. In Germany a community of Baptists also became Jews after studying the Hebraic scriptures.[39] Indigenous people in other areas, notably some African tribes, have also found the message given to them in the older scriptures spoke to them more closely than did those which Christian missionaries believed they were offering.

Notes

1. See Leviticus 26:14ff.
2. In Maori society the concern was not one of impurity at such times, but fear of a woman's powerful connection to the spirit world which could endanger people who came into contact with her.
3. Numbers 19:11ff.
4. F.E. Maning, *Old New Zealand*, p. 136.
5. Leviticus 7:21.
6. Father C. Servant, *Customs and Habits of the New Zealanders, 1838–1842*, pp. 44–45.

7. Deuteronomy 13:1–3; Jeremiah 27:9–10, 29:8.
8. Tuta Nihoniho, *Narrative of the Fighting on the East Coast 1865–1871*, p. 53.
9. Exodus 21:23–5; Leviticus 24:20; Deuteronomy 19:21.
10. Henry Williams, Journal, 3 March 1833. Rogers, *Early Journals*, p. 289.
11. See the example of David in 2 Samuel 11:27.
12. For example, the blessing given by Isaac to Jacob, Genesis 27:26–29. Also Deuteronomy 33:1.
13. Genesis 50:5–13. See too Joshua 24:29–33.
14. Exodus 13:19.
15. Genesis 50:26.
16. Genesis 49:1.
17. See Numbers 20:29; Deuteronomy 34:8.
18. Joel Polack makes reference to these points in various places in *Manners and Customs* vol. 1, pp. 62–127.
19. Marsden, Journal, 9 November 1819. Elder (ed.), *Letters and Journals*, p. 220.
20. 2 Kings 10:6–7. Elder (ed.), *Letters and Journals*, pp. 219–20.
21. Johansen, *Rites and Myths*, p. 78, citing George Grey, in H.W. Williams (ed.), *Nga Mahi a Nga Tupuna*, 3, p. 94.
22. Leviticus 23:10.
23. Best, *Tuhoe*, p. 1063.
24. See Genesis 31:43ff. C.J. Wilson (ed.), *Missionary Life and Work in New Zealand, 1833–1862*, p. 43.
25. T.G. Hammond, Letter to S. Percy Smith, 29 August 1910.
26. Polack, *Manners and Customs*, vol. 1, p. 66, n. 33.
27. Ibid., pp. 24–25, n. 9.
28. Leviticus 20:10.
29. Deuteronomy 6:7–9. Polack, *Manners and Customs*, vol. 1, p. 52, n. 27; vol. 2, p. 145, n. 49.
30. Polack, *Manners and Customs*, vol. 2, pp. 124–29.
31. See Numbers 6:5; Leviticus 21:5.
32. Leviticus 19:28, 21:5.
33. Polack, *Manners and Customs*, vol. 2, p. 42.
34. Genesis 35:22; Numbers 33:9; Samuel 2:15.
35. John Gorst, *The Maori King*, p. 103.
36. See William Morley, *History of Methodism*, p. 68; Henry Williams, Journal, 3 October 1831; Rogers (ed.), *Early Journals*, p. 193.
37. Henry Williams, 3 February 1833. Rogers, *Early Journals*, p. 278.
38. See, for example, Acts 13:45, 50; John 5:16.
39. These cases cited in R.J. Thompson, 'Christian and Jewish Understandings of the Old Testament'; in Hinchcliff, Lewis, Tiwari (eds), *Religious Studies in the Pacific*, p. 76.

7. Rejection and Reformulation

Two broad points have been made and explained so far: firstly, the rejection of European culture, manifested particularly in the rejection of the message of the missionaries; and secondly, the association by Maori of their race as allied with the situation of, and even the descent from, the ancient Israelites — a feeling encouraged by many instances of identification with traditional customs. So there occurred a switch in allegiance, which was in some cases a deliberate and calculated rejection of the Christian Church rather than a gradual persuasion away from one and towards another.

As this occurred there was a wholehearted and enthusiastic acceptance of the Old Testament by a great number of Maori. They took from these scriptures names, ideas and phraseology. The country itself was referred to as Kanana (Canaan) and the people called themselves 'Tiu' or 'Hurai' — both transliterations of the word 'Jew'. As New Zealand was Canaan, then Jehovah was the appropriate and rightful God of the country, and the people of it were therefore his chosen people. Sometimes this meant that the New Testament was merely devalued or not emphasised, but at other times it was rejected completely. John White, Resident Magistrate at Wanganui, wrote to the Colonial Secretary of the Native Department in 1864 that Te Ua Haumene had said the Old Testament may be true, but denounced the New Testament as an entire fallacy.[1]

In several cases Maori identification of themselves as 'Jews' meant that actual members of the Jewish religion living in New Zealand were regarded favourably by them. This was certainly to the distinct advantage

Rejection and Reformulation

of at least one of them, for S.A. Levy probably had his life spared for this reason. Levy kept a store at Opotiki in 1865 when the Pai Marire warriors under the leadership of Patara passed through the district on their way to the East Coast. Patara, who called on Levy and had tea with him, informed the trader that they 'fully intended to take the heads of all ministers, soldiers, and Englishmen' as trophies, to carry back to Taranaki. But, Patara assured Levy, he was not to worry for he would be given written protection guaranteeing his safety. The warrior stated that he was very pleased that Levy was a Jew, 'he being very fond of them, giving, as his reason, that the Jews were once a very grand people, but were now reduced to a very small one through the persecutions they had gone through, the Maoris believing themselves to be undergoing the same.'[2] On this occasion CMS missionary the Rev. C.S. Volkner was killed but Levy was left unharmed as promised.

It is probable that further considerations of nationalism and personal revenge were involved in this matter. After the incident a Maori warden, Wi Maruki of Motiti, reported that when the Pai Marire passed through the Bay of Plenty, Te Tiu Tamihana (Tamihana the Jew) proposed to kill the Catholic priest at Whakatane but then spared him because he was a Frenchman — had he been English he would have died.[3] Because of the recent actions of the British troops, there was much anti-English feeling at the time. In addition, the Rev. T.S. Grace who was also at Opotiki at the time of Volkner's killing was spared, so it seems that the missionary's murder was primarily motivated by revenge for his assumed involvement in earlier incidents resented by Maori. But this does not change the evidence of Maori regard for people of the Jewish faith.

The messenger who brought the message of Volkner's death to the mission station at Turanga (Gisborne) told William Williams:

> *We received our Christianity from you formerly, and now we give it back to you again, having found some better way, by which we may be able to keep possession of our country.*[4]

The same missionary was told by the people of Kokohinau, near Te Teko, that they had given up the way of the Son and had adopted instead the way of the 'Father', meaning that they had renounced Christianity and regarded Jehovah as their spiritual leader.[5]

The 'better way' spoken of by the messenger proved to be through the formation of a series of new religious movements — formed with the purpose of establishing a new theology which related to the thought and situation of the Maori, and to which the people could therefore relate fully.

The Maori Response

Most of these were founded by a prophetic-style leader of the Hebrew tradition, and incorporated aspects of the ancient culture as well as the revival of some practices of the former Maori culture too. While the motivation for the movements was based largely on social need, brought about by the suppression of Maori culture by colonisation and the destruction of the vitality of the people, both physically and spiritually, the response was very much religiously based. The instances of physical acts of rebellion were in response to the alienation of the land, but by far the most widespread reaction was to the alienation of the people from their past beliefs. The response in this area was to be a very long period of adjustment, as Maori sorted out a new system of belief, including both the old and the new teachings.

As Maori movements were a reaction away from the missionary teachings, their emphasis on the Old Testament therefore implied a critique and a rejection of the religion of the missionaries. This does not mean, however, that there was a total repudiation. Most of the various movements were syncretic — keeping aspects of Christianity in differing degrees, with some of the teachings of the missionaries retained because of their appeal or because of parallels with Maori tradition. For instance, the idea of the church itself (that is, the building) was adopted, as was, usually, the pattern for the church service.

While the reaction may have been against the missionaries themselves, this usually did not include a rejection of the Bible. A large part of this book's appeal was due to the fact that it was the means by which Maori learned to read and write — a move which held great appeal to a race with a previous rich heritage as regards spoken tradition, a well-developed mythology, and extensive waiata. In addition to this, the Maori were a naturally religious people, and revered everything in which they recognised any sign of divinity. That it was present in the scriptures they had no doubt, for these spoke of things which were familiar to their own spiritual background and nature.

It should also be clear that the identification of the Maori was with the ancient Israelites, the Hebrews of the Old Testament, and not with the Jewish religion. The view of Christianity was that of nineteenth-century English Christianity as represented by the missionaries and settlers. Problems which arose were not to do with the pure teachings of Christianity (though it has been shown how these were not so familiar, and therefore not thought to be particularly applicable to Maori at the time), but rather with those who practised that religion. So it was not a question of anything like Judaism versus Christianity, with a fight for converts. If a situation of confrontation must be seen it would be, rather, the age-old problem of the dichotomy which often exists between the doctrine of a religion and the followers of the faith, or discrepancies between principles and the way they are put into practice.

As regards the matter of the Jewish religion, none of the Maori religious movements which arose considered themselves Jewish beyond the extent to which they identified with the Old Testament stories. While members of the Jewish religion were favoured and respected, there was no obvious attempt to study the Jewish religion further, and no thought of following its religious traditions apart from the observation of the sabbath on Saturday. Jewish feasts and holy days were not kept as such, and when such concepts as the Passover were referred to, they manifested themselves in a far different form than the original. So Maori took the model of a culture and religion, but without adopting the Judaic religion itself. When they called themselves 'Jews' it was not so much that they had adopted that religion as it was, but it was rather to make the statement that they were not aligning themselves fully with Christianity.

If the Lord had spoken to his people in the past when they were in need, so he would again now — for the Maori were his people. Whereas this idea rose with the belief in genealogical descent, supported by an overwhelming number of religious and cultural parallels, it was wholeheartedly adopted and carried on as a model upon which the Maori fight for self-determination and freedom could be patterned and justified.

And the Lord did speak, and there were many who heard and who arose to lead their people.

Notes

1. John White, Letter, 17 August 1864. *AJHR*, 1864, E-8, 12.
2. William Butler, writing of Levy's account of the incident. W.L. Williams (ed.), *East Coast Records*, p. 91.
3. See *AJHR*, 1867, E-4, 24.
4. William Williams, Journal, 7 March 1865. Cited by Paul Clark, *Hauhau, The Pai Marire Search for Maori Identity*, p. 77.
5. W.L. Williams, *East Coast Records*, p. 80.

Part Three

The New Religions

8. The New Religions

The new religious movements which arose from the 1830s and into the twentieth century are many, ranging from small groups led by a local prophet, to much larger movements which had effect over much of the country. Most had their origin and area of activity in the North Island, and certain areas stand out as being particularly represented — Northland, Gisborne–northern Hawke's Bay, Taranaki, Waikato, and the Bay of Plenty. Two factors are relevant to this: firstly, these were the areas in which mission stations were first set up and where they were always strongest; secondly, they also correspond to those regions which suffered most from the alienation of land either through sale or confiscation.

In some cases the movements were religious responses which were very short-lived, perhaps surviving for a matter of weeks only. Others were influential for a period of a few years, but others are still in existence after more than, or close to, a century. How many of them there have been will never be known, for some have passed away leaving no written record by which they might be remembered. Of others, very little is known — sometimes no more than a brief mention in a missionary journal. In some of these cases it might indeed be preferable had they been in the former group, for often the references are brief, biased and ill-informed. Fewer have been the subject of specific study. While the total number can now be no more than conjecture, references to at least 70 still remain.

A number of these religious responses are examined in the following chapters, to show to what extent each one identified with the Hebraic

The New Religions

system. It is not the purpose of this work to give a full history and account of each of them, but enough general background is given in order to place each of the movements within the wider area of the development of the religious movements, particularly concentrating on how the Maori–Hebrew identification manifested itself in each case.

9. Papahurihia, or Karakia Nakahi
Prophet: Te Atua Wera

The prophet Te Atua Wera — or Papahurihia, as he was first known — is usually regarded as the first of the prophets of the post-contact religious movements, though other movements of adjustment between the two cultures did occur in earlier years. A chief of the Bay of Islands area, Te Atua Wera began his mission around 1833 and it was influential amongst the Hikutu and surrounding peoples over a long period, for although the prophet died in 1875, revivals of the movement arose from time to time.

The name Papahurihia was translated by Henry Williams as 'One who relates wonders';[1] another name was Penetana.[2] Little else is known about the prophet himself, other than he was a chief of Nga Puhi, and was educated at the Rangihoua mission school (CMS) conducted by the missionary John King.[3] He took the name Te Atua Wera — the 'Hot God', 'Burnt God', or 'Fiery God'[4] — and became the foremost religious tohunga of the northern area, acting as adviser to chief Hone Heke in his battles, and gaining a great reputation as a seer.

The Papahurihia movement arose at the beginning of the period in which the Christian gospel started to be accepted by Maori, and was obviously a reaction to it. Te Atua Wera claimed to be inspired through a vision of a spirit called Te Nakahi — a divinity given to Maori by missionaries through the translated scriptures. Nakahi was the Maori form of the serpent of the biblical story of Eden — translated from the Hebrew 'Nahash'. The common Christian interpretation of the serpent is to view it as a snake, a creature unknown to Maori, but its nearest local

The New Religions

equivalent, ngarara, the lizard, already held some awesome significance as it was associated with death. (Taniwha were usually described as great reptiles also.)

As well as the mention of the serpent in Genesis 3, a further reference to Nakahi occurred in the Christian scriptures, in the verse:

And as Moses lifted up the serpent in the wilderness,
even so must the Son of Man be lifted up:
That whosoever believeth in him should not perish,
but have eternal life.[5]

This refers to an act of Moses as related in Numbers 21:8–9 which was not then available to Maori in that language, though the background to it was very likely explained by missionaries. Whether the original reference was fully understood or not, the verse obviously held great significance in the new religion, for it contained the idea of a serpent as protector and healer of the people, and combined it with the appealing promise of no death for believers. This was taken literally by Te Atua Wera.

With the notion of an Atua who was a great leader and protector, the prophet assured his people of immunity from bullets in battle, and in addition gave the promise that their own bullets would hit the mark. In 1845, on the occasion of Heke's war, the prophet was believed to have turned the soldiers' shot and rockets from their course, and kept the people from harm by his miraculous powers.[6] While this idea could have had its background in the instances of protection given by Yahweh to the original 'Chosen People' during their trek to the promised land, so too could it be identified with the protective chants used by tohunga in traditional Maori warfare.

Te Atua Wera also claimed to possess the power to raise the dead — an idea which would appear to derive its inspiration from the Christian scriptures rather than from the older texts or from Maori tradition. In 1843 when a comet was seen in the sky, it was reported that the prophet claimed to have it under his control.[7] Such a notion could be related to biblical inspiration or tradition, for the belief in such a heavenly phenomenon as being religiously portentous is a concept common to all religious systems. Other reported instances of 'miraculous' happenings can be attributed to traditional beliefs and practices of tohunga, though comparisons can often be made with biblical incidents.

Te Nakahi revealed itself through the entranced Te Atua Wera by whistled messages — the traditional way in which atua spoke to humans, being heard as a half whistle, half whisper.[8] The teachings of Papahurihia came from this atua. The object of worship was to be Te Nakahi, and Te Atua Wera was its prophet, being endowed by it with great powers. So the prophet was believed to be able to transport himself from place to place through the air, instantly, and even over great distances. He could call up the spirits of the dead and arrange dialogues between them and the living. It was said he could make himself invisible,[9] and the instance was told of how Heke, going against advice given to him by the prophet, was wounded in battle at Te Ahuahu, and escaped only because Te Atua Wera and others were able to carry him out — all having been rendered invisible through the power of Te Nakahi.[10]

The Papahurihia persuasion was one of many adjustment movements of the early contact period, by which Maori attempted to relate the new teachings to traditional beliefs. It is, therefore, a synthesis of old and new, and includes an element of resentment of the alien culture, seen in its rejection of the missionaries. The Rev. Thomas Buddle recorded the translation of a song which was sung by Papahurihia followers after the assault on Ohaeawai Pa by the British troops, which includes the lines:

You had better stayed at home in Europe
...
He has driven you back to your God.
You may cast your book behind,
And leave your religion on the ground.[11]

But while the missionaries were bypassed, the teachings of the new religion were not thrown out entirely. Charles Baker heard from Papahurihia members in 1833 that the Bible was true, but that the missionaries gave a wrong interpretation of it and thereby corrupted the word of God.[12] Services and baptisms continued to be held, based on the Christian models.

The former belief in an afterlife was extended to include the notion of a heaven and hell, dependent upon judgement and division into good or wicked souls. Heaven was a Christian-inspired paradise — 'You feel there neither the rigours of cold, nor of hunger or thirst; you enjoy unending light' — with the addition of material considerations of appeal to Maori at the time, as it was promised 'Everything is found in plenty, flour, sugar, guns, ships; there too murder and sensual pleasure reign.'[13]

Heaven was closed to missionaries — the alternative, the fiery hell of Satan, being the final abode of such heretics and all those who spoke ill of Te Nakahi. This was a Christian idea, missionaries having given Maori stern warnings that believers in the Christian God would be saved while others were doomed for their unbelief. It was a natural consequence that

The New Religions

the doctrine should be used against those who introduced it, and that the new movement should include the same judgement upon the detractors of Te Nakahi.

So while the Papahurihia movement included some aspects of Christian teachings, it also implied a rejection of the Christian mission. The Rev. Richard Taylor, writing in 1868, stated that at its basis was the conclusion of Te Atua Wera that as 'the Jewish Church preceded the Christian, it must be the mother Church', and therefore 'all who were opposed to the Gospel' immediately followed Papahurihia.[14]

Te Nakahi was not viewed in the same way as the Christian image of God, but was seen as a traditional atua. Even from the standpoint of the new scriptures, this atua must be seen as in opposition to the God of Christianity. If considered the serpent of the Eden story, it persuades the allegiance of the people away from the newly established order. If it is the brass serpent of Mosaic time, it protects its own people against the bites of the 'fiery serpents' which had been sent among the people by the Lord for their sin.[15]

The missionaries themselves saw the movement as opposed to their gospel. Henry Williams said it had sprung up 'in opposition to our instruction' from some who were, after being educated at the missions, 'two-fold more the child of the Devil than they were before', and that the prophet and his party were 'opponents to the Government'.[16] In 1842 the Rev. Thomas Chapman wrote to the CMS that 'the opposers of the truth' were now 'from the very spirit of opposition' being more amenable to the teachings of the Catholic Church because of its less dogmatic stand on some issues.[17]

On the other hand, the missionaries clearly saw the 'Jewish' aspects of the Karakia Nakahi. The Wesleyan missionary William Woon recorded that while the people did not appear very desirous for a missionary to reside among them, members of the movement were called Hurai (Jews) by others as they had imbibed 'Jewish sentiments'.[18] In line with this was the teaching that the Sunday sabbath of the missionaries should be abolished and that Saturdays were to be kept as sacred.

The missionaries' response to Te Atua Wera was sceptical, to say the least, and they referred to his powers as sorcery, ventriloquism and mere sleight of hand. Such tricks, they declared, he had learned from a 'juggling Jew'. This is an interesting accusation, but it does not appear to have any basis in verifiable fact. Joel Samuel Polack, the Jewish trader who lived in Kororareka in the early part of the decade, left the area for a period which he spent in Sydney. He visited Hokianga in 1837 before returning to England. Reporting his experience in New Zealand to the Lords' Committee in London in 1838, he referred to the good work of the Wesleyan mission at Hokianga, but said it was hampered by 'a crusade' continuing among Maori — this being 'a new religion which has sprung up, called Papahurihia'. Polack reported, 'they have made their Sunday on the Saturday, and work on the Sunday.' He also repeated the common rumour that 'the captain of a ship first introduced it', but added his opinion that 'it is impossible to believe it'.[19] Mr Ormond Wilson notes that the prophet's teaching about the sabbath was known two years before he was reported to have any dealings with Jews.[20] In this case, then, the knowledge of the change of the sabbath from the seventh to the first day of the week must have been explained to Maori by missionaries.

Similarly, it was claimed that Te Atua Wera's 'ventriloquism' had been learned from a sailor from a European boat — but this is no doubt an attempt by missionaries to deny the traditional skills of the tohunga. The prophet's lineage was impeccable in this respect — he being the son of a famous tohunga father and a renowned sorceress mother, and was himself married to a descendant of a spirit people.[21] There appears to be no doubt that Te Atua Wera possessed powers which embarrassed the missionaries. John White in 1861 told of how the prophet one night 'saw' two canoes in trouble in a storm and through the agency of Te Nakahi intervened to save a friend who was drowning. The next morning the boat of the friend arrived ashore and he affirmed that he had indeed been in great danger but had been miraculously saved.[22] Europeans, however, preferred to see the prophet as a mere opportunist — using his skills for the purpose of gaining wealth from his people, through his 'pretended conversations with the spirits of the dead'.[23]

Te Atua Wera's Te Nakahi movement came into being less than twenty years after the gospel was first preached to Maori. The intervening years had been marked by very slow progress as regards converts, and the period in which the movement arose was also that of the first real breakthrough as regards conversion. That this opposing message of Te Atua Wera came at this early period shows that the preceding two decades had not been static ones as regards missionary impact on Maori, but perhaps that the influence had been too great.

The movement began as a reaction to the missions — Christian concepts were used against the missionaries, and the aspects of the new religion which were adopted were those that had some parallel in tradition. With the growing feeling of alienation from their own roots felt by Maori from around 1840 onwards, the Karakia Nakahi manifested itself

The New Religions

more and more as a revivalist movement with the purpose of revitalising the mana of the Maori.

Following the death of the prophet on 3 November 1875, the Resident Magistrate at Hokianga reported that he was perhaps the greatest tohunga of modern times known in New Zealand, and that 'for the last twelve years of his life he acted as Warden of Police, and was a useful officer', being highly respected by Pakeha of the district.[24]

Revivals of the movement sprang up many times in the northern region as periods of dissatisfaction occurred. In the late 1890s the people of Waima and Omanaia areas of Hokianga, in reaction to government legislation and land policies, and the Hokianga Dog Tax (1898), actively opposed the law for a short period, invoking the spirit of Te Atua Wera and others. Known then as the 'Blackout Movement' for its spiritualist-type meetings held in darkness, it was motivated by anti-European feelings, and involved a return to traditional practices.[25] In 1896 the Inspector of Native Schools included in his annual report mention of a 'spiritualist' or 'spiritist' craze rife in the Hokianga district. The report mentions only 'table-rapping' but the concern of the inspector was that it was enough to keep numbers of children from attending school. Subsequent reports show that this 'craze' continued for several years, and it was not until 1900 that the 'long alienation from school' gave way to an increase in interest.[26] Revivals have occurred even more recently, with meetings said to have been held around 1930[27] and even in the 1950s in some northern areas.[28]

Notes

1. Henry Williams, Letter to CMS 17 June 1834. Jean Irvine, though, translates it as 'The earth turned over', saying this refers to 'the name in mythology of Papa when after being separated from her husband Rangi, she grieved so much for him that her offspring turned her over so she might no longer see him. This is the Polynesian version of the Fall, a fall not of man alone but of all nature of which we are part. It means the divorce of the spiritual from the material which were once joined . . .' Jean Irvine, 'Maori Mysticism in the North', Peter Davis, John Hinchcliffe (eds), *Dialogue on Religion, New Zealand Viewpoints*, p. 9.
2. See Irvine, 'Maori Mysticism', p. 9, and the report of the prophet's death made by S. von Sturmer, R.M., *AJHR*, 1876, G-1, 19.
3. Judith Binney, 'Papahurihia: Some Thoughts on Interpretation', *JPS* vol. 75, no. 4, p. 322.
4. The name has also been translated as 'Red God', but this is presumably due to confusion of 'wera' and 'whero'.
5. John 3:14–15, which was available to Maori from 1830.

6. F.E. Maning, *Old New Zealand*, pp. 233, 237–38.
7. William Woon, Journal, 18 March 1843.
8. On this subject, see Samuel Marsden, Third New Zealand Journal, 18 August 1820. Elder (ed.), *Letters and Journals*, p. 286 and footnote p. 287.
9. W.E. Gudgeon, 'The Tohunga Maori', *JPS* vol. 16, no. 62, pp. 74–75.
10. Maning, *Old New Zealand*, p. 256. See too Gudgeon, 'Tohunga Maori', p. 75; C.J. Parr, 'Before the Pai Marire', *JPS* vol. 76, no. 1, p. 44.
11. Thomas Buddle, *The Aborigines of New Zealand*, p. 23.
12. Charles Baker, Journal, 3 November 1833.
13. From the MS of Father Louis Servant. Cited by Ormond Wilson, 'Papahurihia, First Maori Prophet', *JPS* vol. 74, no. 4, p. 479.
14. Richard Taylor, *Past and Present*, p. 41.
15. Numbers 21:6–7.
16. Henry Williams, Journal, 15 December 1833 (see too entry for 12 January 1834); Rogers (ed.), *Early Journals*, p. 354; Letter to CMS, 17 June 1834; Letter to CMS, 18 January 1847.
17. Thomas Chapman, Letter to CMS, 19 February 1842.
18. William Woon, Letter to the Rev. J. Beecham, 17 August 1836, citing journal 16 May 1836.
19. Ward, *Information Relative to New Zealand*, p. 91.
20. Ormond Wilson, Letter to ATL, 5 June 1965.
21. Gudgeon, 'Tohunga Maori', p. 74.
22. John White, 'Lectures on Maori Customs and Superstitions', *AJHR* 1861, E-7, 19.
23. James Busby, MS, 'The Occupation of New Zealand 1833–1845', p. 32.
24. S. von Sturmer to the Under-Secretary Native Department, 11 May 1876. *AJHR* 1876, G-1, 19.
25. P.W. Hohepa, *A Maori Community in Northland*, pp. 27–29.
26. *AJHR* 1896, E-2, 11; 1897, E-2, 4; 1898, E-2, 5; 1900, E-2, 6.
27. W.J. Phillipps, Letter 'The Cult of Nakahi', *JPS* vol. 75, no. 1, p. 107.
28. G. Blake Palmer, 'Tohungaism and Makutu, Some Beliefs and Practices of the Present Day Maori', *JPS* vol. 63, no. 2, p. 154.

10. Other Early Movements

Between the 1830s and the 1860s, no large or long-lasting movements arose other than Papahurihia, but it was a period marked by many small and localised responses — linked by their rejection of the religion of the missionaries, to greater or lesser extent.

In 1845–46 another movement enjoyed an enthusiastic, though short-lived, existence in the Warea-Haurangi district of Taranaki. It was mentioned by the Rev. Richard Taylor and others[1] and was known to Maori as Tikanga Hou — a term which has the meanings of the 'New Truth', or the 'New Way'. In this respect it acknowledged that it took much from the gospel, and yet it also rejected some parts of Christian teachings. As such it was yet another attempt to syncretise the traditional and the introduced beliefs into a relevant system.

The people involved, reported Taylor, began by giving up prayer, the observation of the sabbath, and the reading of the scriptures. Though they kept to belief in the Christian godhead, they also became convinced that each aspect of the Trinity had become manifest in a member of their own congregation. A man called Hakopanikau claimed to be the Christ, another one God the Father, and a third the Holy Spirit. The angel Michael and the apostle Paul were also living in the persons of two more of their number. While they still used the Lord's Prayer when rowing their canoes, and made much use of the word Amine (Amen) apparently as a sort of charm, they threw away prayer books and scriptures as unnecessary, and no longer prayed. It was thought there was no longer any need of such practices now that God actually resided among them. Consequently they knelt to the manifestation in their midst.[2]

Other Early Movements

The Rev. H.H. Turton, on a visit to Warea in October 1845, found that the people had 'dreamt dreams, seen visions, and received revelations from the Spirit — that they had personal converse with God, seeing him with their mortal eyes'. Christ, now returned in the form of Hakopa, was to be worshipped by all nations.[3]

The teachings of the new movement were that there was no Bible, no sin, no sabbath, no hell, no Devil, neither a day of judgement nor a future state. It is clear that the Maori were rejecting the doctrines of the Christian Church which had been brought by the missionaries, and which were alien concepts to them. Those who had brought the new ideas were condemned as false prophets who spoke 'lies in hypocrisy', while the people of Warea were, in contrast, angels.

The members of the movement received their revelations directly — going regularly into the bush for this purpose — and paid full allegiance to Hakopa (Jacob) as the returned Messiah. A letter was sent to Captain FitzRoy advising him that it would be appropriate to move the capital and government to Warea, since Christ had set up his earthly home at that place. A Maori teacher who visited the settlements and reported back to Taylor brought back a basketful of their discarded books, and said that Hakopa had prophesied that as Moses struck the Red Sea with his staff and a dry road opened to him and Israel, so too would he strike the sea and cause a dry road, by which he and his followers would go to England.[4]

As the people of Warea had rejected the foreign teachings, so too their concept of the Christ reflected their traditional notions of a spiritual leader. The people in this period wanted a prophet to be a strong leader, a deliverer, and a provider for his people. The Messiah, in this case, took on the aspects of an Old Testament prophet — while he was called by the name of Jesus Christ, his image was, rather, that of Moses of the older scriptures.

The missionaries, who were unable to sway the members of the movement by their arguments, found they had to wait only about three months for their flock to return to orthodoxy — a move which was caused by a follower demonstrating that 'sin' was indeed a reality requiring some reaction from the leaders.

Within a few years further claims of the Advent were made — this time the chosen area being Tauranga, Bay of Plenty. The missionary Alfred Nisbit Brown found the period around 1849 was one marked by much prophetic activity. In February of that year he noted in his journal that the residents of the village of Matarawa[5] were in a great state of excitement 'in consequence of a woman having declared to them that our

Saviour was about to descend from the clouds at their village.'[6] The 'Matarawa delusion', as it was referred to by the missionary, apparently died out in only a few days as the promised appearance did not take place, and Brown took the opportunity to preach to the people on false prophets and spirits.[7]

Two months later the missionary noted in his diary that he hoped his workers would not be led astray again by pretended visions and signs from heaven[8] but did not appear to appreciate the depth of feeling behind the incident. The villagers attributed the non-appearance of the Saviour to the unbelief of the missionary, showing quite clearly that their belief in the message of the mission was greater than their trust in and respect for the messengers and the society they represented. Some weeks later Brown's worker at Matarawa begged the missionary for a prayer book, pleading, 'It is with my heart as with your garden. If you had no spade the weeds would cover the ground. So also if I am kept without a book, sin will flourish in my heart till it is choked.'[9]

The dissatisfaction continued, for in September that year the same people were 'again led captive by Satan, or rather have become, I fear, his willing captives.' This time the prophecies were voiced by Te Witu, judged by Brown as 'a boy so ignorant that I have been obliged to refuse him baptism'. The new prophet convinced many of his tribe, including two teachers and several communicants. Te Witu told the people that while some parts of the scriptures were the words of God, much of it was merely manmade. Brown does not record which parts were accepted by Te Witu, but does say the boy claimed to have received 'a revelation from our Saviour that a fire will descend from Heaven on Friday next and destroy their pa as well as our Settlement and the houses of the Natives who disbelieve his prophecy.'[10]

More prophecies followed, including one that a woman called Caroline would be taken up to heaven without dying, and that five members of the tribe who had died recently would soon be resurrected. Even after the day predicted for the descent of the heavenly fire had passed without fulfilment of the prophecy, many of the people of Matarawa continued to follow the words of Te Witu.

It is notable that now, as the Christ had failed to return according to the revelation of the prophetess some months before, the new instructions took on more of the flavour of the Old Testament. Te Witu persuaded many people not to plant their seed potatoes, for God would feed them miraculously. The plantations of the disbelievers would be destroyed by a whirlwind, and heavenly fire would now come to dry up all the streams so that those who did not believe would die of thirst. Te Witu and his followers, however, would be supplied with gushing fountains of water.[11]

As the month of October progressed the Matarawa residents gradually returned to the mission services, though Mr Brown noted that some still seemed unwilling to acknowledge that there was no truth at all in the visions. Clearly the people were finding the new ways were not suited to their way of thinking.

A number of other movements — including the Wahi Tapu, the Wairuarua, and spiritist responses, and many led by individual 'healer' figures — arose in the 1850s in an effort to combat the diseases which took disastrous toll of Maori communities in this period of exposure to European settlers. These were primarily attempts to combine the new Christian teachings with Maori tradition for a specific purpose — protection from the introduced diseases. All of these movements were small and localised, lasting for as long as the need for them existed.[12]

Being still in the early period, none of these identifies primarily with the Hebrew culture and situation, though Te Witu's assurance of manna-like provisions from heaven and the water which would gush forth for the believers, as well as the destruction of the enemies by the elements, are more than merely reminiscent of the exodus of the Israelites from captivity.

Together, though, they reveal much about Maori feeling of the time. Firstly, they make the point that the people were now being profoundly affected by the Christian missions. Secondly, the responses show growing dissatisfaction with those missions, with Maori often feeling that they themselves possessed a more superior grasp of true religion than did those who would be their teachers. Thirdly, the pattern of the prophets shows how the reaction developed with the aid of charismatic leaders who arose to give voice to that dissatisfaction with the formation of a continuing movement of protest based on the idea of divine aid and justice. It was a pattern directly relatable to that of Old Testament times with the people given spiritual leadership by prophets.

Another tantalising account of a further Maori response to the culture and religion of the Europeans in the mid-1850s is given by the Rev. Richard Davis, who tells of a 'deception' among the people of the Mangakahia area of Northland. In brief, someone was said to have been distributing drawings of a 'flying dragon' among the local people, 'a look at which would preserve people from the fatal disease with which the world was to be visited.' The original of this drawing was said to have come from a visiting steamer, but its history beyond that cannot be known. Perhaps it was indeed an image with an occult significance, or maybe it

The New Religions

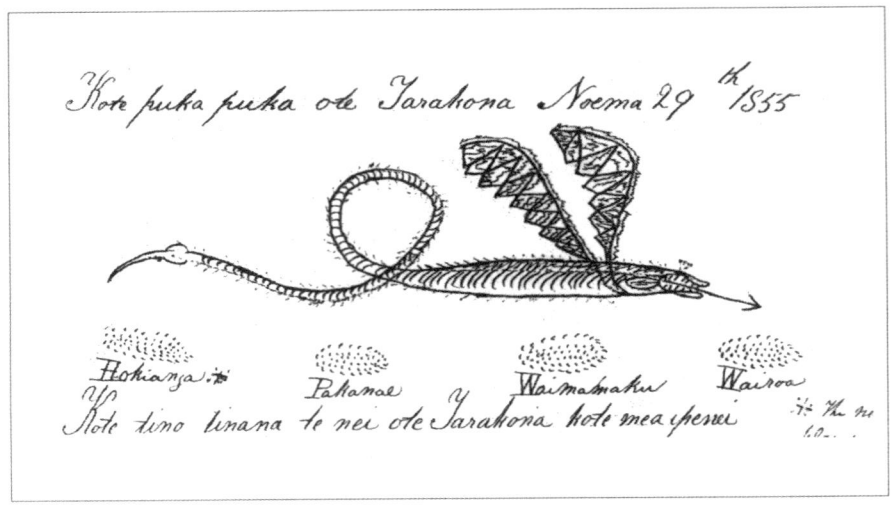

A drawing of the 'Flying Dragon'. Text with the drawing explains that the dragon symbolises evil which is to come to this country — it being the same evil that afflicted the ancient Israelites.
(Webster Collection, C-10624, Alexander Turnbull Library, Wellington)

was no more than the imaginative work of a seaman. Whatever the truth, a man who professed to be both a doctor and a priest was now dispensing medicine, and a picture of the dragon was to be copied and hung in each house as a protection. The name of the man was known to Davis, but unfortunately he did not record it in his account. The healer was also known to communicate with spirits and obtain his remedies from the sea by diving where directed by the spirit.[13]

This example of one of the very many movements of the 1850s which were motivated by the European-brought diseases sweeping through Maori communities in that period, is interesting because of several factors. It gives an example of the stories of doom which abounded at the time — based upon the twin notions that the atua maori had deserted their own people because of their allegiance to a new God and their corresponding neglect of the old ways, and that the European Atua had nevertheless failed to protect and sustain his new followers. It also illustrates the people's desire for some form of supernatural deliverance from the ills which had befallen them, a wish wholly in keeping with former tradition.

But perhaps the most intriguing part of all, from the point of view of this study, is that Richard Davis noted that the picture of the dragon had 'a direct reference to the brazen serpent in the wilderness'.[14] Putting the three points together, the inference must have been clear to Maori that while their problems had been brought about by the Christian missions, their deliverance might lie in the older Hebraic tradition.

The Wairoa district in Hawke's Bay was another area where the phenomenon of the rejection of the missions manifested itself from an early time. William Williams tells how, in October 1840, on the way from Ahuriri (Napier) to the mission station at Turanga (Gisborne), he arrived at Wairoa to find the former believers at that place no longer considered themselves Christians. In fact, recorded Williams, they went by the name of Jews, having come to a determination to have nothing more to do with Christianity. Williams had heard previously of this matter, and learned now that the reasons for it were threefold. A chief told the missionary that some of the people had lost faith because 'they could get nothing by it', others because 'some of their relatives had died', and because they did not believe the missionary's earlier promise that he would send them a teacher if they put up a house ready for the mission worker.[15]

In this case the reasons show that the dissatisfaction with the new system was based more on cultural factors than theological ones. The people felt that the religion had not lived up to the promises it had at first appeared to give — the European Atuanui had not showered material blessings upon the new believers and had failed to protect them from death as they had inferred from the scriptures. In addition, or perhaps as a consequence, the mission itself was not trusted fully enough to keep its word and send a teacher.

This response was apparently fairly widespread in the area, for Williams on another journey the following month found several more villages where the inhabitants, disillusioned with Christianity, called themselves Jews or unbelievers.[16] In one instance Williams says the cause was 'the misconduct of a baptized native from Hokianga' who had been living in the area. While it is possible that the influence could have come from a follower of Te Atua Wera, there is no reason to suppose that this was so, for Williams, who would have been familiar with that movement, makes no reference to it in connection with this matter. It could, more simply, be attributable to a bad example set by a professed Christian, or merely tales told against the missions in the northern area by someone with a grudge.

During these early years other missionaries also reported instances of Maori villages where the residents regarded themselves as Jews — using the terms 'Tiu' or 'Hurai'. In May 1844 in the Taranaki area, the Rev. Richard Taylor noted that two Hikurangi families were holding out against the mission teaching, calling themselves Jews and singing their own songs each evening 'in imitation of the believers'.[17]

The New Religions

It is certain that in such cases the claim to be Jews did not mean that the people had come under the influence of members of that religion and had converted to those beliefs — few of them would have had the opportunity. Their profession of Jewishness was, rather, merely indicative of their rejection of the Christian mission — they were unbelievers who chose not to adopt the new teachings.

Notes

1. Richard Taylor, Journal, 18 December 1845, 24 January 1846.
2. Taylor, *Past and Present*, pp. 41–42.
3. H.H. Turton, Letter to WMS, 30 May 1846. Cited by Parr, 'Before the Pai Marire', p. 41.
4. Taylor, Journal, 24 January 1846.
5. That area near the Waikareao estuary of the Tauranga Harbour now known as Judea.
6. A.N. Brown, Journal, 12 February 1849.
7. 1 John 4:1. Brown, Journal, 13, 16 February 1849.
8. Brown, Journal, 26 April 1849.
9. Brown, Journal, 7 June 1849.
10. Brown, Journal, 29 September 1849.
11. Brown, Journal, 6 October 1849.
12. Fuller details of these movements and others mentioned in this chapter can be found in Elsmore, *Mana From Heaven: A Century of Maori Prophets in New Zealand*.
13. John Noble Coleman, *A Memoir of the Rev. Richard Davis For Thirty-Nine Years a Missionary in New Zealand*, pp. 380–81.
14. See Numbers 21:6–9.
15. William Williams, Journal, 20–21 October 1840.
16. William Williams, Journal, 21, 23, 24 November 1840.
17. Taylor, Journal, 24 May 1844.

11. Pai Marire
Prophet: Te Ua Haumene

Te Ua Haumene was a prophet who arose in Taranaki in the early 1860s — a time when Maori grievances were approaching their peak owing to disenchantment with European rule, dissatisfaction over land alienation, and despair following their rapidly declining numbers.

Prior to his prophetic revelation, Te Ua had studied scripture under the missionaries — firstly at Hokianga, where he had been taken as a slave when a child, and later in his home area of Taranaki to where he returned.[1] Upon his baptism by Wesleyan missionary the Rev. John Whiteley, he was given the name Horopapera from the biblical name Zerubabbel (literally 'Shoot of Babylon'). The original Zerubabbel was appointed Governor of the colony of Jews allowed by Cyrus to return from captivity in Babylonia to their land, and the task he undertook was the rebuilding of the temple in Jerusalem in the sixth century BCE.[2] It was a somewhat appropriate name for a man who also attempted to raise a new structure on the ruins of the old.

In 1862, following a domestic dispute in which Te Ua was bound with ropes by a tribesman with a grudge against him, the angel Gabriel appeared to him and gave him the power to burst his bonds. Te Ua himself attested that the angels Gabriel and Michael, with an innumerable host of ministering spirits, had appeared in the area.[3] This happening was repeated, and soon afterwards in an Abraham-like incident a voice from heaven commanded Te Ua to kill his son. There are several accounts of this event, differing a little in the details, but the basic story is that Te Ua went to comply and broke the boy's leg in several places (or cut off a hand

The New Religions

and foot with an axe) before he was stopped by a further command. Gabriel then instructed the man to wash his son in water, whereupon the boy was instantly and completely made whole.[4]

In the early period after his visions, Te Ua's family regarded him as a madman and kept a watch on him, but his teachings at this time were very much along the orthodox Christian lines of love and peace. In early 1863 he urged his new followers to:

> *Return and go home in peace, for the Lord has spoken to me twice and urged that his people, his forsaken . . . flock, return as did Abraham of Israel.*[5]

A new movement arose around the prophet. Te Ua's instructions to his people were to be 'good and peaceful' — hence the name Pai Marire. He was instrumental in preventing skirmishes on several occasions, and published circular letters urging Maori and Pakeha to live together in peace. Speaking of the appearance of Gabriel in 1862, Te Ua later attested:

> *It was the day . . . of returning to the house of Shem. For the oppressing yoke had been flung off. The message of Gabriel was that I should reject the heavy yoke of the flints of the rifles, that you might be glorified by God, that you might stand here on the roof of clouds.*[6]

The message of Te Ua's Pai Marire mission spread rapidly in the Taranaki, Waikato and Bay of Plenty districts, then to the East Coast and Poverty Bay. Letters expressing the love and goodwill of a number of chiefs to government officials included the blessing 'Pai Marire'.[7]

The tensions between the two races, though, were running high, and as troubles over the land question escalated, the prophet found it more and more difficult to reconcile Christian teachings to the plight of the Maori people. In the much publicised incidents involving Captain Lloyd in Taranaki, and the Rev. Carl Volkner at Opotiki, blood was shed at the instigation of Te Ua's disciples Hepanaia, Patara, Raukatauri, and Kereopa Te Rau. Such men became the effective leaders of the movement while Te Ua, described as 'of a mild and inoffensive disposition', appears to have become more of a figurehead leader.

After the killing of Captain Lloyd, his head was used ritually for a ceremonial drinking of blood, then it was buried. A few days later, the angel Gabriel appeared to those who had taken part in the ceremony and the spirit of Captain Lloyd ordered them to disinter the head, cure it, then take it right around the country. On the carrying out of the first instruction, the head appointed Te Ua to be the high priest, and gave him the tenets of the new religion. From this time on, the head became the medium of communication with Jehovah, and Te Ua was regarded as an infallible prophet.[8]

While Te Ua saw himself as a new Abraham or Moses, his followers called themselves Tiu, or Jews. They identified themselves as the Chosen People of God, with New Zealand being the new Canaan. The end of the world would come about with the expulsion of the last European, after which the dead would rise again in an atmosphere of peace and Te Ua would appear in the guise of Moses. The deaf would hear, the blind would see, the lame would walk, and every species of disease would disappear.[9]

There is much evidence to show that Te Ua Haumene identified himself and his people with the ancient Hebrews. On 30 May 1864 he wrote a letter signing himself 'Te Ua Jew Te Ua'.[10] His writings contain copious scriptural references, as seen in his allusions to New Zealand as Canaan, and in such instructions to his followers as:

Remember the sayings of the past — seek you the salvation of Israel and live in peace.

and:

Remember the saying — your word is a lamp unto my feet and a light unto my pathway.[11]

John White, Resident Magistrate at Wanganui, reported in 1864 that Te Ua regarded the religion of England, as taught by the scriptures, as false, later quoting the prophet as stating that the Old Testament may be true, but that the New Testament was an entire fallacy.[12] The following year William Williams wrote that Pai Marire members on the East Coast recognised only the Pentateuch, the Psalms and the Revelation of John as the word of God.[13] While Revelation was said to be the favourite text of Te Ua, it can be noted that this book is apocalyptic writing in the Judaic tradition, with the content being strongly in the millennial tradition.

The chiefs of Opotiki wrote to the government on 6 March 1865, following the death of Volkner, stating that the missionary was killed according to the laws of the New Canaan, and condemning the Church because of the deception it had practised upon the New Zealanders. While the Church had said its gospel was sent by God, the people were now clear that it was really sent by the 'knowing society of the Church of England'. In addition, the atrocities perpetrated by government troops in shooting women at Rangiriri and Rangiaowhia (Rangiaohia) were further specific reasons for the rejection of the faith and culture of the Europeans and the setting up of a new religious and social system.[14] A Pai Marire letter circulated to the chiefs of New Zealand referred to the angel Gabriel as 'the sword of Samson and Gideon; the sword by which the Philistines and the Midianites were overpowered' — a weapon given to the Maori by the Lord of Hosts. The letter also referred to an assurance from God that they were his people.[15]

The Pai Marire identified with the Israelites as follows: they were descended from the sons of Shem, and the Pakeha from the sons of Japheth,[16] so the God of the sons of Japheth was Jesus, while that of the sons of Shem was Jehovah.[17] God had chosen the Maori as his special people and so the intruders must be driven out. John White, Wanganui Resident Magistrate, reported to the government that Te Ua was promising that should all Maori believe in his message, then New Zealand would be rid of Europeans. Members of every Christian denomination, reported White, had given up their Christian names and reverted to their old Maori names.[18]

The victory was not to be brought about by Maori themselves — and Pai Marire supporters were urged not to fight, though this command was not heeded. Rather, the action would be divine — the angel of the Lord would be the agent of destruction, and Maori living near military posts were advised to move away for fear they would be destroyed together with Europeans. Some accounts said that 'Auckland will be burned by the fire of the angel', and others promised that Gabriel would drive the Pakeha into the sea.[19] Such ideas of divine retribution were very much of Hebraic patterning, with the notion of Pakeha being driven into the sea particularly striking in its analogy to the destruction of the Egyptians in the waters of the Red Sea by the hand of Yahweh.

But while Europeans were to be driven from the country, a certain few found themselves amongst the 'chosen' also. Writing to Mr Nathan, a Jew of Wanganui, Te Ua assured him:

> *Great is my love for you. Hearken I am the Jew; I am the Hau Marire standing on the half of Canaan which has ascended up out of the darkness and peace. . . . Enough from Te Ua a peaceable Jew.*[20]

At the Opotiki incident of 1865 in which the missionaries Volkner and Grace were captured, two Jewish merchants — brothers by the name of Levy — were allowed to go free because of their faith. As the Pai Marire regarded themselves as Jews, so the Levy brothers were of their kin.[21] Also on this occasion, the disciple Kereopa is reported to have said:

> *Hear, O Israel, this is the word of the God of Abraham, Isaac and Jacob. We are the Jews who were lost and have been persecuted.*[22]

At the beginning of Te Ua's mission, the angel Gabriel instructed him in the building of a niu — a tall pole with yard-arms like a mast, and with trailing ropes rather reminiscent of those from a maypole. This had its traditional antecedent in the small niu, divinatory rods, which were used in communicating with the atua by divination. To Europeans, however, it was thought to be symbolic of Christianity — with its yard-arms it was considered to be not unlike a cross or a steeple of a church, and it was said that the niu symbolised the crucifixion of Maori at the hands of Pakeha.[23]

But if the niu must be regarded as having some religious significance in addition to that of Maori tradition, then, bearing in mind the rest of the movement's doctrine, it would be more likely that the model would be taken from the Old Testament, in which case the examples of the rod of God held by Moses, or the pole entwined by the brazen serpent, could be considered again.

According to Te Ua, the angels (anahera hau) came to the people on the winds of heaven — their means of descent and ascent being the ropes trailing from the yard-arms of the niu. So the niu was a means of communication from Jehovah to people — just as the earlier niu had the same purpose of aiding communication with the transcendant. Gabriel had also said that the niu would enable the believers to speak the language of all the races on earth — perhaps a reference to Genesis 11:1, 'And the whole earth was of one language and of one speech.'

In their ceremonies the Pai Marire chanted in languages they believed to be English, German, French and Hebrew, though:

> *'Scotch' and Hebrew were the most important for they likened their own trouble with the pakehas over land to the captivity of the Israelites and their escape to the wilderness and to the Scottish fight to keep independence of England.*[24]

European opinion of the Pai Marire gift of 'tongues', however, was that it was gibberish.[25]

Study of the *Ua Rongopai* of Te Ua shows that the teachings of the prophet are a synthesis of New and Old Testament ideas, together with teachings inspired by the perceived situation of the 'forgotten and deserted people'. From the New Testament came the pattern of apostles, the Christian ideal of love and peace between the races, and references to the 'Lord of Peace', the 'God of Peace', and the Holy Spirit. A prayer of Te

The New Religions

Te Ua Haumene, founder of the Pai Marire religion. Note the characteristic gesture of the raised hand.
(5495 1/2, Alexander Turnbull Library, Wellington)

Ua's included in the text, though it begins with the words of Psalm 23, is Christian in its patterning:

The Lord is my shepherd. I shall not wrong that which is right. Forever remain before us in all that we do, and forever bless us in all that which begins and ends according to your laws so that we may love and adore you. O God, bless and keep us who stand before you. Yours is the Glory. Glory be to you. Glory. Glory be to Thee.[26]

But it is also quite clear that while aspects of the religion of the missionaries is retained, there is also rejection of the missionaries themselves, who are thought to be misguided. Such restrictions as applied by the missions are abrogated by Te Ua — for instance, those on card-playing and liquor — and a return to such 'worthwhile' traditional practices as 'the quiet waiata and haka, the lullabies, the moko of the chin and lip' is encouraged.

Old Testament warrant is given for the condoning of polygamy, with Abraham and Solomon given as examples. The situation was given as the justifying factor — 'The reason is that Canaan may be peopled in great numbers.' Although in the text the section on this topic is headed 'Rules for Adultery' and it is often believed that this was freely allowed, or even encouraged, in the Pai Marire system, examination of the rules shows that this is not so. Free sexual relations were allowed between men and women, and sleeping together was recognition of the state of marriage, with no ceremony necessary — this being a return to traditional Maori custom. But Rule Two makes it clear that a high price must be paid for adultery:

Tamper not with another man's wife. The sword will strike you for should a child be born, the price will be you. Your dwelling place is not sufficient price. You yourself will be the price.

Rule Five tells that this was the cause of 'our destruction during the great flood of Noah'.[27] So while adultery remained forbidden, the new rule was one of polygamy — another example of a rejection of Christian customs in favour of the earlier Hebrew practices, and a return to tradition.

While the Pai Marire movement was led by twelve appointed men designated 'apostles' — these being consecrated to their task on Christmas Day, 1865 — their allegiance was to be to Jehovah. The ceremony included aspects of traditional rites as well as newer additions, and the instructions were couched in biblical terms:

The New Religions

> ... they will select the first fruits of the soil and those of the trees, the well-conditioned creatures that roam and creep upon the land and float in the waters, together with the flesh of man and silver, also from the winged animals, the likeness or photo of the Governor, the honey and stone of the wilderness, and the cloak and the broom [signifying that all this was to be swept away] will be placed by the altar [or niu or sacred pole].[28]

Several of the leaders of the Pai Marire movement were called 'prophets' at various times, because they led a group of adherents in various parts of the country. One such was Tamihana, who called himself Te Tiu (the Jew) and led a party of Tauranga and Waikato men through the Bay of Plenty. Tamihana Te Tiu claimed no Pakeha could approach the Pai Marire niu or god under penalty of death. Prayers were held daily, with God being invoked to cause an accident to befall the horses or men of the government troops so they would not have access to the travelling party. God had promised these believers knowledge of arts, sciences and technology — becoming the Provider figure which was very much a Maori conception of the God of the Old Testament.[29]

Another report of Pai Marire activities said that a party of '80 prophets, and 500 men to support the prophets' was travelling to Hawke's Bay from Waikato.[30]

It is generally considered that the greater significance of Te Ua's movement centred on its Hauhau or political aspect, rather than on the Pai Marire or religious one. Certainly with physical defeat the movement declined — in 1866 Te Ua renounced his earlier visions as delusions, whereupon he and most of his leaders were pardoned by the Governor. But to Maori the religious and secular aspects of life were inseparable, so while a situation of dissatisfaction remained, the religious manifestation could not be more than dormant. It was to be revived in further forms in the following years.

Notes

1. Letter of Hone Te One, R.M., 9 July 1864. *AJHR*, 1865, E-4, 39.
2. See Ezra 1–6.
3. Letter of the Assistant Native Secretary, Taranaki, 8 December 1864. *AJHR*, 1865, E-4, 5.
4. Rawiri Te Kakawaero to Dr Nesbitt, R.M., *AJHR*, 1864, E-8, 8.

5. *Ua Rongopai* (The Gospel of Te Ua), Grey Corrections, p. 27. Cited by Paul Clark, *Hauhau, The Pai Marire Search for Identity*, pp. 122–23.
6. 1 September 1863, in He ohaki no te kingitanga o Potatau Te Wherowhero, o Tawhiao, 1860–70 (Some pronouncements in the time of kings Potatau and Tawhiao concerning the Maori King Movement, 1860–70). Cited by Clark, *Hauhau*, p. 10.
7. See examples in *AJHR*, 1864, E-8, 9.
8. For more details, see Clark, *Hauhau*; and S. Barton Babbage, *Hauhauism*, pp. 27ff.
9. Daniel P. Lyon, 'An Analysis of Three Maori Prophet Movements', I.H. Kawharu (ed.), *Conflict and Compromise*, p. 64.
10. Cited by Clark, *Hauhau*, p. 17.
11. See Psalm 119:105. Te Ua Rongopai. Cited by Clark, *Hauhau*, p. 126.
12. John White, R.M., to Colonial Secretary Native Department, 29 April and 17 August 1864. *AJHR*, 1864, E-8, 10 and 12.
13. William Williams, to CMS, 22 May 1865.
14. *AJHR*, 1865, E-5, 9–10.
15. *AJHR*, 1864, E-8, 7. See too William Williams, *Christianity Among the New Zealanders*, p. 367.
16. Genesis 10.
17. Babbage, *Hauhauism*, pp. 33–34.
18. *AJHR*, 1864, E-8, 11.
19. *AJHR*, 1864, E-8, 7; E-4, 39–40.
20. Cited by Clark, *Hauhau*, p. 17.
21. See William Greenwood, *The Upraised Hand*, pp. 14–16, and Lazarus Morris Goldman, *History of the Jews*, pp. 86–88 for two accounts of this incident. Regarding the evidence of Captain Levy, Clark (*Hauhau*, p. 39) sheds some doubt on his description of the incident, saying it may have been exaggerated. However, the fact remains that Jews were well treated by Maori owing to a belief in their common ancestry.
22. Greenwood, *The Upraised Hand*, p. 15.
23. Lyon, 'Analysis of Three Movements', p. 63.
24. Robin W. Winks, 'The Doctrine of Hauhauism', *JPS* vol. 62, no. 2, p. 230.
25. See, for example, evidence of Lieutenant Herbert Meade, who witnessed a Pai Marire ceremony. Meade's description of the event was first published in the selections from his journals and letters, *A Ride through the disturbed districts of New Zealand*.
26. See translation in Clark, *Hauhau*, p. 121.
27. Clark, *Hauhau*, pp. 121–22.
28. Ibid., pp. 130–31. The bracketed words are explanatory additions by Sir George Grey who acquired the original manuscript in the 1880s.
29. *AJHR*, 1865, E-4, 15–18.
30. *AJHR*, 1865, E-4, 20.

12. Ringatu Prophet: Te Kooti

From a prophecy made by a seer before the birth of Te Kooti, he was given the name Rikirangi (Arikirangi), meaning 'Lord of the Heaven'.[1] This name was not used by Te Kooti himself but was often used by his followers. His full name was Te Kooti Rikirangi Te Turuki. Te Kooti, who was probably born about 1830, was educated at a mission school near his home in the Turanga (Gisborne) area, and apparently became a proficient reader of translations of the Old and New Testaments. It has been claimed that his wish to become a mission teacher was opposed by Bishop William Williams of that area.[2]

During the wars of the 1860s, Te Kooti was employed as an ammunition carrier by Government forces opposing Pai Marire rebels, and in 1865 was arrested on a charge of spying for the enemy. There appears to be no basis in fact for this accusation, and Te Kooti himself insisted that his only contact with the rebels was in attempting to persuade his brother Komene, who fought on the Pai Marire side, to defect and join the Government side. It was a defence he was never able to put to the court, for Te Kooti was condemned without trial and exiled to the penal settlement on the Chatham Islands with other prisoners.

It was here in 1867 that, following a severe illness, Te Kooti went through a series of religious experiences in which he was spoken to by the spirit of God. This marked the beginning of the Ringatu religion. The year after this, Te Kooti escaped with a boatload of his followers and returned to New Zealand where he became feared for his retaliatory campaigns against those who had wronged him. He was hunted by the Government for almost four years before retiring to the King Country.

A sketch of Te Kooti made by J.H. Kerry-Nicholls after a meeting with the prophet. *(31751 1/2, Alexander Turnbull Library, Wellington)*

It is often stated that the Ringatu religion of Te Kooti is an offshoot of, or the successor to, the Pai Marire movement of Te Ua Haumene. Although some of the early members of Te Kooti's party had been Pai Marire supporters, and though the injustice of his arrest could well have turned his allegiance to the other side, the evidence does not point in that direction.

The New Religions

The belief in the similarities between Maori and Hebrew was common to both, but this was a notion which was accepted by far more of the Maori race than were involved in the two movements. The gesture of the upraised hand was used in each, though there was a difference in the significance — in Pai Marire this was a practice invoking protection, while in the Ringatu faith it became a sign of homage to God.[3]

There are, though, similarities in the manner of revelation to the two prophets. As Gabriel appeared to Te Ua, so the Spirit of God spoke to Te Kooti who was gravely physically ill and in great spiritual despair. The first message of the Spirit to Te Kooti was:

Arise, God has sent me to bring you to life to make known his name to his people who are in captivity in this place so that they may know that Jehovah drove them out into this land . . .[4]

Other visions followed, affirming Te Kooti's special mission to his people. In the most dramatic of these he was given two signs — that of a reptile (ngarara),[5] and of fire which did not burn, nor even singe the hand or clothes of the newly appointed prophet. Te Kooti thereafter identified himself with Moses, and saw his mission as the deliverance of his people from foreign oppression.[6]

As the prophets before him had done, Te Kooti fully identified the Maori people with the Children of Israel, and the plight of his people with that of the Hebrews. The spirit of the Lord speaking to the new prophet had assured him of this fact:

Fear not because thy cry hath reached unto God, and God hath heard thy crying, hearken I will strengthen thee and will cause thee to know the things whereof I had spoken unto your forefathers, to Abraham to Isaac to Jacob and all their children down to David . . .[7]

In the services instituted by Te Kooti in the Chatham Islands, the first section of panui (scriptural verses) to be chanted included the verses Jeremiah 31:16–17:

Thus saith the Lord; Refrain thy voice from weeping, and thine eyes from tears: for thy work shall be rewarded, saith the Lord, and they shall come again from the land of the enemy.

And there is hope in thine end, saith the Lord, that thy children shall come again to their own border.

While the verses are especially significant because of the escape from the Chathams, they also clearly show the doctrinal emphasis on the parallel between the Israelites and the Maori exiles. It was an emphasis which was to continue throughout the mission of the prophet. While still a prisoner on the island, Te Kooti used the scriptures of exile — concerning the years of bondage in Egypt and the exodus, the Psalms of David, the story of Jeremiah. Psalm 64 became the exiles' daily devotion.[8] A prayer written by Te Kooti at this time invokes the protection of Jehovah for the deported people:

> *O God, if our hearts arise from the land in which we now dwell as slaves, and repent and pray to Thee and confess our sins in Thy presence, then, O Jehovah, do Thou blot out the sins of Thy own people, who have sinned against Thee. Do not Thou, O God, cause us to be wholly destroyed. Wherefore it is that we glorify Thy Holy Name.*[9]

In the structure and doctrine of the Ringatu Church in its early days, the parallels with the old Hebraic system are striking. That Te Kooti saw himself as an Old Testament-style prophet is undoubted. As already noted, he identified himself with Moses in his task of leading the people. Like Moses, he had apparently considered himself an unlikely candidate for prophethood. As the ancient prophet had protested that he did not have the necessary attributes, so Te Kooti attested after his calling:

> *God then began to strengthen his servant and to prepare my voice and my body and I lost all fear of the great and of all those things that he had spoken to his servant.*[10]

His spiritual designation was marked by a ceremony anointing him with oil. More signs of the power of God were given to Te Kooti and to his people, and knowledge of ancient times additional to that given in the scriptures was revealed to the new prophet.

Te Kooti's escape with his band of followers from their place of exile, over the sea to their native land, was to their mind very much a latter-day flight out of Egypt, with the ship (the *Rifleman*) a veritable ark of deliverance. It is said that the prophet stated when he boarded the boat, 'The day, the vessel, the salvation, are from God'.[11]

Back in the homeland Te Kooti exacted an eye for an eye and a tooth for a tooth from those he felt had wronged him — a response not only in line with Maori tradition, but also, it seemed, ratified by scripture. While still on the island Te Kooti had been inspired to take note of a verse in which Samuel instructs Saul to destroy the Amalekites for that people's domination over them:

Now go and smite Amalek, and utterly destroy all that they have, and spare them not; but slay both man and woman, infant and suckling, ox and sheep, camel and ass.[12]

In a month's preparation for the time of the fulfilment of the promises, the prophet inspired his men with messages from the words addressed to the former people so long before:

And the Lord your God, he shall expel them from before you, and drive them from out of your sight; and ye shall possess their land, as the Lord your God has promised unto you. Be ye therefore very courageous to keep and to do all that is written in the book of the law of Moses, that ye turn not aside therefrom to the right hand or to the left.[13]

After an early victory against the Government forces, Te Kooti held a service of thanksgiving based on two verses from Exodus:

Thus the Lord saved Israel that day out of the hand of the Egyptians; and Israel saw the Egyptians dead upon the sea shore.

And Israel saw that great work which the Lord did upon the Egyptians: and the people feared the Lord, and believed the Lord, and his servant Moses.[14]

Throughout his ministry Te Kooti continued to prophesy according to divine inspiration, and as much of what he foretold did come to pass, his predictions were believed and followed. The people of Te Teko, Whakatane, and Ruatoki areas of the Bay of Plenty, for instance, following a prediction by the prophet that they would die if they ate food grown on land affected by the dust of the Tarawera eruption, moved in a mass to the Galatea and Ruatahuna districts. While they didn't stay in these places for the stated three years, the mana of Te Kooti was more than sufficient to convince them of the danger.[15]

As in the Papahurihia movement, the Saturday sabbath was instituted by Te Kooti. Here the reason given to justify the change is because of the historical accuracy of Saturday as the seventh day, though it is probable in this case too that at least a good part of the motivation was a rejection of missionary practice.

The 'Christian' calendar was also set aside for that of the Old Testament, for the feast days of Ringatu were based on those commanded in scripture.[16] But while the significant days of the new religion — New Year's Day and the first day of the seventh month — were taken from the feasts of the Hebrews, the European calendar was kept, so these were celebrated on 1 January and 1 July rather than on the corresponding days of the Hebraic almanac. Planting and harvest festivals were reinstituted — these being traditional practices as well as scriptural commands. A Feast of the Passover was inaugurated, though the purpose of this was to commemorate not the passing over of the Lord as in Egypt, but the deliverance of the exiles from the Chatham Islands.

Services in the new movement were held on the twelfth of each month, the number twelve being chosen for its biblical precedence, being significant in the social organisation of the Israelites and also referring to the twelve gates and twelve pearls of the new Jerusalem.[17]

That Ringatu in its early days implied a rejection of the Christian Church was undoubted by the missionaries of the time, who noted a dropping or reorganising of the practices of baptism and communion, and of the doctrine of the atoning sacrifice of Christ. William Leonard Williams (later Bishop of Waiapu) attested that, according to Ringatu practice, believers at morning and evening prayers chanted 'a cento of verses from the Old Testament', and read prayers addressed to Jehovah. In Te Teko the people told the clergyman they had now 'given up the way of the Son and . . . adopted instead the way of the Father'.[18] The Rev. J. Laughton who claimed he had heard hundreds of Ringatu 'sermons', said the religion did not include those 'cardinal and central doctrines of the Christian faith . . . the Gospel of salvation from sin, and of the glorious hope of immortality.' The God of the Ringatu was 'at best . . . a God envisaged in portions of the Old Testament, rather than the God and Father of our Lord, Jesus Christ.' Therefore, concluded Laughton, their conception of God was very different to that of Pakeha, and 'the place that he has filled in their life system has been precisely a place filled by the gods of their fathers, whose empty shrines had not yet been removed from their psychology when Ringatuism was established.'[19]

Some years later, however, the Church was to notice that the name of Jesus and the Virgin Mary were incorporated in Ringatu scriptures, though Williams was to state what while they had introduced the Saviour's name into their prayers, they 'reject Christian doctrine and make no pretence of adopting Christian practice'.[20] The ceremony of communion is directed to Jehovah, with no intermediary in Christ. The bread and wine which symbolise this intermediary in the Christian Church are consequently not a part of the service.

Ringatu prayers were also generally addressed directly to God, though one of the six prayers of Te Kooti quoted by William Colenso invokes the

The New Religions

trinity — 'O Jehovah, O Christ, O Holy Ghost . . .' The hymns and scriptural passages used in Ringatu devotions and services were all rearrangements of scriptures — mainly Old Testament but also from the New — selected by Te Kooti. One such passage, Panui 7, reads:

Come my people enter thou into thy chambers and shut thy doors about thee.

And none shall go out the door of his house until the morning.

And the Lord will pass over the door and will not suffer the destroyer to come into your houses to smite you.

I laid me down and slept, I awakened for the Lord sustained me. Now the Lord is that Spirit and where the spirit of the Lord is there is liberty.[21]

This panui was constructed by Te Kooti, under inspiration, from several separate verses — mainly from the Old Testament, but one from the New.[22]

It should be noted that Christian aspects of Ringatu have been emphasised more and more since the early years of the religion, so that the present form of the faith of Te Kooti is a Maori Christian Church. It is in accord with the very purpose of the religion that such a shift should have occurred. At its beginnings it was an attempt to fit the introduced teachings to the circumstances of Maori people at that point in history, and as those circumstances and needs altered, the movement adapted to cater for them — had it not, the religion would not be active now after more than a century. Even after that period, however, it is notable that Ringatu doctrine and liturgy still reflect the liberation theology of Old Testament times.

Notes

1. Wi Tarei, 'A Church Called Ringatu', in Michael King (ed.), *Tihe Mauri Ora*, p. 62.
2. J.A. Mackay, *Historic Poverty Bay and the East Coast, N.I., N.Z.*, p. 299.
3. There is scriptural warrant for this — see Nehemiah 8:6; Psalms 28:2, 63:4, 134:2, 141:2; and particularly in the lifting up of the hands by Moses in the protection of the Israelites — Exodus 17:11.
4. Te Kooti manuscript, entry dated 21 February 1868. Extracts from this MS are cited in W. Hugh Ross, *Te Kooti*, pp. 30–33; and in Peter Webster, *Rua and the Maori Millennium*, pp. 104–6.
5. Compare this to Papahurihia.
6. See Exodus 3:2–5, 7–9.

7. Te Kooti MS. Cited by Ross, *Te Kooti*, p. 31.
8. Ross, *Te Kooti*, p. 34.
9. Translated by William Colenso. Colenso, *Fiat Justitia*, p. 23.
10. From Te Kooti's notebook. Ross, *Te Kooti*, p. 33; Webster, *Rua*, p. 107.
11. Ross, *Te Kooti*, p. 39.
12. 1 Samuel 15:3. See Gilda Z. Misur, 'From prophet cult to established church, the case of the Ringatu Movement', in Kawharu (ed.), *Conflict and Compromise*, p. 103.
13. William Greenwood, *The Upraised Hand*, p. 25.
14. Exodus 14:30–1. Ross, *Te Kooti*, p. 52.
15. See reports of R.S. Bush, R.M. *AJHR*, 1887, G-1, 10; 1885, G-5, 5.
16. See Psalm 81:3–4.
17. Revelation chapter 21.
18. W.L. Williams, *East Coast Records*, pp. 79–80.
19. J.G.L. Laughton, *Ringatuism: The Ratana Church*, p. 3.
20. W.L. Williams, *The Maori Mission Past and Present*, p. 8.
21. Quoted by Wi Tarei, 'A Church Called Ringatu', p. 64.
22. Isaiah 26:30; Exodus 12:22; Psalm 3:5; and 2 Corinthians 3:17.

13. Parihaka Movement
Prophets: Te Whiti-o-Rongomai, Tohu Kakahi

Te Whiti-o-Rongomai, popularly celebrated as the pacifist of Taranaki, was, in his youth, very influenced by Christianity, and remained a believer in the message of the Bible all his life. In 1864–65, being then in his thirties, Te Whiti and his brother-in-law Tohu Kakahi joined in the activities of the Pai Marire religion of Te Ua Haumene, participating in the rites centred on the niu, and in several battles — though apparently not bearing guns. The association lasted probably only about a year.[1]

While Te Whiti is not claimed to have founded any distinct religion, the response of the Parihaka Movement was very strong in its religious element — this forming the basis for its political policy. The spiritual message and influence which emanated from the settlement of Parihaka was very great, not only in the Taranaki area but even further afield, from the mid-1860s.

Te Whiti was of the Ati Awa people to the north of Taranaki proper, and Tohu was of Ngati Ruanui to the south, but both also claimed Taranaki connections. The village of Parihaka grew around two marae — one headed by each of the leaders.

The motivation for the movement was, again, the land. Much of Taranaki had already been alienated by the sale of larger blocks — some of it subject to disputes over ownership. This led to open warfare between Maori and Europeans as the tangata whenua fought to retain land which had been sold to settlers, often without the legitimate owners' agreement.

As more and more people came to live at the village of Parihaka, it became a thriving settlement which was marked by its good organisation

Te Whiti-o-Rongomai. The prophet refused to sit for portraits, and it is said this photo was taken when Te Whiti was unaware of the camera.
(Taranaki Newspapers Ltd)

and healthy conditions.² To begin with, European foods were excluded from the village, and the people returned to a wholly traditional diet, but this policy was later relaxed. European forms of learning were rejected also — writing was the method by which Maori had been defrauded in the past — and traditional skills were revived and taught to children.

Te Whiti, as did many in those years, dropped the use of his 'Christian' name given at baptism, Eruera or Erueti (Edward), and reverted to his birth name Te Whiti-o-Rongomai.³

The beliefs of Te Whiti regarding God and his relationship to Maori followed those which were now common in the period — the New Zealanders were of the race chosen by the great Lord of the ancient days, who would lead them and deliver them in their time of need. Te Whiti recognised the twelve tribes of Israel in the members of different peoples to come to Parihaka — 'Great are you amongst people,' he assured them. 'You are as a heavy stone not to be moved.'⁴ All the promises of God, as made in the scriptures of the Old Testament, applied to Maori, but whereas that people were descended from Jacob, Europeans were regarded as taniwha (monsters) or Gentiles.⁵

The prophet saw his community as a haven for his broken people — the remnant remaining after diseases and war had taken their toll — and a home for the now homeless. The selling of land was wrong, he instructed; the only biblical case of land selling was the purchase of the field of Machpelah for use as a burial place.⁶

At Parihaka, readings from Old Testament prophets were chanted, the following verses from Isaiah being an example:

> *And the days of thy mourning shall be ended . . . Thy people shall inherit the land for ever . . . A little one shall become a thousand and a small one a strong nation.*⁷

Te Whiti addressed his people in 1881, drawing copiously on biblical imagery in his message of assurance of God's protection:

> *There are two roads, one to life and one to death. God said, in the days of Noah, the earth will be destroyed; build an ark, or all will perish. Noah did as he was commanded and this was an example for us to follow. God said to Moses, do not strive against me, or you will die; by faith only can this tribe be saved. This also is an example to us. Our salvation today is stout-heartedness and patience . . . You must believe in my teaching, or you will die . . . Let us all remain here at Parihaka, which came from heaven, and none shall be taken.*

The new message, while it was one of resistance to foreign pressures, was also one of peaceful response:

> *Do not think I am fighting against men, but rather against the devil and all wickedness, that he may be destroyed. Let us not use carnal weapons. Listen. Do not let us seek that which is lost — not look back to what is left. This is a day of teaching to this assembly of what shall guide us in the future. The ark by which we are to be saved today is stout-heartedness, and flight is death. Let this sink into the ears of all, even the children. There is to be nothing about fighting today, but the glorification of God, and peace on the land. Many generations wished to see this day; but we, a blind, small, and a despised people, have been chosen and glorified this day . . . Obey God and glorify Him; do not be distracted by the shouting, laughing and gathering together . . . My gun of today is not my gun of former years. All fighting is now to cease. Do not follow your own desires, lest God's sword fall upon you . . . . The canoe by which we are to be saved is forbearance . . . . It will save us all. The land we spoke of is the old land; but if we choose a new land we shall be saved . . . . Put both your hands and your feet on the new land, and stand in the ark of patience.*[8]

William Baucke, who knew Te Whiti, attested that the prophet interpreted the Bible literally — 'To him a strong man smiting a host with the jawbone of an ass presented fascinations incomparably beautiful — aye, beyond all things to be copied.'[9] John Ward, who spent a year with the two prophets during their time in the South Island, often made similar remarks.[10] In October 1882 when a comet was in the sky, Te Whiti's view of the phenomenon was that a comet is a world that is being destroyed by fire, having been judged for the transgressions of its people. The earth would, before long, be in a similar condition. Ward added that study of 'the Book of Revelation, and its peculiar language as well as the wild imagery of Isaiah' occupied a great part of the time of the two prophets.[11]

Through their respective genealogies, both Te Whiti and Tohu commanded great respect. With their learning and their spiritual messages in addition, their mana and authority were unquestioned — the people of Parihaka had unfailing faith in both their leaders. Knowledge of the old arts of the traditional tohunga were known to the two. Te Whiti is said to have possessed the gift of healing, and he was well known for his prophecies, though in European circles this became a further source of ridicule of the man.

According to the evidence of many Europeans who met Te Whiti, the prophet was an imposing figure — being a fine-looking man, and having the undoubted bearing and manner of a rangatira. As such a leader he took on a similar function to the Hebrew prophets. Both he and Tohu claimed they had been raised up by God to lead their people in this time. Their teachings were not from themselves, but from God above who moved them; and in this function they were to be obeyed, for whatever they foretold or spoke reflected the will of God. And whatever was ordained by God would surely come about.

The parallels are clear in the choice of words used by Te Whiti when he addressed his people in March 1880:

The place I have measured out shall remain sacred for my people.... I tell the assembled tribes that they shall not be lost. If you have taken silver, then indeed you will be lost. What good have you got when you stretched forth your hand for it? Did it not turn to poisonous drink which maddened you? And then where was the land of your fathers?[12]

Te Whiti claimed to have experienced visions of Moses and other Old Testament figures, and to know them from these. When the prophets visited Dunedin in 1882, the Jewish Rabbi called on them and invited them to the synagogue to view copies of the ancient laws as were delivered to Moses. The pair did not go, Te Whiti saying he was not well enough, and their companion John Ward noted that 'Te Whiti does not evince the interest in this matter which one would have expected'.[13] Once again it is clear that while Maori saw themselves as descended from the Hebrews, and in a similar situation to the ancient peoples, their response was their own and was not indicative of an interest in the Jewish religion itself.

Melchizedek, the Priest-King of the early Hebrews, was said to have appeared to Tohu in a vision, asking him for the offering of a son. Tohu had no son, but Te Whiti said one of his would be offered if acceptable to the priest. A meeting was called and the boy was laid on a mat in the middle of the meeting house. As he lay there he quietly died. This was considered a sure sign that the offering was accepted, and the two prophets were inspired thereafter.[14]

Te Whiti extended his belief in the descent of the Maori from the Israelites to claim kinship with other races also. He was impressed by members of the Chinese race whom he met, and considered that the two races were one and the same long before. Their common ancestor was Shem, son of Noah, so before the two peoples had gone their separate ways, they were the same. John Ward noted that Te Whiti regarded the Chinese 'with a very loving eye and fraternal feeling'.[15]

Strong millennial beliefs were a part of the Parihaka Movement. Jehovah had entered into him, claimed Te Whiti, and he was the 'King of Peace'.[16] When his work was completed, and the chieftainship returned to Israel, there would be a time of peace, happiness and prosperity. Parihaka was the New Jerusalem. In the millennium, money would not be the circulating medium, but it would be preserved as property to adorn the person, as did greenstone ornaments.[17]

The idea of the prophethood of Te Whiti appears to be based on a blending of traditions. He attested that Jehovah was God, and he himself was the mouthpiece of Jehovah. As such, he was under the protection of divine will — 'If thousands of people black, white and red try to close my work they shall not succeed, only myself can do it.' Te Whiti also said that there was only one man able to wash out the sins of the wicked, one arbitrator, and one conductor. That was himself. 'The world has been given unto me,' he stated, 'to work out its conversion,' and if he spoke falsely on this matter it was God who lied, for He put the words into his mouth.[18]

The Rev. T.G. Hammond claimed that Te Whiti said there was no true Christ but himself. The prophet said he was 'not Christ Jesus, but a small Christ'. From his further comments — that Queen Victoria could be a true Christ also if she eased the burdens of the people — it is clear that he saw the station of a Christ in a somewhat different way than did the missionaries.[19] A 'Christ', then, in this view appears to be perhaps less divine and more a leader who protects and cares for his people, having their welfare as his primary concern.

Hammond further claimed that 'Te Whiti and his people know nothing of religion, have no religious observances and simply make use of the Bible as a profane history which they say is corroborative of the tradition handed down to them by their ancestors.' He added that Te Whiti said he did not believe in Moses, Adam, Noah, Abraham, the Governor, the King and the Queen; but that the people of Parihaka read the Bible only in order to discover passages proving Te Whiti in the right and identifying themselves as the 'lost sheep of the house of Israel'.[20] Te Whiti's reported reply to the allegation that they had no church and did not pray — '. . . prayer is useless and resultless and no man was ever benefitted or healed by prayer. . . . We are all in the same hole and the rain wets the praying and prayerless alike' — reflects a view closer to the Hebraic position than to the Christian.

Such a blending of the traditions is entirely in keeping with the principle of Te Whiti that Maori should be free to take whatever parts of

The New Religions

European culture suited them, and reject what would not appear to be to their benefit. His argument with Pakeha was that Maori had not been free to do this — new conditions and values had been imposed on the indigenous people, often against their will.

Traditional beliefs and practices were also a part of this blend, as shown by the importance attached by Te Whiti and Tohu to a sacred carved stone at Puniho. Ceremonies at this ahurewa, or sacred place, included regular anointing of the stone with oil, and the lighting of a fire in order to determine omens from the column of smoke — incidentally, both practices which can be seen to have some parallel in the scriptures of the Old Testament.[21]

Both prophets died in 1907 — Tohu in February and Te Whiti in November — and their burial services were conducted along traditional lines. The offer of a Christian burial service for Te Whiti, by the Rev. T.G. Hammond, was refused, and in both cases the bodies were laid to rest without coffins — a final rejection of the unwanted customs of the Europeans, or 'Gentiles'.

Te Whiti's vision was not as in an Old Testament-style defeat of the usurpers of the Promised Land, as had been preached before and would be again. His idea was for Maori and Pakeha to live 'side by side in peace, Maori to learn the white man's wisdom, yet be the dominant ruler.'[22] The biblical prophecy of the wolf and lamb, leopard and kid existing together, meant that the two races would live side by side, but Maori would have chieftainship.[23] William Baucke was assured by the prophet that while he resented the greed of Europeans since their arrival — 'greed of land, greed of women, greed of good fishing grounds, greed of everything one has and the other has not' — and the consequent evils, still he had no bitterness against the individuals as men.[24] W.E. Gudgeon noted that although the teachings of the new movement included millennial hopes with Europeans banished from the country, an exception was to be made in favour of Pakeha born in New Zealand.[25]

In these beliefs there is a parallel with the story of the Children of Israel who wished to return to and gain domination over their former land, having ascendancy over the Canaanites. But again, the action was to be in the hands of God — the millennium would be brought about by divine rather than human agency. Here too there is more than coincidental similarities with the position of the Hebrews.

Te Whiti taught the principle of suffering, as a necessary part of the working out of God's plan. It was an atonement for sins perpetrated, and therefore must be endured before the promises and blessings of God could

'Te Whiti and Tohu (1882)'. After a sketch by G. Sherriff, at Parihaka, 5 November 1881. *(43078 1/2, Alexander Turnbull Library, Wellington)*

be fulfilled. Again, in this view, there is more than a trace of the Hebraic position and point of view, in which the suffering of the Chosen People is generally accepted to be an inevitable corollary to their exalted position.

The pacifism attributed to Te Whiti has been seen as a Christian rather than a Judaic teaching, but the reason behind the principle is clear. The prophet taught his people that it was not only not right to fight but, more importantly, it was both unnecessary and inappropriate. Justice was firmly in the hands of God, and no human agency was needed to help see justice done. By having faith in the omnipotence of the Lord, their salvation would be ensured.

The white feather of the albatross became the emblem of the Parihaka Movement. It signified glory to God on high, peace on earth, and goodwill to all mankind. While Te Whiti was often regarded by the European community as something of a religious maniac, his critics would have done well to appreciate his response in an undoubtedly explosive situation. His message was one of peace and obedience to God, based firmly on the scriptures brought by those who opposed him. Once again this demonstrates Maori cultural inability or unwillingness to separate the secular and the religious. What was seen by Europeans as a social or political problem was always motivation to Maori for a religious response.

The Parihaka Movement was to give rise to several other movements, each including a slightly different religious response.

Notes

1. Bernard Gadd, 'Teachings of Te Whiti O Rongomai, 1831–1907', *JPS* vol. 75, no. 4, p. 447.
2. Evidence of this was given by many visitors to Parihaka, though Archdeacon Walsh, 'The Passing of the Maori', p. 168, says that at times of meetings at the settlement, the overcrowding caused by so many visitors was the cause of the spread of diseases through the Taranaki communities.
3. Dick Scott, *Ask That Mountain*, p. 31. This book remains the fullest source on the Parihaka Movement.
4. *NZH*, 21 June 1881. Cited by Gadd, 'Teachings of Te Whiti', p. 449.
5. T.G. Hammond, 'Te Whiti and Parihaka', TS ATL, p. 8.
6. See Genesis 23. Hammond, 'Te Whiti and Parihaka', p. 8.
7. Isaiah 60:20–2. 'Chanted to the rhythm of the poi at Parihaka to the present day.' Scott, *Ask That Mountain*, p. 185.
8. *AJHR*, 1863, A-4, 9–10.
9. Baucke, *NZH*, 30 November 1907. Cited by Scott, *Ask That Mountain*, p. 187.
10. See, for example, John P. Ward, *Wanderings With the Maori Prophets, Te Whiti and Tohu*, pp. 15–16.
11. Ward, *Wanderings*, p. 129.
12. G.W. Rusden, *History of New Zealand*, p. 219. Cited in Caselberg (ed.), *Maori Is My Name*, p. 134. The reference to silver is probably from the sin of some of the Israelites at Jericho. See Joshua 7.
13. Ward, *Wanderings*, pp. 24, 68.
14. Hammond, 'Te Whiti and Parihaka', p. 24.
15. Ward, *Wanderings*, p. 55–56.

16. Hammond, 'Te Whiti and Parihaka', p. 24.
17. Ibid., p. 8.
18. Ibid., pp. 25–26.
19. Ibid., p. 29.
20. Ibid., p. 34.
21. Hammond, letter to E. Best, 9 March 1924. ATL MS, Best Scrapbooks, vol. 8, p. 46.
22. *NZH*, 30 November 1907. Cited by Gadd, 'Teachings of Te Whiti', p. 450.
23. See Isaiah 11:6. Hammond, 'Te Whiti and Parihaka', p. 8.
24. Baucke, *Where the White Man Treads*. See the whole account 'Taranaki', pp. 163–67.
25. Gudgeon, 'Maori Superstition', pp. 177–78.

14. Tariao
Prophet: King Tawhiao

In the late 1870s, in the King Country, a further religion, the Tariao faith, was being practised. The King Movement had been set up in 1858 — its basis and its aim being to unite the tribes of New Zealand into one people in order to give the Maori a strengthened voice in their opposition to the continuing alienation of their land.

Wiremu Tamihana, a chief of Ngatihaua, led the movement to elect a king, and so earned the name 'the Kingmaker'. Tamihana could see that the Christian Church, as judged by European settlement and rule, had failed in its mission to Maori. It had, however, provided them with a pattern for an appropriate response. Tamihana was said to be 'a diligent student of the code of laws contained in the Pentateuch', which he appeared to find 'better adapted to the wants of an uncivilized nation than English law' — he always quoted Levitical Law 'upon any doubtful case'.[1]

The books of the Old Testament spoke to the New Zealanders, giving them the model for a new nationalistic feeling. In particular, two verses in Deuteronomy gave a clear answer:

> *When thou art come unto the land which the Lord thy God giveth thee, and shalt possess it, and shalt dwell therein, and shalt say, I will set a king over me, like as all the nations that are about me;*
>
> *Thou shalt in any wise set him king over thee, whom the Lord thy God shall choose: one from among thy brethren shalt thou set king over thee: thou mayest not set a stranger over thee, which is not thy brother.*[2]

The divine mandate was clear. Tamihana went to his people with the words of the Israelites — 'make us a king to judge us like all the nations'[3] — and eventually the first king was elected. While it is usually said that the king was crowned according to traditional and 'Christian' rites, the facts remain that the idea arose from the Hebraic scriptures, the Church had generally opposed the idea, and when the Bible was placed upon Potatau's head, it was the words from the verses in Deuteronomy which were spoken by Tamihana.

Whereas Maori and missionaries could not stop the flow of blood in the country, once the king was set up, the blood at once ceased, claimed Tamihana in 1861.[4] European critics were quick to point out that the Israelites acted against the will of God by choosing a king; and the following decade was to show that years of warfare were still to come. But there can be no doubt that without the influence of the principles of the King Movement, the results would have been even more regrettable.

The first king, Potatau, was said to follow the Io religion, finding solace in the traditional cosmological beliefs of his people.[5] With the death of Potatau, his son Tawhiao succeeded in 1860, the second king's reign lasting until his death in 1894.

At the rise of the Pai Marire religion, Tawhiao, together with many Waikato chiefs, travelled to Wanganui to learn about it. John White, the Resident Magistrate, reported that they had all been convinced as to the truth of Te Ua's teachings, and all, including King Tawhiao, bowed to a small flag representing the traditional atua Rura. The prophet, he added, had told the king that New Zealand was Canaan, the Maori were Jews, and that the books of Moses were their law. A scripture called The Book of Rura contained a chapter titled 'A Lament for King Tawhiao'. Containing eleven verses, the chapter confirms Tawhiao as holding kingship by divine sanction of Rura. The text includes much Old Testament-style imagery, and Rura emerges as the Maori conception of Yahweh.[6]

From this time (1864) Tawhiao took the step of dropping his 'Christian' name Matutaera (Methuselah). In the following years, however, the king became influenced by the pacific teachings of Te Whiti, and in 1867 sent twelve 'apostles' to live at Parihaka.

Following this, Tawhiao founded his own form of religion, which was called Tariao — Tariao being the forerunner or herald star of the dawn star.[7] This faith gave yet another emphasis to the predominant beliefs and feelings of the time. While including the more peaceful responses of the Parihaka Movement, it developed as a sort of synthesis of Christian and traditional teachings. Tawhiao as their leader and high priest had the role

The New Religions

King Tawhiao (Potatau II), second Maori king, and founder of the Tariao religion. *(48131 1/2, Alexander Turnbull Library, Wellington)*

of overseer of peaceful relations between Maori and Europeans. A revival of traditional forms of worship included the invocation of some of the atua maori — Tawhirimatea, Tanemahuta, Tiki, Uenuku, and the stars Matariki (Pleiades), Tawera (Venus as morning star), Tautoru (Orion's Belt), and a number of other gods of myth.[8] Such traditional concepts were intermingled with passages of biblical scripture.[9]

Some aspects of the Christian religion were retained — the patterning of services followed the faith of the missionaries, and a Government official present at one attested he was favourably impressed by it, and that there was 'not a single word or act of fanaticism' in any of the prayers or psalms. Rather, God was asked to give Tawhiao strength to preserve peace between Maori and European, and to assist the people in obeying their king.[10] The religion included a form of clergy, each settlement having two men and two women functionaries designated 'Ngehe' (presumably from the meaning 'peaceful' or 'calm').

Again millennial expectations were held, but this time in a different form, for at one time at least the Tariao believed that their deliverance would come in a new age ushered in by the return of Christ. Both Major W.G. Mair and Mr B.J.F. Edwards reported separately in 1871 that when they visited Tawhiao on 20 September, the king greeted Mair at the door asking whether the Major was Christ, for whom they were waiting, and who had been called to come.[11]

The Tariao response, therefore, was a syncretism between several strands of religious thought, from traditional Maori beliefs and from the introduced scriptures.

Notes

1. John Gorst, *The Maori King*, p. 173.
2. Deuteronomy 17:14–15.
3. 1 Samuel 8:5.
4. Wiremu Tamihana to the Governor, June 1861. Richard Taylor, *Past and Present*, pp. 133–34.
5. Pei Te Hurinui, *King Potatau*, p. 246.
6. White to Colonial Secretary, 7 September 1864. *AJHR*, 1864, E-8, 12–13.
7. The name of the dawn star was Kopu, and is probably Venus, though some tribes called Jupiter by that name. Tariao is probably Mercury, which can be seen only just before sunrise or after sunset because of its proximity to the sun. James Cowan, *The Maori Yesterday and Today*, pp. 85–86, 90. See also Elsdon Best, *The Astronomical Knowledge of the Maori*, pp. 38–42.
8. From an article 'Hauhauism, or the New Superstition Called Tariao' published in the newspaper *Te Wananga*; reprinted in *BOPT*, 2 September 1876.
9. From an anonymous one-page biographical sheet 'King Tawhiao of the Royal Tribe of Waikato, the Ngatimahuta', printed by the *Daily Telegraph*, Napier, undated.
10. R.S. Bush to the Hon. Sir D. McLean, *AJHR*, 1876, G-1, 6.
11. *AJHR*, 1872, F-3A, 15 and 17.

15. Arowhenua Movement
Prophet: Te Maiharoa

The Arowhenua Movement[1] of Te Maiharoa, like other responses to European settlement, had a strong religious element. Unlike the others, however, this one arose in the South Island.

Like tribes in so many other areas from the mid-nineteenth century onwards, the Kaitahu and Katimamoe people of Arowhenua (close to Temuka) held a strong grievance against Europeans over land issues. When the land of the South Island was sold, Maori understanding of the agreement was that the area sold extended inland from the coast only as far as the base of the nearest mountains which could be seen.[2] They were to have adequate reserves and the right to continue using their traditional hunting grounds. But the reserves allotted to them proved to be poor and small, and the holders of the stations which enclosed the important weka grounds now barred them from their hunts. The Rev. J.W. Stack, reporting to the Native Department in 1878, said, 'There can be no doubt that they ought to have had more land assigned to them originally — the amount reserved for them per head is ridiculously small when compared with the average holdings of the colonists . . .'[3]

Te Maiharoa, a chief of the Kaitahu, was very much a leader of the old tradition, being a tohuka (tohunga) of great mana. He sometimes used the name Hipa as a secondary name, this being 'the name of some God or Karakia with the Uruao crowd of Matiti in Hawaiki'.[4] He spoke for his people against the europeanisation of the Southern Maori, but against the Pakeha rule his words could have little effect, and therefore he was sometimes known ironically as 'Patu-whenua' (beating the ground).[5]

In 1866 the tohunga Piripi, from the North Island,[6] was invited to Arowhenua in order to remove all tapu in the area. This followed a similar practice in many parts of the North Island in the previous decade, as Maori, seeing their numbers drastically reduced by disease, sought to destroy all vestiges of the traditional religion. Being told that the European God was punishing the people for clinging to the old ways or, alternatively, believing that the atua maori were punishing them for turning their allegiance to a foreign God, Maori often made a decision to destroy the old system completely in the hope that their lot would improve.[7] Before Piripi left Arowhenua, he gave instructions to Te Maiharoa so this tohuka could continue to carry out the work.[8]

It appears, however, that the relevance of the old traditions, no doubt supported by growing disillusionment with European rule, and therefore the Christian Church, was re-established in the mind of the people, and they reverted to the old ways. During the following years Te Maiharoa was involved in addressing meetings on the subject of pressing claims for land ownership. By 1877 it was reported that all the pa of Canterbury, except Rapaki and Tuahiwi, had 'reverted to tohungaism as taught by Te Maiharoa'.[9]

It seems too that within this period a change took place in the person and function of Te Maiharoa himself. By 1877 he emerged as a prophet figure, though with the emphasis on the role of the traditional tohunga ahurewa (high priest). He was surrounded by very strong tapu, and lived in a house by himself — no one ate with him, only his wife could give him food, and even the doors of the house were tied up. It is said that one of his sons once touched some of the tohuka's food and was later found drowned as a consequence. Te Maiharoa was also said to be the only person to have swum across Lake Tekapo, for he was the only one whose power was great enough to keep the taniwha from doing anything to stop him.[10]

Many miracles were reported to be performed by Te Maiharoa. One story is told of how a baby disappeared from a house while its mother was out fetching water. Te Maiharoa instructed the people to observe silence and not eat anything, and the mother was told to sit in a field until she saw a white cloud approaching. Te Maiharoa prayed, the cloud came close to the woman, and she jumped up and took the child from it.[11] Many other such tales are told.[12]

Few details survive of the actual religious beliefs of Te Maiharoa at this time, but from several brief references, it appears that he too formed a faith based on the books of the Old Testament. Herries Beattie says that

The New Religions

the old Maori religion had gone, so Te Maiharoa improvised one from the Bible and adapted it to suit Maori.[13] A contemporary of the prophet said that Te Maiharoa was 'a religious man and one who pondered things. He was not an orthodox Christian, but was some sort of Israelite.'[14]

The 'reversion' to the former ways noted by observers was, as in other movements, not so much a wholesale return to Maori tradition as a reformulation of culture and beliefs based on an amalgamation of old and new values. The people of Te Maiharoa were forged into a tight community conducted on a set of regulations for the running of a God-fearing society, as were the Israelites in the earlier time. Strict rules included prohibitions on alcohol, gambling, lying, blasphemy and fighting. In a speech in Parliament in 1873, Captain Fraser said that whereas formerly the South Island Maori had been morally low, a great change had taken place. Being entirely neglected by the Provincial and General Governments, they had 'formed laws for their own guidance' and 'created a creed, the due performance of which has worked a great change in the natives of three or four of the principal settlements . . .'[15] Daily services of worship were conducted by the prophet, as in many other Maori religious movements where the pattern of regular services was the main aspect of Christianity retained.

During this period Te Maiharoa began to develop his powers, again apparently an amalgamation of those of the tohunga and the prophetic figures of old. He became known for healing, and it is recorded that one visitor from the North Island, an Ati Awa called Tuhaha, was so grateful for being freed from makutu by the prophet, that he sold land he owned in Nelson and elsewhere and gave the proceeds of £2,000 to Te Maiharoa to establish his planned settlement.[16] Te Maiharoa chose twelve disciples, and to these he passed on his powers so that they too could heal. His prayers were directed to 'Almighty God'.[17]

The occurrence for which Te Maiharoa is most remembered is a migration of a large number of his followers under the leadership of the prophet, and in this there is again a strong similarity to a Moses-like figure leading his people to a promised land.

The purpose of the heke (migration), according to Fraser, was for the people to withdraw from all association with Europeans, and the plan was to 'retire into the desert'. The original aim was to travel to that area of the country between lakes Hawea and Wanaka, where they would put a fence across the peninsula and be isolated as though on an island. On this poor land, which they believed had never been sold, they would live and be free to follow their own beliefs.

The heke began in June 1877. In the years previous to this, Maori from many tribes had joined Te Maiharoa at Arowhenua, including some from North Island peoples.[18] A newspaper account of the time said the people of the heke numbered 150, having with them 101 horses, 20 carts, and 30 tons of flour, potatoes and other goods,[19] though a member of the party stated there were 12 drays and 10 traps.[20] The travellers journeyed from Arowhenua southwards, across the Waitaki River to meet the road running inland, then westward towards the ranges. More people joined the party on the way.

The journey took about eight days, and during the period of travel the prophet conducted his people in a strict fashion. No eating or smoking was permitted, and should someone in the party infringe this rule, Te Maiharoa would sense it, stop the group, and lift the tapu temporarily until the people were refreshed and ready to travel on.

The station of Te Maiharoa as priest and prophet is further illustrated in accounts of this journey. It was later agreed by many that when the party reached the Waitaki River on the second day of the heke, the gate across the bridge was shut, it being a combined road and rail bridge and a train was due. Te Maiharoa, at the front of the party, recited some karakia and the gate opened of its own accord. The people drove onto the bridge, crossed the river, and the gate at the southern end was opened in a similar fashion to allow the vehicles to pass off the bridge. Before all the party was over, however, the train approached from the south. The prophet then got down from his trap and stood praying. Mitai Tuture attested:

> . . . *the wheels of the engine were going round but were not going forward. The engine driver and the stoker got off to see what was the matter and they looked at the wheels in a puzzled manner. When all the carts were off the bridge, Te Maiharoa released his power and the train went forward. As far as I know it was only two or three chains from the bridge that the train stopped and our carts were alongside the train, but as far as I can remember the train men and the Maoris exchanged no conversation although both races thought it a most peculiar thing. As the train went forward the Maoris all got out of their carts and assembled for prayer.*[21]

If that account sounds very much like a modern day equivalent of an Old Testament example of deliverance of a chosen people, other incidents of the journey illustrate the traditional function of the prophet. The same witness tells of how Te Maiharoa stopped the party on two occasions in order to deal with the forces of evil spirits that were endangering his

The New Religions

people. The offending atua were 'killed' in a ceremony involving fire as well as karakia.

The heke did not travel to the proposed destination, but stopped at Omarama. Here, the people believed, they were within their rights to settle — they being well beyond the limit of the land sold to the Government.[22] They built a settlement of sod houses, including a church/hall named by the prophet 'Te Whakaahua-a-raki', the likeness or resemblance of heaven. Extensive gardens were planted, and the people lived for two years in this place — hunting birds for meat, and running some cattle. But local station holders opposed their presence, claiming that dogs belonging to the party were worrying their sheep. At the same time reports were received that in the North Island settlers' land was being ploughed up by parties of Maori.[23] Proceedings were being taken against the offenders there, and Police Inspector Thomson was ordered to do the same in the south. A force was gathered, and the Inspector proceeded to Omarama where the people were moved on and their houses destroyed. On this occasion some of the men of the heke were ready to fight, although their weapons were few and unsuitable, but the prophet forbade them to resist, saying, 'I do not wish to shed blood'. So a potentially explosive situation passed off peacefully.

The story is told that during the Omarama period Te Maiharoa took some of his leading men to a steep mountain to the east of Lake Ohau. There the prophet left his followers at the foot of the mount, and proceeded to climb up alone. On the top he had a vision, and in that vision saw a new place where he and his people would reside after Omarama. Because of this insight he knew they were to leave, and for this reason did not oppose the order to quit the village.[24] Pita Paipeta, who visited the mountain later, said it is 'very steep and unclimbable from one side and it was from some religious motive Maiharoa ascended it'.[25]

The displaced people started another trek back the way they had come. Apparently a message had been sent by the Government giving the people of Te Maiharoa permission to settle at Omarama permanently, but the agent arrived too late to stop the exodus. Meeting the party near Duntroon, he tried to persuade them to return, but they refused as their houses had been destroyed, conditions were hard, and relations with the station holders had not been favourable.[26]

Instead, they were offered land at Waitaki, on either side of the river mouth. Here Te Maiharoa recognised the site of his vision, and a new village was set up — named Korotuaheka after an ancient settlement of that name in the area. Here the 'Israelites' stopped their wandering and made their home. In time the prophet and most of the older people died and were buried at Korotuaheka, and the village eventually declined.

Before his death, Te Maiharoa prophesied that 'A very little child will come forth from under Taranaki mountain (Egmont); he will finish my words for Jehovah.' Some believed that T.W. Ratana later fulfilled the prophecy, though others considered that the child was still to come.[27]

From the few details now known of the religious aspects of the Arowhenua Movement, it seems reasonable to include it among those which were inspired by the scriptures of the Old Testament. While Te Maiharoa appointed twelve disciples and gave them power to join him in his healing work, there remains very little further evidence of Christian influence. On the contrary, Te Maiharoa emerges as, rather, a prophet of the earlier times — leading his people from place to place in search of land where they could settle permanently in peace, away from the usurpers of their homeland and apart from alien domination.

That the movement incorporated a strong element of traditional beliefs and practices is undoubted, and these were always far more compatible with the religion of the Hebrews than with Christianity. The people were known as Israelites, and there is some link with the Parihaka community, for visitors from there joined Te Maiharoa, and one of the ploughmen arrested in Taranaki was an Arowhenua man.[28] In addition, they were sometimes called 'Hauhau' by Europeans. Although this must be inaccurate, it nonetheless suggests that the movement included an element of rejection of Christianity in favour of the earlier religion — particularly considering that prayers were directed to 'Almighty God' rather than through the mediumship of Christ.

The name of the church/hall at Omarama suggests some belief in either a coming millennium or else a notion that the separatist settlement itself constituted a state of heaven on earth.[29] In the matter of the vision of Te Maiharoa when, leaving his men at the foot of the mountain, he climbed, as did Moses, to receive divine inspiration, there is no doubt that the link is with the Old Testament; and in image and function the prophet must be seen in the same light as those of ancient times.

Notes

1. There appears to be no proper name for this movement, so I have called it this in order to identify it. A fuller study of the history of the movement is available in Buddy Mikaere, *Te Maiharoa and the Promised Land*.

2. Herries Beattie, 'A Celebrated Trek. Maori Migration from Temuka to Omarama in 1878', MS Hocken, p. 2. See petitions made by Te Maiharoa and others, *AJHR* 1883, 1-2, 18, 19, 27; and also A. MacKay's report to Parliament on the matter of land sale in the South Island, *AJHR*, 1891, G-7.
3. *AJHR*, 1878, G-1, 17.
4. Beattie, MS, Notebook 'General Maori Information' Book 2, p. 10.
5. Beattie, 'Celebrated Trek', p. 2.
6. It is likely he was Ati Awa. See Bill Dacker, 'Chapters in South Island Maori History', p. 32, for consideration of this. This author is indebted to Bill Dacker for his help in regard to the Arowhenua Movement.
7. This response is generally referred to as 'Wahi Tapu'. See brief mention of it in 'Other Early Movements', or more fully in Bronwyn Elsmore, *Mana From Heaven*, chapter 18.
8. Dacker, 'S.I. Maori History', p. 33, citing W.A. Taylor, Notebooks, vol. 11, p. 31.
9. Taylor, *The Lore and History of the South Island Maoris*, p. 166. Cited by Dacker, p. 35.
10. Personal recollections of Mrs Rickus and Mrs Fowler, Temuka. Maud Goodenough Hayter, *Folklore and Fairy Tales of the Canterbury Maoris*, pp. 32–35. Mrs Rickus also says that Te Maiharoa had three wives.
11. Personal recollections of Mrs Fowler. Hayter, *Folklore*, p. 33.
12. See examples in Teone Taare Tikao, *Tikao Talks. Traditions and Tales Told to Herries Beattie*, pp. 83–85.
13. Beattie, 'Celebrated Trek', p. 2.
14. Tikao, *Tikao Talks*, p. 85.
15. *NZPD*, 1873, vol. 14, p. 640. The settlements referred to are probably Moeraki, Timaru (Arowhenua), and Waikouaiti. See Dacker, p. 38.
16. Beattie, MS, Notebook 'General Maori Information' Book 2, HL, Herries Beattie Collection, MS 582/E, 271, p. 10.
17. Mrs Rickus. Hayter, *Folklore*, p. 35.
18. Beattie, 'Celebrated Trek', p. 2.
19. *North Otago Times*, 27 June 1877. See Dacker, 'S.I. Maori History', p. 39.
20. Mitai Tuture's account. Beattie, 'Celebrated Trek', p. 11.
21. Beattie, 'Celebrated Trek', p. 11. See too Mrs Fowler's account, Hayter, *Folklore*, p. 32.
22. Pakeha understanding of the transaction, however, was that the New Zealand Land Company had bought the entire South Island, with the exception of some reserves. See 'Omarama Maoris, 1879. An Official View' (Inspector Thomson's Report), Beattie, 'Celebrated Trek', p. 21.
23. See 'Parihaka Movement'.
24. Beattie, 'Celebrated Trek', p. 8.
25. Beattie, MS, 'General Maori Information' Book 6, p. 2. Herries Beattie Collection, MS M.1.582 E/16, Notebook 275.
26. See Beattie, 'Celebrated Trek', pp. 13, 17.
27. Beattie, MS, 'General Maori Information' Book 2, p. 10.
28. *NZPD*, 1882, vol. 41, p. 187. Cited by Dacker, p. 50.
29. It is possible, though, that it was named for the second canoe from Hawaiki to New Zealand in Waitaha tradition — a canoe said to be ferried by fairy folk. This author is indebted to Bill Dacker for this idea.

16. Tekau-ma-rua
Prophet: Te Mahuki Manukura

The religion of the Tekau-ma-rua — literally, the Twelve — was founded by a follower of the prophets of Parihaka, the new movement being based on their teachings.

While the tribes of Waikato and Taranaki were formerly enemies, their common opposition to the sale of land and their distrust of Europeans had helped to unite them. Te Mahuki Manukura, a chief of the Ngati Kinohaku subtribe of Ngati Maniapoto, together with his people went to join the protestors at the village of Parihaka in the late 1870s, and he and many of his men were among the ploughmen arrested and jailed. Following the entry of European forces into Parihaka in November 1881, and the subsequent dispersal of more than two thousand people belonging to tribes outside the Taranaki area, Te Mahuki's band returned to their home at Te Kumi in Waikato. At this time Te Mahuki was aged about 33. He was described by the Government Native Agent as being a consumptive, cunning-looking man, of unprepossessing appearance, but gifted with considerable glibness of speech.[1]

Te Mahuki now assumed the function of prophet to his people, basing his teachings on those of Te Whiti. At Te Kumi he constructed a village which was a replica of Parihaka, building the houses in the same way and in the same relative positions as those at Taranaki. The Government Agent reported that the people worked hard to provide food for their settlement.

A little to the north, in the 'King Country', the tribes united under King Tawhiao were keeping themselves separate from European rule. Southwards in Taranaki, under the leadership of Te Whiti and Tohu,

The prophet Te Mahuki Manukura at Te Kumi, the village he modelled on that of Te Whiti and Tohu at Parihaka. *(Burton Brothers Photo. 613474 1/2. Alexander Turnbull Library, Wellington)*

protestors continued a policy of peaceful disruption in order to upset government projects and further settlement. At Te Kumi the people of Te Mahuki did the same. Their motivation was twofold — the protection of the land, and the protection of their race and culture from the less beneficial aspects of settler society. To effect these aims they kept themselves apart from European influence, yet periodically engaged in episodes to disrupt settlement.

In 1883 Te Mahuki and a band of his men attempted to stop the surveying of the proposed main trunk railway. At Te Uira they tied up the surveyors Charles Hursthouse and Mr Newsham, and treated them poorly, apparently leaving them without food for several days. The party received a short term of imprisonment. Shortly afterwards, the prophet led his men into the township of Alexandra (now Pirongia) as a protest. They arrived in force, but without arms. Apart from tying up one of the residents they met outside the town and keeping him a prisoner in some scrub, they caused no harm, but the townsfolk were put in fear of what might happen next. The people of Te Kumi then made many shows of returning to Parihaka — marching southwards to the limit of the boundary imposed upon them at White Cliffs (now Pukearuhe), before being turned back again by the constabulary. These were peaceful protests — the party having walked for four or five days to this point, would rest for a while, then begin the several days' journey home again. In October 1890 the prophet and his followers earned a further twelve months' imprisonment with hard labour for taking forcible possession of Mr Ellis' store in Te Kuiti, 'and generally alarming the people of this district by their fanatical actions'.[2] In 1897 Te Mahuki set fire to a store in Te Kuiti, and was sentenced to seven years' hard labour; but his health broke down during this term and he died in 1899.[3]

The religion of the Tekau-ma-rua was again based on the Old Testament, with the 'Twelve' referring to Te Whiti's likening of the peoples visiting Parihaka to the tribes of Israel. Mr Wilkinson, the Government Native Agent, reported that they read the older scriptures continuously — 'the New Testament, with the exception of the book of Revelations, does not form any part of their religion.'[4] Faith in God was the answer to their grievances. Te Mahuki realised that no hope lay in physical force, for Maori were now greatly outnumbered by Europeans, and far outstripped as regards technological aids. Neither was the answer in argument or dialogue, for the new rule was primarily designed for the settlers' benefit. The deliverance of the people of God, therefore, lay only in the hands of the Lord — the scriptures told how he had helped his people in ancient times, and now they had been assured he would do so again.

Te Mahuki regarded himself as the representative of Te Whiti to his people. At his trial in Auckland in 1897 he referred to Te Whiti as his father, and said that he acted according to the spirit of the other prophet. He had, though, claimed some revelation of his own, for in 1890 Te Mahuki prophesied that the millennium would begin on 2 November that year. The 'occupation' of Te Kuiti in October was in anticipation of the coming of the promised time of the Lord.

External sources claimed that the spirit of the people of Te Kumi was broken by the unfulfilled prophecies of their leader and the apparently ineffectual protests — but the fact remains that Te Mahuki was instrumental in giving his people guidance and direction over two decades, in a time when it was desperately needed.

Notes

1.   G.T. Wilkinson, report to Native Department, 11 June 1883. *AJHR*, 1883, G-1, 5.
2.   For reports of these incidents, see *AJHR*, 1883, G-1, 5; 1884, G-1, 7; 1892, G-3, 4.
3.   Scott, *Ask That Mountain*, p. 179.
4.   *AJHR*, 1883, G-1, 5.

17. Maketu Movement
Prophet: Himiona Te Orinui

Himiona Te Orinui was of the Patuwai people, of the Whakatane district, but came to the Maketu–Motiti[1] area of Bay of Plenty and settled there. He came from a very influential family, and his brother, Rihara Te Reke, was well known in Bay of Islands as a tohunga.

It appears that the 1870s were years of reassessment of religion at Maketu and Motiti, as elsewhere. The Maketu news correspondent reported in 1876 that the local people had become 'more religiously inclined', and were apparently looking at various forms of religion. As well as the social problems of Maori at the time, differences between the Christian churches may have played a part in this too, for Anglican and Catholic doctrines were being compared by Maori of the area, and at Maketu the practice of confession was added to the services of the Church of England. The correspondent predicted that the people would eventually join 'either the very High Church party or the Roman Catholic Body'.[2] At the same time, there was also influence from the Tariao faith and the Ringatu religion, so it was inevitable that some form of synthesis would result.

Himiona was extremely well acquainted with the Bible, and in the late 1870s received revelation and became known as a prophet. The prophet himself attested that his inspiration came when he was in a kind of trance and saw a rupee floating in the air, passing backwards and forwards before his eyes. He remembered the letters written on the coin, wrote them down, and thereafter realised they referred to certain chapters of the Bible.[3]

The new beliefs attracted a following in the Bay of Plenty, for in 1880 a church was erected on Motiti Island for the followers of Himiona.

Himiona Te Orinui, the prophet of the Maketu–Motiti area.
(Nuku family collection)

Newspaper reports at the time referred to the prophet and his people as 'followers of the Old Testament',[4] and it was said that in their worship they concentrated on Old Testament scriptures. By January 1882 'nearly the whole of the native inhabitants of Maketu' belonged to the new sect, including the great Arawa chief Te Pokiha Taranui — who was also known as Major Fox and had led his men on the side of the government against Te Kooti — who 'renegaded from the Church of England' to join it.[5]

In 1883 King Tawhiao and his followers were invited to Maketu by Te Pokiha, apparently for the purpose of cementing peaceful relations between the Arawa and Waikato peoples who had formerly been opposed over old disputes.[6] But whereas many Maketu residents were supporters of King Tawhiao, it appears that the religion of Himiona was not the same as Tariao — despite the fact that European reports sometimes referred to the movement by that name.

Rather, there is definite evidence of Ringatu influence. The Resident Magistrate R.S. Bush reported in 1883 that the majority of Maketu Maori 'adhere to Te Kooti's form of prayer', and he had not heard the Tariao or Kingite form of prayer in the district at all.[7] Much later, in 1888, Bush said the religion of Himiona was 'somewhat similar to Te Kooti's', though there were three or four different sects in the area, judging by the number of church bells that rang morning and evening.[8] New Year's Day was celebrated in the Ringatu manner, for in 1882 it was reported that a 'Po Takoto' had been held, consisting of prayers and devotions throughout the night before New Year.[9]

It is probable, though, that Himiona used the Ringatu movement as a pattern rather than showing allegiance to the person of Te Kooti himself. When Te Kooti stayed a night at Maketu in 1884, he was reported as feeling slighted at 'not being made more of' by the chiefs of the area.[10] Later in the decade the Motiti movement was described as in 'opposition to Te Kooti's' being 'somewhat similar to his, but yet quite different in form'. There was, however, talk of the two faiths uniting.[11]

The religion of Himiona, as had many before it, celebrated the sabbath on Saturday,[12] and included the belief that Maori were descended from Israel. The Psalms of David were used extensively, reflecting the belief in the similarities between the situations of the ancient and later peoples, though portions of the New Testament were also read.

The prophet again emerges as an Old Testament-style figure. Early in his ministry he received a divine command to offer up his daughter as a sacrifice, but the girl did not agree and left her home to stay with friends.[13] Himiona became a noted healer and seer, using prayers and

The New Religions

immersion in cold water to effect his cures.[14] In serious cases of makutu, he was sometimes assisted by his brother, Rihara Te Reke, who visited from the Bay of Islands on occasions — Rihara being a tohunga of the old tradition.[15]

Following the eruption of Tarawera in 1886, Himiona and 70 followers visited the Rotorua people, and in the manner of an ancient prophet in his functions of admonisher and warner, reproved them for their drunkenness and evil doings which he stated had been the cause of the tragedy. Because of their wicked ways the area had been destroyed, as a latter-day Sodom or Gomorrah. The residents, however, were unwilling to take the blame, and Himiona and his attendants were badly received and even cursed for their warnings.[16] Following this, the prophet predicted a further eruption of the mountain, to be preceded by the appearance of a comet in the sky. The comet appeared, and he predicted the eruption would occur between the first and tenth of February 1888. The calamity would be preceded by thunder and lightning, and the mountain would erupt in the direction of Whakatane.[17]

This prediction is very similar to one made two years before by Te Kooti, when shortly after the original eruption, that prophet similarly warned the residents of Whakatane, with the result that some two hundred moved from there to Matapihi near Tauranga.[18] Now on this later occasion the people of the Maketu district made feverish preparations for the coming calamity, gathering food, wood and water, and securing their livestock. Services were held, and when the appointed time came and passed uneventfully, it seemed that the prayers had been answered, for Himiona stated that because of God's love for his people he would not allow them to be destroyed.[19]

European sources said that Himiona's mana suffered from this incident, and he was less in evidence over the next few years. But the prophet's powers of healing ensured that his prestige was soon restored, and he was very widely renowned in the district until his death.

Te Pokiha Taranui, the chief who had converted to the new faith some years before, remained firm in his belief and was an effective leader over a long period — in fact the movement was often known by Europeans as 'Pokiha's Karakia'. It was always strongest among the Patuwai of Motiti and the people of the Ngati Pikiao hapu at Maketu.[20] In January 1887 Te Pokiha led a revival gathering attended by representatives from a wide area of the Bay of Plenty. At this time ministers of the religion were appointed from different ranks, and rules were laid down for the guidance of the believers.[21]

Rihara Te Reke, the famous tohunga of the Bay of Islands, brother of Himiona the prophet. *(Nuku family collection)*

The New Religions

Himiona died at Motiti in April 1904, a victim of a severe epidemic of influenza then sweeping the area.

In the years that followed, many of the people of his movement joined the Ringatu Church, while others reverted to membership of the Church of England. Finally, it is interesting to note that the name of the church built at Motiti Island in 1920 was dedicated to Te Nakahi Parahi — the brazen serpent of Moses, used as a protection by the people of Israel in their wanderings in the wilderness.[22]

Notes

1. There appears to be no proper name for this movement, so for convenience I am referring to it by the name of the area in which it existed.
2. *BOPT*, 8 November 1876. This author is indebted to Alister Matheson for his help regarding newspaper references regarding this movement.
3. *BOPT*, 16 January 1882.
4. *BOPT*, 30 October 1880.
5. *BOPT*, 16 January 1882.
6. See report of R.S. Bush, R.M., *AJHR*, 1883, G-1A, 7; 1884, G-1, 16.
7. *AJHR*, 1883, G-1A, 6.
8. *AJHR*, 1888, G-5, 6.
9. *BOPT*, 16 January 1882. The correspondent, however, refers to this as Tariao.
10. *AJHR*, 1884, G-1, 16.
11. *AJHR*, 1889, G-3, 6.
12. F.W. Williams, *Through Ninety Years*, p. 254.
13. *BOPT*, 16 January 1882.
14. *Auckland Weekly News*, 14 December 1889, p. 8.
15. *BOPT*, 20 May 1898; 2 December 1898; 11 April 1900.
16. *Auckland Weekly News*, 10 March 1889.
17. *BOPT*, 1 February 1888.
18. *BOPT*, 21 September 1886.
19. *BOPT*, 18 October 1899.
20. Subtribe of Arawa, led by Pokiha.
21. *BOPT*, 15 January 1887.
22. Numbers 21:9.

18. Upper Waihou Movement
Prophetess: Remana Hi
(also Maria Pangari, Ani Karo)

This was actually a group of three movements which followed one another in quick succession and which, together, quite neatly illustrate the process of change which occurred throughout the prophetic period.[1]

The first prophetess of the three, Maria Pangari was, in 1885, a young woman of about 25 when she had a vision of Christ. Following the commands he gave her, Maria made burnt offering sacrifices, and kept a fourteen-day silence, then announced the return of Christ. The Advent was to take place at the end of March. In a period of millennial expectations people disposed of their possessions and waited for the fulfilment of the promise. Following the given date another was prophesied, and after this passed uneventfully the prophetess announced the time was postponed, and a little later travelled south for the purpose of visiting the prophets of Parihaka. She took ill and died before reaching her goal.

This was primarily a Christian-inspired response — ideas of an expected Return of Christ and the establishment of the Kingdom of God on earth being teachings of the missions from the time of contact.

Following the death of Maria Pangari, Ani Karo, who was travelling with the prophetess' party, assumed leadership, and on her return to Upper Waihou after visiting Parihaka, spread the teachings of the Taranaki prophets.[2] Concern over the loss of land was the main emphasis, and some rejection of the message of Christianity was shown by the dropping of the observation of the sabbath.

Within a short time, however, there appears to have been a rival claim made by a third prophetess, and a movement led by Remana Hi, a sister

The New Religions

of the first prophetess Maria Pangari, was gaining ground. Relations between the two women deteriorated, and after some incidents disturbed the peace of the area Ani renounced her claims to prophethood. Remana now received the support formerly given to her two forerunners.

A further change of ideas is evident. In this later movement the Christian content declined and it came to reflect a greater influence from the older scriptures. The sacredness of the New Testament was denied as it was not divinely inspired — rather, the Old Testament was to be followed.[3]

Remana and her followers built a settlement on a rise near the river at Upper Waihou, and set up an exclusive community. A sacred area was marked out according to instructions revealed to the prophetess in a dream. The boundaries of the area were marked by a line of flagpoles bearing streamers of white calico. All the people inside the tapu area had to wear white, symbolising purity and which was, in the reported words of Remana herself, 'an emblem of peace'. Black, on the other hand, was bad and signified lawlessness, so anything of that colour was forbidden. Black clothes were not permitted, and black animals which strayed inside the markers would be killed. The site of this new camp was known as Mount Zion.[4]

Following an incident in which a settler was accosted after straying into the sacred area, apparently by mistake and wearing black clothes, a party of police also entered the enclosure. They too were clothed in black and so were attacked by the residents. Twenty-three were arrested and tried, with sixteen convicted and sentenced to terms of imprisonment with hard labour of up to three months, served at Mount Eden jail in Auckland.[5] These included the prophetess Remana Hi, her father Aporo Pangari, Wiremu and Kokou Pangari, her husband Hipiriona Hi, sister Mata Kuku, and nephew Tame Kuku.

While the main figures were away local leaders demolished the camp and persuaded the remainder of the residents to disperse. On their return, however, the movement revived and while it conducted itself quietly it attracted adherents from some neighbouring areas.

In this period the group took to marching along roads in processions, dressed in their white robes, carrying flags and blowing horns. As they marched they chanted the Psalms of David, and one local clergyman said that 'they worked themselves into a state of frenzy.'[6] There was also an accusation that the prophetess attempted to sacrifice a child — an action needed to ensure the assistance of God. As in the case of the Hebrew prophet Abraham's intended sacrifice of his son, the act was stopped at the

Upper Waihou Movement

last moment when the Atua showed he was satisfied with the display of faith. The Waihou prophetess told her people that God was waiting to come down and endow them with a knowledge of all things, but that a proper offering must be made to him. Though this time it was avoided, it might be necessary in the future.

As in other movements during this period, the prophetess and her followers used the scriptures of liberation to speak to their people in a time they felt they were socially disadvantaged by the loss of their land to European settlement. They saw themselves as a dispossessed race and, as in other responses with similar motivation, this was reflected in their concentration on Old Testament books such as the Psalms.

From the stories of the Israelites, particularly in their time of wandering in the wilderness under the prophet Moses, they found the model for their exclusive community of believers and the idea of the sacred enclosure. The insistence on the colour white was likely inspired by biblical references, and two possible sources are interesting because of their contexts. The verse Ecclesiastes 9:8, 'Let thy garments always be white', quotes a Hebrew text which presents God as an austere judge who is to be approached with care and appeased by evidence of righteous living; and Revelation 3:4–5, which speaks of those who are worthy and clothe themselves in white, is an apocalyptic and prophetic work following the pattern of earlier pre-Christian Jewish writings which address issues of liberation from oppression. The very wearing of robes was a deliberate adoption from scripture of a tradition of past times — it being neither a Maori nor an observed European custom.

The practices of marching and blowing horns also show biblical influence. The Hebrew prophet Joshua and his people marched around Jericho blowing trumpets made of rams' horns, with very effective results against their enemies. The older scriptures also mention the horn of salvation — a reference to the Lord as fortress and deliverer.[7] Psalm 18, which contains a repeated reference to 'the horn of my salvation', tells of King David's cry to the Lord in his sorrow and distress, together with God's response — deliverance from enemies, and continuing mercy to the people of the Lord.

Though the tradition of human sacrifice was not part of the Israelites' code, the recorded response of the prophet Abraham to the test of faith demanded by God[8] was apparently at least considered in other Maori movements (Pai Marire, Parihaka, and Maketu movements)[9] — and the response associated with Parihaka would have been well known to the Waihou prophetess.

The New Religions

Other biblically inspired ideas which were present in former movements — divine revelation, the agency of angels, the transfer of knowledge of languages, protection from bullets, and preservation of the faithful from their enemies — all also formed part of the reponse at Upper Waihou. In addition, the conclusion that the Old Testament was inspired while the Christian scriptures were not, and the changing of the sabbath from Sunday to Saturday, were also quite common responses to mission teachings during the second half of the nineteenth century.

The many obvious borrowings from the Hebrew scriptures illustrate the spreading dissatisfaction of the period. The three responses together show the change from a Christian-based millennial movement, through a decline in confidence in New Testament ideas, leading to a movement in which the newer scriptures and teachings were rejected in favour of those of the Old Testament.

Notes

1. Much fuller details can be found in Elsmore, *Mana From Heaven*.
2. For more details of Ani Karo, see Elsmore, *Mana From Heaven*.
3. Gudgeon, 'Maori Superstition', p. 179.
4. See *Northern Luminary Extra*, 26 July 1887.
5. For a full description of the incident, see evidence of the trial held 23 July 1882, P1:89/1545; also *Northern Luminary Extra*, 26 July 1887, though this account does vary from the court records in some details. Also McGovern, Telegrams sent 26, 27 July, 1 August 1887, Letter 27 July, 1887.
6. T.A. Joughin. See McGovern, Letter, 9 March 1889.
7. Joshua 6:13; 2 Samuel 22:3; Psalms 18:2.
8. Genesis 22:1–13.
9. See the earlier chapter on these movements.

19. Kohititanga Marama
Prophet: Te Matenga Tamati

With the death of Te Kooti in 1893, it became obvious that the period of physical protest by Maori was over. Social conditions were improving as a group of well-educated indigenous youths entered the professions, and began to make their mark, particularly in Parliament. By now the people had acquired some immunity to introduced diseases, and while they were outnumbered fourteen to one, by the end of that decade the population would again start to rise. It was still, however, a time of great spiritual need.

In 1894 God spoke again — this time to a member of the Ngati Kahungunu at his home near Wairoa, Hawke's Bay. Te Matenga Tamati was an elder of Putahi Pa, and was a man respected for his spiritual qualities and quiet leadership. He was already known for his gift of healing, and often helped people by means of the water from a spring on his property.[1]

To Matenga it was revealed that while God numbered the Maori among his own people, full blessings would not be given to them until they had raised a temple to the Lord in their midst. This was a task which had been kept back from Te Kooti because of the blood on his hands. But now the time for the temple had come, and Te Matenga's mission was to oversee its construction.

With divine confirmation of the command, Te Matenga announced his call to his people, and many believed him and came to follow him. To them he revealed that God had renewed his covenant with them, and had promised a period of peace and prosperity to come. It would be a new age.

The people called themselves Kohiti, from the phrase Te Kohititanga Marama — a reference to the new moon as symbolic of that new age. An alternative name for the movement was the Church of the New World. As knowledge of Matenga spread throughout the district, more and more came to join the Kohiti and offer their support.

Just as in ancient times Moses received full details from Yahweh as to the building of the first tabernacle or tent of meeting in the wilderness, and just as the Lord also gave instructions to Solomon, for the building of the first temple in Jerusalem, so now were details of the new one given to the prophet Matenga.

It was to be built of twelve posts — each 40 feet in length, 4 feet square at the base and tapering to 3 feet square at the top (12.2 metres long by 1.2 m square, tapering to 0.9 m square). These pillars were to be named for the twelve children of Jacob, and were to be erected in a square. The tabernacle was to remain as this simple structure — merely the twelve pillars forming a square, without roof or walls, for the natural elements (rain and wind) would be kept out by divine will. Inside the sacred area there was to be an Ark of the Covenant — the dimensions of this being 6 feet by 4 feet by 4 feet (1.8 m by 1.2 m by 1.2 m). When the temple was built, the Ark was to be dragged into the sanctuary by two cows.

Finally, when the whole structure was completed according to instructions, God himself would speak to the people from the temple.

The preparations for the materials of the building were carefully carried out. From a stand of giant totara at Mangatawhiti, in the foothills of the Waikaremoana ranges, twelve trees were chosen, and accompanied by the appropriate karakia they were felled and trimmed at the site to the specified dimensions. Then came the extremely difficult task of moving the giant logs some miles across rough country to the bank of the Mangaaruhe Stream. Matenga promised the men that should they have sufficient faith, the pillars would be moved by divine will — the Kohiti were merely to guide them to where they should go.

The workers were under strict regulations throughout this period, and no one was permitted to do anything which might result in violating the sacred nature of the task. Everyone worked naked, as was the traditional practice in work relating to strictly tapu rites. There was to be no smoking, drinking of alcohol, or spitting, and even the use of inappropriate words was condemned. Anyone who broke any of these rules was fined, or set out of the camp for a time.

The shifting of the pillars proved to be an immense task, and consequently a great test of faith. At one stage the project was postponed for a few months to allow time for more faith to build up. Ropes and tackle were necessary at times — such as when the leader log, Joseph, was stuck firmly in a gully. But eventually, some years after the start of the venture, all the pillars were waiting by the stream for the last stage of their journey.

From this point on, said Matenga, there would be no need of physical human help. The pillar named Joseph would lead his brothers to the chosen land — the site selected for the new temple, at Korito (Corinth), a beach a few kilometres from the township of Wairoa. Te Matenga and a large band of followers gathered at Erepeti in the Ruakituri Valley, where they prayed under the guidance of the prophet.

Their faith was amply rewarded in a dramatic fashion, for the region soon experienced heavy rain which quickly flooded the watershed. Such a result was more than sufficient to float the twelve totara, and these rode down the Mangaaruhe Stream to join the Wairoa River, southwards down the river, then across the bar into the sea.

This occurrence excited much interest in Wairoa. A great surge of water approached the town down the swollen river, and riding the crest of the surge were the giant pillars. A notable incident occurred as a result of this. As the timber was coming down the river, two men from the town paddled out in a canoe intending to claim and secure one of the pillars. Their canoe was capsised as it bumped the wood, and both climbed on top of the log. When the timber was swept close to the shore, one of the men jumped off and managed to reach safety, but the other stayed aboard and was drowned at the bend of the river when the log rolled.

This incident was notable because of the drowning, but even more so because of the consequences of the breach of tapu which occurred when the men sat on the sacred pillar.

Eleven of the logs eventually beached themselves right on target at the chosen spot of Korito. But the twelfth, Joseph, was found to have followed the lead of his namesake and travelled into a distant land. Joseph was located some miles to the east, near Waikokopu. This time there was no hope of the missing brother finding his way back unaided, and a boat was chartered to pull it back to join the rest.

The date was then 1904, for the task of cutting and trimming the timber and bringing it from the hills to the sea had taken seven years. The pillars lay ready for the building of the temple at Korito, and on completion the Ark of the Covenant would be placed inside. When this was accomplished God would talk to his people from this spot. Due to the fact that things had not gone entirely according to plan — the difficulties

The New Religions

encountered during the moving of the pillars, and Joseph's going astray being evidence of this — the prophet was now forced to tell his people that this generation would not be the builders of the temple. Instead, another leader would have to come to fulfil this work. So the people abandoned the project temporarily, awaiting the appearance of another prophet yet to come.

This was not seen as any lack of fulfilment of a promise, but rather recognised by the believers as a sign that the faith was not yet sufficient, the time not right, the conditions not yet fulfilled. It was accepted that with the completion of this stage, Te Matenga's work was ended. He had been given the task of overseeing the building of the temple to this point, and this was now accomplished. The time was not yet come for the final stage, but this would surely come to pass. It would not be achieved by this generation, but maybe the next, or the one after. Or perhaps it would be several generations. But it would come about.

Meanwhile, a small meeting house was built at Korito, close to where the pillars waited. This site was known as Te Karauna, the Crown, and it was on this spot that the promised temple would eventually be built. Te Matenga Tamati died in 1914 and was buried at Korito.

The Kohiti met at Te Karauna each month at the time of the new moon. They would gather on the evening before the first appearance of the moon, hold services throughout the next day and until the morning of the third day. Te Matenga counselled his people to keep faith in God and his promise to them. The new age would be brought about by the unity of the people. To effect this they should gather together at the time of the new moon and at these meetings they should play harps so that the earthly congregations would resemble those in heaven, and a harmony would be established between the two. When the people of New Zealand, Maori and Pakeha together, met in this way, then would commence the new age.

During these years Te Matenga became more and more renowned for his spiritual gifts. People from around the district, and further afield, came to him for healing and help. Using remedies of his own making, and through the agency of blessings and the application of water from his spring, he healed all manner of illnesses, and straightened bent and broken limbs. To the childless he gave special blessings, with the result that formerly barren couples were afterwards able to have children. It was said that he knew the problems of those who came, before they arrived, and none went without comfort.

The Kohiti religion was based on a threefold assurance that there was an all-powerful God who was creator and sustainer of the world; that

The pillars of the temple to be built by the people of Te Kohititanga Marama lie on the beach at Korito. The stake standing at left is about two metres high.
(Ken Elsmore)

The end sections of some of the totara pillars destined for the temple of the Lord, to be built by the followers of Te Matenga Tamati.
(Ken Elsmore)

Maori were his people; and that God had made a covenant with his people by providing them with a prophet to lead them. The message given by Matenga was marked by being non-exclusive — the hope for the future was in a great millennial period of peace and prosperity for all. It would come about when the people of New Zealand, Maori and Pakeha together, all gathered at the new moon to praise God, and played their harps to create a harmony on earth which would resemble that in heaven.

Te Matenga fulfilled the role of spiritual leader in very much the same manner as did the prophets of the Old Testament. He received revelation from God, and was given divine assistance in the form of powers of prophecy and healing. The laws governing the Kohiti, particularly those in regard to the sacred nature of the temple, were comparable to those incumbent upon the Hebrews. Like the Old Testament prophets Matenga was a strict leader and enforced rules for the protection of the people and their purpose.

As in the case of the Israelites, the Kohiti had a covenant, made between Jehovah and his people. Should the Kohiti follow their instructions faithfully and build the temple to the Lord, God would then speak to them directly, just as had been promised in the earlier time when Yahweh was present at the mercy seat.[2]

The tabernacle or temple itself provides numerous parallels when considered alongside the biblical accounts of the tabernacle of the Mosaic period, and the later temple at Jerusalem. Though neither of these provides the identical model for the Kohiti temple, that at Jerusalem is obviously the conceptual model, and there is no doubt of the influence of the Hebrew scriptures.

The pillars were named for the twelve children of Israel, with Joseph as their leader. Instructions were given that the structure should be built and the Covenant of the Lord placed inside it before full blessings would be given to the people.[3] While the dimensions given for the temple are no longer known, it seems likely that they would closely resemble those of the inner sanctuary of Solomon's temple.[4] The idea that the Ark was to be drawn into the Kohiti temple by two cows has its parallel in the history of the Ark of the Covenant of the Hebrews also.[5]

The period of seven years taken to bring the totara from the hills to the sea corresponds to the seven years taken for the building of the temple in Jerusalem;[6] likewise, the cedars and cypresses from the hills of Lebanon were also floated southwards in the sea to cover the greater part of their journey.[7] While the temple of the Israelites was first mentioned to David by God,[8] David was later to learn that he would not be the one to see to its construction, but that this must be done by another. So too was Matenga told that the task must be undertaken by a future leader. It is interesting that the reason David could not build the temple was because of the blood on his hands — the reason why the task had not been given to Te Kooti.⁹

Te Matenga decreed that the Kohiti follow the lunar calendar, and meetings were held on the first of each lunar month, at the time of the new moon. In doing this he was not only putting aside the European calendar and returning to the traditional Maori system, but he was adhering to the old Hebraic custom, for that people also celebrated the new moon as the beginning of the month. The meetings followed the Ringatu pattern, beginning on the night before the new moon, continuing for the whole of the day of the new moon, and ending on the morning of the third day.

The purpose of the Kohiti religion, and therefore the task of the prophet Matenga, was to act as a spiritualising or revitalising force to the people who were at their lowest ebb culturally, socially and spiritually. Once more it was to draw heavily on the Hebraic scriptures as its model for a message to a depressed people. The religion of Matenga brought them a positive approach to the problems of the day, teaching as it did that the answer was in the unity of the people. While this inclusive message had a definite social purpose, it is also clear that the manner of the response was very much a spiritual one. Rather than becoming a political leader, Te Matenga led his people in building up a new spiritual system from which they could gain inner strength.

Notes

1. The sources of information on this movement are almost all oral. For a full account of Kohititanga Marama, see Bronwyn Elsmore, *Te Kohititanga Marama: New Moon, New World*. The oral informants are acknowledged in the preface of that work.
2. See Exodus 25:22; 30:6.
3. See Exodus 25:8–9.
4. For further details on this, see Elsmore, *Kohititanga Marama*, p. 66.
5. See 1 Samuel 6:7–16.
6. 1 Kings 6:38.
7. 1 Kings 5:9.
8. 2 Samuel 7:5–7.
9. See 1 Chronicles 22:8.

20. Iharaira
Prophet: Rua Kenana

In the years following the death of Te Kooti, a number of people made claims to be his successor. While Te Kooti had left a number of prophecies regarding a future leader, no one candidate managed to gain unanimous support.

Rua Kenana Tapunui was one of those who made the claim to be this awaited figure. Born in the Urewera district in 1869, he was of both Tuhoe and Ngati Kahungunu parentage, being the posthumous son of Kenana Tumoana who had died fighting for Te Kooti at Makaretu the previous November. As a child he was sent to live with relatives of his father in Hawke's Bay, returning thereafter to his early home when he was about nine years old.[1]

In 1904, when working in the Bay of Plenty district, Rua underwent mystical experiences in which the voice of God spoke and Christ appeared to him. Following this receipt of revelation and his consequent personal development to the state of charismatic leader, many people became devoted to the new prophet. The power of his personality and persuasion can be shown by the fact that miraculous cures were reported from his healing ability, and some believers in his millennial prophecies readily sold all their possessions in order to follow his command. Rua established his 'New Jerusalem' at Maungapohatu in 1906, and this settlement in its heyday (c. 1907–1908) was sometimes the home of up to 800 people.[2]

Once again the alienation of land, by sale and government confiscation following the Pai Marire battles, was the prime concern. Rua is reported to have answered the call of God to prophethood with the words,

Rua Kenana, who established a New Jerusalem at Maungapohatu for his Israelites.
(7800 1/2, Alexander Turnbull Library, Wellington)

'If your wish is for me to save only people, I won't help, but if it is to save the land, then I shall carry out this task.' Rua's explanation of this reply was, 'I shall save the land, for if I save only people, there will soon be no land on which they can live.'[3] It was a call to which Rua responded as a true leader, becoming friend, protector and prophet to thousands of people for over 30 years.

His religious teachings largely followed those of Te Kooti before him. Like his predecessor he identified himself with Moses, and his followers took the name Iharaira, Israelites. Rua drew a parallel between himself and the exiled people, saying that in his childhood he was 'rejected and despised' by his people 'so that the Bible words were fulfilled,'[4] presumably a reference to the prophecy pointing to the Redeemer of Israel who was to be '. . . despised and rejected of men; a man of sorrows, and acquainted with grief . . .'[5]

The move back to Maungapohatu under Rua was a symbolic return of the people to their homeland. This ancestral land he called 'Peura', Beulah, a poetic name for the land of Israel in its future restored condition.[6] In the way of an Old Testament prophet, Rua had prophesied that a flood would wipe out all those who failed to follow him, but this did not come to pass. There was also a sound political reason for the move — by returning to occupy the land and bring it into production, as the Iharaira did by clearing hundreds of acres for cultivation and grazing for cattle, they would also save it from being designated wasteland and so taken over by the government. Like the nation of Moses, the settlement led by Rua was very well ordered, for the prophet proved himself an astute leader and involved the help of apostles and councillors in the ongoing affairs of the community.[7]

In 1904, at Maungapohatu, Rua claimed to have had a mystical experience on the sacred mountain of the Tuhoe people.[8] Parallels with the Old Testament and New Testament can be seen in accounts of the incident, as well as original occurrences. Briefly, Rua, accompanied by his wife Pinepine (some accounts say a dog also), climbed Maungapohatu after he was called in a manner similar to the Hebrew prophet Samuel and instructed by an angel. There they spent some days, meeting with Christ and a woman, and were shown a large diamond said to have been buried by Te Kooti. A rainbow leading down from the mountain was seen as a renewal of the Covenant of God made with his people. Because of this experience the mountain can be compared to Horeb where Moses conversed with the Lord. To some of the Iharaira, Maungapohatu was seen as Zion, and Lake Waikaremoana as the Sea of Galilee.[9]

At the New Jerusalem in the Urewera country, under the sacred mountain, Rua erected two buildings which were inspired by stories of the Hebrew King Solomon. One also named Hiruharama Hou (New Jerusalem) was a large house apparently constructed with the idea of being a gift to the Lord in the manner of Solomon's building — a conceptual likeness, though with some physical parallels. A further large building of circular construction, used as meeting house and courthouse, was named Hiona, Zion. Hiona was a two-level structure, which could have been associated in Rua's mind with the tower of Babel.[10] The hall was brightly painted in the colours blue, white and gold — colours included among those of sacred and priestly significance to the ancient Israelites.[11]

Rua's name, then, takes on added significance. With Rua (two) together with Kenana (transliteration of Canaan), the combination alludes to a 'second Canaan', in line with his millennial teachings. The name Tapunui, also, was appropriate to his sacred designation and powers — the word denoting great sacredness, or very sacred. In addition, he took the name Hepetipa from Hephzibah (My delight is in her), this being symbolic of Zion or the restored Jerusalem in the land of Beulah.[12]

Like the Nazirites — Israelites who took a special vow of separation and abstinence in order to dedicate themselves, either temporarily or permanently, to some special service[13] — the Iharaira let their hair grow long without cutting it, and no tobacco or alcohol was permitted.[14] Following the return of Rua from his jail sentence in 1915, however, the long hair of the Iharaira was ceremoniously cut and most of the tapu lifted. The period of 'separation unto God' was now over, and so the New Jerusalem was made desolate — but this time at the hands of the faithful. The buildings Hiona and Hiruharama Hou were demolished, and the timber was used to build a new meeting house and residence at Maai, a short distance to the west.[15]

Along with Rua's identification of himself with Moses was an additional claim to be the second Christ. This was made at the beginning of his career as prophet, for at Pakowai near Gisborne in 1904, soon after his initial calling by God, he claimed to be 'the second Christ', having a predecessor such as John the Baptist in the person of Te Kooti.[16] It is in this context that he called himself and was acclaimed by his followers as Te Mihaia Hou — the new Messiah.

It was said that Rua not only saw himself as a messiah to his people, but claimed to resemble Jesus Christ physically.[17] In 1906 he was baptised as the Messiah by a Ringatu tohunga in the Waipaoa River. However, he

Hiona (Zion), the meeting house and courthouse modelled on the idea of the courthouse of the Hebrew King Solomon, and constructed at New Jerusalem for the Iharaira (Israelites).
(F-2915 1/2, Alexander Turnbull Library, Wellington)

is reported as saying that there are three good religions — that of the Father, that of the Son, and that of the Holy Ghost. His religion was the third, for the Holy Ghost spoke through him.[18]

In the minds of many of the followers present on the day of the taking of Maungapohatu by the constabulary in April 1916, the identification of Rua with Christ was so accepted that many believed he was shot but miraculously healed. Several close followers would swear that later a wound in his side would often bleed and he would sometimes display the stigmata, and that a wound to his forehead represented the crown of thorns.[19]

Rua's stated aim, however, reveals him more in the line of an Old Testament prophet, for he said his task was to deliver his people who were now living in bondage. The reason for this was based in the history of the ancient Israelites. Rua explained that Adam had two children, Cain and Abel, Cain being the Pakeha and Abel the Maori. In this time, as in old, the people of Cain continued to attack those of Abel. The prophet also stated that there were two Jacob's ladders leading to heaven — one for the white people and one for the dark people.[20]

Seeing himself as the 'brother of Christ',[21] Rua selected twelve disciples, but this was more from an Old Testament model than Christian, as they were drawn from different areas, and were therefore roughly symbolic of the twelve tribes of Israel. Moreover, they were known as Riwaiti (Levites), and strict rules were applied to them, as had been also to their Old Testament counterparts.

The religion of the Iharaira also included elements of rejection of the Christian Church. As did several of the Maori prophets of the past, Rua followed the practice of the Saturday sabbath, and while Christmas was recognised as a Christian ceremony, it was not celebrated by the community as a whole. Instead, a festival period was held from 20 December, culminating on the twenty-third with a celebration marking Rua's 'name-day'.[22]

The church's teaching of monogamy was set aside for the prophet himself, for following the prophecy of Isaiah, Rua took seven wives.[23] The number eventually rose to a total of twelve, though not all of these lived with him at once. Rua apparently compared himself to King Solomon in regard to his many marriages, and his favourite wife was referred to by the Iharaira as the 'Queen of Sheba'. In addition, Pinepine, the prophet's first wife, who was designated as highly tapu because of her sacred experiences on Maungapohatu, lived alone in a separate house, as did Solomon's wife, the daughter of the Egyptian Pharaoh.[24]

Like the other prophet-leaders, the teaching of a great millennium to come, following the destruction or departure of the Pakeha, was part of the teachings of Rua. But the way in which this was to be achieved differed in this movement. Whereas in the former movements the agency for bringing about the Pakeha-free state was the intervention of Jehovah, in Rua's system the emphasis altered from God to man. Now deliverance would come through the law, Rua taught, but no doubt this was thought to reflect divine will nonetheless, for Rua was lord of the earth by heavenly designation.

According to Rua, King Edward would arrive in Gisborne and present back to Maori the land which had been taken over by Europeans. In 1906 Rua rode to Gisborne with a box said to contain jewels from an unknown place, to be presented to the King. On the journey the box was placed in a special tent at night, this being compared by the party of travellers to the Ark of the Covenant of the Israelites. Rua and his followers waited on the Gisborne wharf for three days. When the King did not arrive, Rua revealed that he himself was the king. So his role of prophet then became one of Saviour-king — through him would the millennium be ushered in.

The following year he prophesied that catastrophic upheavals would precede the millennium. Whakaari (White Island) in the Bay of Plenty

The New Religions

would first erupt, then an earthquake and tidal wave would destroy the coastal lands.[25] Many of the prophet's believers sold their properties and moved inland, up to the new settlement at Maungapohatu.

In the later period of Rua's mission, his millennial prophecies were revived, though there was now a difference. The Covenant had been defiled and the separation had ended — now what was awaited was the return of Christ. The end of the world would come either before or during the year 2000. With the foretelling of two weeks of darkness, to be followed by deluge and flood, then fiery storms, more people sold property and moved to Maungapohatu where the New Jerusalem was rebuilt. Followers there during this period tell how they read the scriptures through, from Old Testament to New Testament, under Rua's instruction.[26]

The missionary John Currie recorded that the ailing prophet, before his death in 1937, told him that he would rise again on the third day after death, a prediction that prompted 600 would-be witnesses to pour into Matahi where the prophet then lived. But the verses quoted by Rua on this occasion were from Ezekiel 37, beginning:

Behold, O my people, I will open your graves, and cause you to come up out of your graves, and bring you into the land of Israel....[27]

The scripture refers to the vision of Ezekiel that the nation of the Israelites, previously divided because of the sins of the people, and now seemingly extinct, would again come to life. It was an assurance that God, who had seemed to abandon his people, had not really done so, and when the period of purification was over, they would be restored. In addition, Rua, before his death, gave money for his funeral to his family, and left instructions for the burial.[28] In this case too, therefore, it appears that the prophet was not seeing himself as Jesus Christ in person, but rather in the station of a prophet with a similar function as leader to his people. This is in line with the statement of Rua that he resembled all the prophets of Israel.[29] The reference is also a reassurance that the millennial period foretold by the prophet would still come about, and the people come into their own.

The story of this extraordinary leader adds a further fascinating chapter to the account of the identification with the Old Testament within the Maori religious movements. While parallels with the Hebraic system are at least as strong here as in any of the other movements, those with Christianity are also present. Rua's movement, then, can be seen as a changing point in the response to European culture, though this had been pointed to by Te Kooti in his later period. It was a change which reflected

Iharaira

the growing maturity of Maori in that understanding of the message of Christianity, and perhaps a growing realisation that rejection of the religion of the Pakeha might not be the most appropriate response to the present social need.

Notes

1. Judith Binney et al., *Mihaia, The Prophet Rua Kenana and His Community at Maungapohatu*, p. 18.
2. See Peter Webster, *Rua and the Maori Millennium*, p. 205, for more details on such figures.
3. Webster, *Rua*, p. 158. Webster gives an interview with F. Teka as his authority.
4. *Hawkes Bay Herald*, 15 June 1908, or *Poverty Bay Herald*, 16 June 1908. Cited by Binney, *Mihaia*, p. 18; Webster, *Rua*, p. 156.
5. Isaiah 53:3ff.
6. See Isaiah 62:4.
7. Webster, *Rua*, pp. 198, 186.
8. For details, see Binney, *Mihaia*, p. 18; Webster, *Rua*, pp. 188–90.
9. Webster, *Rua*, p. 188.
10. Binney, *Mihaia*, p. 50.
11. See Exodus 25:3–9; 28:5–6.
12. Isaiah 62:4.
13. See Numbers 6:1–5.
14. Binney, *Mihaia*, p. 32, Webster, *Rua*, p. 161.
15. Binney, *Mihaia*, p. 80.
16. *Te Pipiwharauroa*, July 1906, p. 6. Cited by Binney, *Mihaia*, p. 29.
17. Webster, *Rua*, p. 210, quoting *NZH*, 20 April 1908. See also Binney, *Mihaia*, p. 73.
18. *PBH*, 16 June 1908. Cited by Webster, *Rua*, pp. 160–61.
19. Binney, *Mihaia*, pp. 119–21; Webster, *Rua*, p. 274.
20. *PBH*, 16 June 1908. Cited by Webster, *Rua*, pp. 160–61.
21. Webster, *Rua*, pp. 160, 283.
22. Binney, *Mihaia*, p. 56.
23. Isaiah 4:1.
24. 1 Kings 7:8. Binney, *Mihaia*, pp. 57–58.
25. Compare this prediction with that of Te Kooti, and of Himiona Te Orinui, both of whom prophesied the second eruption of Mount Tarawera in the 1880s. None of the three predictions was fulfilled.
26. Binney, *Mihaia*, pp. 156–59.
27. Ezekiel 37:12. See Binney, *Mihaia*, pp. 174–75.
28. Binney, *Mihaia*, p. 177.
29. *PBH*, 31 December 1908. Cited by Binney, *Mihaia*, p. 49.

21. Ratana
Prophet: Tahupotiki Wiremu Ratana

A further candidate for the title of successor to Te Kooti, and also to Te Maiharoa, was to arise 25 years after the earlier prophet's death, when a Taranaki farmer received knowledge of his appointment as a spiritual leader to his people. Ancestrally, Tahupotiki Wiremu Ratana had Ngati Apa, Ngati Raukawa and Ngati Hine connections; religiously, he had both Church of England and Methodist backgrounds from his parents.

As a young man, however, Ratana was to be more influenced by an aunt, Mere Rikiriki, prophetess and healer, and founder of Te Hahi o te Wairua Tapu (the Holy Ghost Mission), centred at Parewanui on the Rangitikei River. When Ratana was 39, Mere Rikiriki revealed to her followers that her nephew was the one for whom they had been waiting — a leader who would act for the welfare of his people. The prophecy was repeated several times over the following year, and Ratana began to feel the stirrings of the spirit within and voices speaking to him. In 1918 portentous signs were given to him, climaxing with a vision on 8 November of that year.

On this occasion the bewildered farmer, standing on the verandah of his home, saw a cloud rising from the Tasman Sea, and swirling about him; then a voice spoke, claiming to be that of the Holy Ghost, and appointing Ratana as the 'Mouthpiece of God' for Maori. His mission was to 'unite the Maori people, turning them to Jehovah of the Thousands, for this is His compassion to all of you.'[1]

The message of Ratana's mission spread quickly and widely, particularly as a result of his gift for healing. Individuals, families, and parties of people travelled from all over New Zealand, many settling around the Ratana home, so that shortly a thriving village was established at the spot. As hundreds of aids such as crutches, spectacles, walking sticks and wheelchairs testified as they were left behind or donated by grateful patients who no longer felt the need of them, the new prophet healed the physical ailments of his own people, and others who sought his help.[2] But, more importantly, he provided healing for their spiritual ailments and wounds.

From the Waikato village of Te Kumi, where the prophet Te Mahuki Manukura had founded his Tekau-ma-rua movement 40 years before, a thousand people travelled to Ratana, as they had to Parihaka before, and returned inspired to build a church for the worship of God in the Maori language.[3] Members of other Maori movements, as well as those of Christian Churches, came too, and those who did not become followers of the new prophet were renewed in their own faith. Ratana also undertook journeys around the country, preaching of the oneness of God and of his love for his people. As a result, noted one church historian, many were 'seized with intense religious conviction, and everywhere Maoris could be found earnestly studying the Word of God.' Hundreds who had been slaves to alcohol were transformed, the moral stimulus of the movement being 'more wonderful even than some of the marvellous physical healings which undoubtedly took place.'[4] Also pleasing to the churches was Ratana's denunciation of the traditional practices of the tohunga in their invocation of the atua.[5]

But the teachings of Ratana were not always to be accepted so well by the established churches. In the first few years relations between the two were very positive as the churches recognised the good results of the new prophet's teachings. But a dimension of popular mythology arose around the person of the prophet as the followers saw him as a divine figure, so causing some consternation in the churches. During the same period an element of nationalism was developing in Ratana's mission, and the gap between the new movement and the established order widened.

From the beginning of his ministry Ratana referred to God as Ihoa (Jehovah) rather than as Matua (Father), and included 'Nga Anahera Pono' (The Faithful Angels) in the divine hierarchy. The basis for this was the prominent part played in the scriptures by angels as supporters of Jehovah and mediators between God and humans. While discouraged by the orthodox churches, the new doctrine was not made a definite issue of contention, but the later addition of Ratana himself as Mangai (Mouthpiece), and the replacement of the Trinity with a quinary of God,

Son, Holy Ghost, Faithful Angels, and Mouthpiece, caused great theological dispute.

The one-time head of the Presbyterian Maori Council, the Very Rev. J.G. Laughton, wrote some years later that the names 'Jesus' and 'Christ' had been dropped from Ratana liturgy:

> *These names never occur now in the services of the Ratana Church. All the prayers now end in this way, 'For the Mouthpiece is leader, now and forever, Amen.' Only the title 'The Son' is retained and there is good reason for believing that Ratana is being identified with that divine cognomen.*

Laughton, seeing this as a 'perversion of the everlasting Truth of the Gospel', continued:

> *Recently we heard a Ratana preacher claiming with vehemence that the second coming of Christ is fulfilled in Ratana. Little else is now preached but the glorification of Ratana and of the movement, and the Treaty of Waitangi, and the wrongs of the Maori people, and all the movement is going to do for the amelioration of these evils. When Scripture is used it is quoted in such a way as to support these subjects . . .*[6]

By 1925 the gap between the established churches and the new movement was too wide to be bridged and Ratana registered the faith as a separate church. It was a 'schismatic sect' in the opinion of the Church of England. The Church warned that any Anglican joining would be excommunicating themselves from the Church of Christ.[7] The Methodist Church took a more liberal attitude towards the Ratana movement, and retained links with it, though not agreeing completely with the elevation of the station of the Mangai.[8]

There can be no doubting the Christian basis of the Ratana Church. The creed, formulated in 1925, states the belief:

> *Jehovah sent His Son in the human form of Jesus Christ to redeem man and to conquer the power of sin, of darkness and of death . . .*
>
> *I believe that in Jehovah is the light and the great joy for my spirit and for my body. This fact is experienced through union with Christ in the Infinite Love of the Father and the power of the Holy Ghost and the Faithful Angels, and active fellowship with the true Christian believers.*[9]

Tahupotiki Wiremu Ratana, prophet and noted healer, and founder of the Ratana Church. *(16602 1/1, Alexander Turnbull Library, Wellington)*

The New Religions

The organisation of the Christian Church was also the basis for the administration and the patterning of Ratana services. Before the registration of the new Church, Ratana services included the practice of incorporating aspects of worship from each of the Christian denominations, for the people present were from every background.[10] Hymn singing, the repetition of the (Ratana) creed, and the recitation of prayers were included in services as in the more orthodox churches, being most similar to Methodist practices.

Because of the Christian background, Sunday was retained as the day of worship. Christian festivals of Christmas and particularly Easter were also kept, with the commemoration of Ratana's birthday on 25 January, and the day of his revelation, 8 November, being added to the calendar of festivals. An order of Apostles under the leadership of a President was formed to administer the affairs of the Church.

Other differences in doctrines also point to an element of rejection of the established churches. Ratana, reflecting traditional Maori beliefs, criticised casual Pakeha attitudes to the sacred, seen in such practices as paying the clergy for the performance of religious duties, and using the name of Jesus Christ in oaths. Such acts desanctified the holy, and by engaging in them Pakeha had forfeited the right to assume the religious leadership of Maori.[11] This is the real reason for the lack of emphasis on the name of Christ within the new Church. 'Whakatapungia te ingoa o Te Karaiti', instructed the Mangai, 'Make the name of Christ sacred', and he attempted to do this by removing it from everyday use and abuse; so restoring the feeling of sacred reverence. For the same reason the sacrament of Holy Communion was removed from regular Ratana services, being observed only occasionally and by Church leaders only.[12]

But there was much in the new Church which was also based firmly on the same identification with the Old Testament as in previous Maori religious movements.

Once again the new movement included the notion of descent from the Israelites, and an often-used term for the followers was 'Morehu' (survivors), linking them with the surviving 'remnant' of the Hebrew nation.[13] The foundation stone of the temple built by Ratana is inscribed, 'I establish the Church of the Morehu on this rock which will never be shaken.' Pakeha were referred to as Tauiwi (foreign tribe), or Gentiles. The brightly coloured vestments of the Ratana orders — blue, white, red, purple and gold — are identical with those of the priesthood of the ancient Hebrews.[14]

Ratana himself can be seen as a charismatic Old Testament-style prophet, with he and the Anahera Pono being intermediaries between God and people as in the Hebrew tradition. Signs and visions were given to him to prepare him for his mission. The 1918 influenza epidemic which devastated the population[15] immediately before the announcement of his priesthood was seen by some Maori as indicative of the wrath of God, and comparable to the plagues which Yahweh unleashed upon the Egyptians and the erring Children of God. As many a prophet before him, Ratana went through a time of mental testing before he accepted his spiritual designation.[16] Mere Rikiriki had once commanded him to 'Go with the God of your forefathers, the God of Abraham and of Jacob,'[17] and Ratana in his denunciation of the practices of tohunga took on a role similar to that of both Abraham and Moses in their fervent demonstrations against former polytheistic practices. Like Moses he stressed the importance of a Covenant between God and people — Jehovah would protect them if they kept His worship pure.

Ratana himself testified to his Church's allegiance to the Hebrew religion, for in the Mangai's foundation of faith, made two days before his death, the following passage occurs:

Reverent worship of Jehovah was the genesis of my effort that the Pa might be a reflection of the House of Israel and that all those therein might not be contaminated by materialism, clever sophistries, or the devil. O Jehovah the Father, O the Lord Jesus Christ, the tree has grown of which I sowed the seed to the four winds. We beseech Thee come, govern the whole of it that it may bear good fruit for the salvation of both the body and the soul.[18]

Since the turn of the twentieth century, a number of Maori-oriented churches arose in order to minister to the specific needs of Maori. The Ratana Church has undoubtedly been the greatest of these, for more than 70 years after its inception it is still very active.[19] The period was a more positive one as regards the situation of the Maori — the birthrate was again rising, Maori leaders such as Carroll, Ngata, Buck, Pomare and others had helped to raise the situation and the morale of their people, and the burning question of alienation of land was largely settled, though former injustices over confiscation were yet to be repaired. That the series of indigenous movements continued is in itself a definite indication that Maori still could not identify fully with the system of the Pakeha.

After the Ratana response, several others have arisen, most being localised to a limited area, and often not long lived, but all of them attempting to relate the Christian message to the situation of Maori at the time. It should not be surprising, therefore, that while these movements

The New Religions

are primarily Christian, elements of traditional beliefs are often retained, and scriptural emphasis frequently rests on the books of the Old Testament.

Notes

1. J.M. Henderson, *Ratana. The Man, the Church, the Political Movement*, pp. 24–25.
2. See Henderson, *Ratana*, pp. 31–36 for details of Ratana's healing mission.
3. Ibid., p. 27.
4. John Rawson Elder, *The History of the Presbyterian Church of New Zealand, 1840–1940*, p. 267.
5. See George I. Laurenson, *Te Hahi Weteriana*, p. 217.
6. J.G.L. Laughton, *Ringatuism: the Ratana Church*, pp. 3–4.
7. Information contained in a pastoral letter to Maori clergy, from the press report; cited by Henderson, *Ratana*, p. 48.
8. See Laurenson, *Te Hahi Weteriana*, pp. 218–19.
9. Statements 3 and 9, the Creed of the Ratana Church. Cited by Henderson, *Ratana*, pp. 118–19.
10. Moana Raureti, 'The Origins of the Ratana Movement', King (ed.), *Tihe Mauri Ora*, p. 49.
11. Maharaia Winiata, *Changing Role of the Leader*, p. 99.
12. Henderson, *Ratana*, p. 76.
13. See Isaiah 10:20–23, 11:11; Zephaniah 3:13; Zechariah 8:12.
14. See Exodus 28:5–6, 8, 15.
15. Of 21 family members of his generation, only Ratana and two sisters survived. Henderson, *Ratana*, pp. 23–24. For more details about this epidemic in New Zealand, see Richard Collier, *The Plague of the Spanish Lady*, p. 97.
16. Henderson, *Ratana*, p. 25.
17. Ibid., p. 77.
18. Cited in Henderson, *Ratana*, p. 100.
19. The 1996 census figures give the number of members as 36,450, making the Ratana Church the seventh largest specific religious denomination in the country.

Conclusion

The religious response of the Maori of New Zealand does not present a unique reaction by an indigenous people to colonisation by another. On the contrary, the features of the movements which arose in this country have been duplicated in other places. In several African nations, prophets reminiscent of those of the ancient Israelites have arisen in the same manner and for like purpose, in similar reactions to colonisation. One Nigerian 'Moses', in 1934, founded 'God's Kingdom Society' — a movement which included emphasis on the Old Testament scriptures at the expense of the New, the commemoration of a Feast of Tabernacles rather than the Lord's Supper, and millennial promises, just as was done in New Zealand. Other examples of 'Hebraist' movements can be found among many other peoples — the 'Nunamuit' religion of the Alaskan Eskimos, the 'Israelites' among the Papago Indians of Arizona, the 'Aaronista' among the Quechua in Peru, the 'Universal Family of Yahweh of the Firstborn' in Manila.[1]

But while the New Zealand response is not unique, it is notable for the large number of such movements occurring in a comparatively small population and over an extended period. This very fact must disprove the judgements of early missionaries who stated the Maori had no religion — on the contrary, the belief system must necessarily have been well developed if the race was not to put aside the old ways easily and needed to find movements of adjustment to bridge the former and the new.

Examination of all the numerous Maori religious movements of the past century and a half reveals a pattern that occurs in their development.

Without being too schematic, it is possible to divide that time into four parts to produce four periods, each with its emphasis on a different aspect of response.

The earliest phase, between 1830 and 1850, can be termed the 'Early Adjustment Period', being a time when Maori attempted to adjust to the growing influence of Pakeha on their world.[2] In this time Maori explored the new religious views and reconciled them to their own beliefs. New movements in this period included Christian concepts laid upon a foundation of old tradition. In some cases, as is probably inevitable in any such clash of cultures, the teachings of the missions were turned against those who had brought them. However, Maori who called themselves Jews in this period were not so much rejecting the Christian message totally, but making a statement about the differences between the two cultures, and perhaps pointing to some failing in the mission itself. Towards the end of this time the movements are clearly inspired by the new teachings, the most dramatic of these involving the fulfilment of millennial hopes and expectations as Christ was prophesied to return to earth in the new colony.

For the decade of the 1850s, the emphasis was squarely on healing as the Maori race was devastated by the introduced diseases. The religious bases to the healing movements, though, differed, with some reverting to traditional methods and karakia, while others again turned further from the old ways believing the atua to be the cause of their ills, and so followed the European God.

The 'Prophetic Period' can be dated as between 1860 and about 1900, and it is generally within this time that the movements led by a charismatic 'prophet' figure arose.[3] The prophets were people of action as well as spiritual leaders, as were the former rangatira-tohunga figures and, coincidentally, the great prophets of the Old Testament stories. They were a result of the great need of Maori at this time of the rapid decline of the race — numerically, culturally, socially and spiritually. With the rise in understanding of the religion of the Pakeha taking place at the same time as a disillusionment with European society, the religious responses of Maori became more and more complex. During these years each one of the numerous movements included elements of traditional belief and ideas taken from the introduced religion in varying degrees.

It is in this period that the similarities between the new movements and the Old Testament scriptures are most marked. Whereas earlier the idea of genealogical descent from an ancient race appealed to Maori, in this time they were convinced of its truth because of the overwhelming weight of apparent evidence supporting the notion. The similarities between the two primal cultures provided sufficient 'proof', and the comparable social situations of the peoples confirmed it and presented a pattern of response. Prophets were modelled on their ancient counterparts, and scriptural parallels seen in uncounted cases.

From about 1900 onwards came the 'Period of the Maori Churches'. By this time Maori realised that the continuation of a Pakeha-structured society was inevitable, so the time of active protest was past. In a more positive light their lot was improving and the future looked much brighter for the indigenous race. The passing of a further generation or two also meant that the introduced religion had become far more familiar, and therefore much more acceptable. While there was still a need for Maori-oriented worship, doctrines which had previously been excluded, or at least de-emphasised, became incorporated more into the structures of the movements, and the result was the setting up of Maori Christian churches. Many of these, however, retained definite links with the past periods through their particular emphasis on the scriptures that contained the liberation theology of the Hebraic faith.[4]

There is some irony in the fact that the Christian Church took so much of the blame for the depressed condition of Maori in the initial century of contact. In the first place the Church Missionary Society opposed the colonisation of New Zealand at such an early time in their mission work — a stance with the interests of Maori in mind. While the methods and attitudes of some of the mission workers can now be seen as unfortunate, it must be remembered that these people were as much the product of their own social conditioning as were Maori, and their sincerity as regards their purpose is without question.

Undoubtedly the greatest irony must occur in the fact that missionaries, in providing their sacred scriptures to Maori for the express purpose of converting the race to the Christian faith, handed them the materials by which the mission could be judged, and at the same time provided them with an almost made-to-measure model for an alternative response. Even further, they gave the New Zealanders the idea that they were descended from the people of Israel. It is no wonder that Maori responded in the way that they did.

In fact, it was not only Maori who were affected by the inevitability of the conclusion. James A. Stack,[5] residing at his mission station at Rangitukia, East Cape, in 1846 found the life of a missionary rather too demanding and also reacted in a similar manner. Stack proclaimed himself a prophet, saying God had visited the district, that the hearts of the people were subdued by Divine grace, and the lion had been changed into a lamb. It had been revealed to him by God, stated Stack, that the Maori of Waiapu were Jews and that they would be returned to their former land in ships of war within the coming six months. Stack was sent to Auckland for medical help, but his mental condition deteriorated even more, he being judged not fit for New Zealand work.[6]

While to the missionaries it must have seemed at times that their efforts had been in vain, from the point of view of hindsight the reaction of Maori was perhaps an inevitable happening. As the gap between the two cultures and the religious beliefs was far too wide to allow an easy slide from one into another, intermediate steps were no doubt necessary. Certainly according to the history of the Christian religion this would appear to be so, for the message of Christ could obviously not have been accepted in the times of Abraham and Moses, but those earlier steps and centuries were required to prepare the people for the later dispensation. It is, rather, to be wondered that Maori made the transition in such a relatively short period of time.

Notes

1. These few examples of a widely occurring phenomenon are taken from 'The Maoris and the Jews. Maori Religious Movements Since 1830', one of a series of Burns Lectures delivered at Otago University in 1976, by Dr Harold W. Turner. This writer is indebted to Dr Turner for the script of this lecture.
2. All Maori religious movements that have arisen from the time of first contact and until the present day can, however, be considered movements of adjustment.
3. The divisions cannot be exact. Rua Kenana, who belongs to this category, did not found his movement until 1904. Likewise, The Church of the Seven Rules of Jehovah, which belongs more properly to the fourth period, was established in the decade before the turn of the century.
4. A much fuller work on Maori religious movements including explanation of the periods in the response, and the influence of the published scriptures, is found in Elsmore, *Mana From Heaven: A Century of Maori Prophets in New Zealand*.
5. Not to be confused with his son, Canon James West Stack, who served the Anglican mission in many parts of New Zealand, and who is referred to elsewhere in this book.
6. Charles Baker, Journal, 28 September to 2 October 1846. See also J.W. Stack, *Early Maoriland Adventures*, p. 142, in which Canon Stack says his father's condition was the result of excessive pressure caused by the insistence of his parishioners for him to preach and pray for long hours in anticipation of the coming Day of Judgement, the subject of a series of sermons given by Stack.

Glossary

Aotearoa — a traditional name for New Zealand.
Ariki — high chief; chief of a whole waka (canoe) or tribal area.
Atua — deity, God. Following general practice, in this work a capital denotes the single deity of a system, such as the God of Christianity. When used without a capital it refers to one god among many.
Atua maori — the gods of the Maori.
Atua pakeha — the God of the Pakeha.
Atuanui — great God, Supreme God; as the God of the Pakeha.
Haka — a fierce dance with a chant.
Hapu — subtribe of a large iwi (people).
Hui — gathering, meeting.
Hurai — (transliteration) Jew.
Ihoa (Ihowa) — (transliteration) Jehovah.
Karakia — traditional invocation or chant; prayer; worship. Used in narrow and broader senses to mean a prayer or a system of worship, e.g. 'Karakia Nakahi', the faith of the Nakahi, or Nakahi Worship.
Kiwa, ocean of — Pacific Ocean.
Makutu — a spell, or curse.
Mana — prestige, influence.
Marae — the ground of a Maori settlement; strictly, the plaza or meeting area.
Matakite — second sight, prophecy.
Mate — sickness. Mate maori – indigenous illnesses; mate pakeha – introduced illnesses or diseases.
Mauri — life principle, spirit.
Moko — chin tattoo.
Ngarara — lizard.
Niu — small divinatory sticks used by tohunga in rituals.
Noa — not sacred, free of tapu.
Pa — village; originally meaning a fortified village.
Pakeha — non-Maori New Zealanders.
Po Takoto — a night of readiness. Traditionally a night of watching by warriors before a battle.
Pou rahui — prohibition markers for tribal boundaries.

Pu — gun.
Ra Tapu — sacred day, i.e. sabbath.
Rangatira — chief.
Tangata whenua — local people.
Taniwha — monster.
Tapu — sacred; and therefore often forbidden.
Taua — war party.
Tiu — (transliteration) Jew.
Tohunga (**Tohuka** in South Island dialect) — expert, specialist, priest.
Tohunga ahurewa — highest class of priest.
Utu — revenge; price; reciprocity.
Waiata — song; psalm.
Waipiro — 'stinking water', i.e. alcoholic drinks.
Whakapapa — table of genealogy or ancestral descent.
Whare wananga — school of higher learning.

Bibliography

Unpublished manuscripts

BAKER, CHARLES.
  Journals 1827–1867, AML TS (6 vols).
BEATTIE, HERRIES.
  'A Celebrated Trek. Maori Migration from Temuka to Omarama in 1878', HL, MS M.1. 582 E/21 Notebook 286.
  Notebooks 'General Maori Information', HL, MS Herries Beattie Collection.
  'Racial Comparisons and the Maori', HL, MS M.1. 582/E9 Notebook 65.
BEST, ELSDON.
  Best Scrapbooks, ATL MS.
BROWN, A.N.
  Journal, D.H. Maxwell TS, Tauranga.
BULLER, JAMES.
  Letters to WMS, SJC TS.
BUSBY, JAMES.
  'Occupation of New Zealand 1833–1843', AML TS MS46 (2 vols).
DACKER, BILL.
  'Chapters in South Island Maori History', Dissertation in partial fulfilment of the degree of B.A. (Hons), Otago University, 1980.
GREY MANUSCRIPTS.
  Auckland Public Library.
HAMLIN, JAMES.
  Journal, ATL and NML MS.
  Reports to CMS, ATL and HL, CMS microfilm C.N./O 50.
HAMMOND, T.G.
  'Te Whiti and Parihaka', ATL TS MS73.28 'Taranaki Material'.
HOBBS, JOHN.
  Letters and Journals 1824–1849. AML TS.
LAWREY, W.
  Letters to WMS, SJC TS.
SMITH, S. PERCY.
  Letters, ATL MS Papers 1187, Folder 260.
TAYLOR, RICHARD.
  Journal, AML TS.
TURNER, HAROLD W.
  'The Maoris and the Jews. Maori Religious Movements Since 1830. Some Repercussions of the Christian Contact', Burns Lectures 1976, Series Two, Lecture 8.
TURTON, H.H.
  Letters to WMS, SJC TS.
WHITELEY, JOHN.
  Letters to WMS and others, SJC TS.
  Journal, ATL TS.
WILLIAMS, HENRY.
  Letters to CMS, ATL TS (5 vols).

WILLIAMS, HENRY (Jnr).
  Williams Letters, ATL MS.
WILLIAMS, WILLIAM.
  Journal ATL TS.
  Letters to CMS, ATL.
WILSON, ORMOND.
  Letter to ATL 5 June 1965.
WOON, WILLIAM.
  Journal and Letters, SJC TS.

Official Papers
Appendices to the Journals of the House of Representatives.
Missionary Register.
New Zealand Police Department Records.
New Zealand Statistics Department, Census Records.

Newspapers
Auckland Weekly News.
Bay of Plenty Times.
Hawke's Bay Herald Tribune.
New Zealand Herald.
Poverty Bay Herald.
Daily Southern Cross.
Northern Luminary Extra.

Books, Monographs, Pamphlets
ADAMS, PETER.
  The Fatal Necessity: British Intervention in New Zealand 1830–1847. Auckland/Oxford University Press, Auckland, 1977.
ANONYMOUS.
  King Tawhiao of the Royal Tribe of Waikato, the Ngatimahuta. Printed *Daily Telegraph*, Napier, not dated.
'ARISTOBOULOS'.
  The Universal Destruction of Aborigine Races by Colonizing Nations, and Eventually of the New Zealanders: The Cause of This Evil and its Sure Preventive. Smith, Elder, & Co., London, 1846.
BABBAGE, S. BARTON.
  Hauhauism. Reed, Wellington, 1937.
BAGNALL, A.G. and G.C. PETERSON (eds).
  William Colenso. Reed, Wellington, 1948.
BARTON, R.J. (ed.).
  Earliest New Zealand, Journals and Correspondence of the Rev. John Butler. Author, Masterton, 1927.
BAUCKE, WILLIAM.
  Where the White Man Treads. Wilson and Horton, Auckland, 1928.
BEST, ELSDON.
  The Astronomical Knowledge of the Maori. Dominion Museum, Wellington, 1972.
  Christian and Maori Mythology: Notes on the Clash of Cultures. The N.Z. Worker, Wellington, 1924.

The Maori. (2 vols) Harry Tombs, Wellington, 1924.

Tuhoe: Children of the Mist, vol. 1. Thomas Avery, New Plymouth, 1925.

BIBLE.

(King James Version used throughout.) Also Maori translation, *Paipera Tapu,* 1868 and 1924 editions.

BINNEY, JUDITH.

The Legacy of Guilt: A Life of Thomas Kendall. Auckland/Oxford University Press, Auckland, 1968.

Judith Binney, Gillian Chaplin, Craig Wallace, *Mihaia, The Prophet Rua Kenana and His Community at Maungapohatu.* Oxford University Press, Wellington, 1979.

BRITTAN, S.J., G.F. GRACE, C.W. GRACE, A.V. GRACE (eds).

A Pioneer Missionary Among the Maoris, 1850–1879. Bennett, Palmerston North, 1928.

BUDDLE, REV. THOMAS.

The Aborigines of New Zealand. Williamson and Wilson, Auckland, 1851.

BUICK, T. LINDSAY.

The Treaty of Waitangi. Thomas Avery, New Plymouth, 1936.

BURROWS, R.

Extracts from a Diary kept by the Rev. R. Burrows During Heke's War in the North, in 1845. Upton & Co., Auckland, 1886.

CASELBERG, JOHN (ed.).

Maori Is My Name. John McIndoe, Dunedin, 1975.

CHURCH MISSIONARY SOCIETY.

Documents exhibiting the views of the Committee of the Church Missionary Society on the New Zealand Question. London, 1839.

Further statement of the committee of the Church Missionary Society relative to the New Zealand mission. London, 1840.

CLARK, PAUL.

Hauhau: The Pai Marire Search for Maori Identity. Auckland/Oxford University Press, Auckland, 1975.

COLEMAN, JOHN NOBLE.

A Memoir of the Rev. Richard Davis For Thirty-Nine Years a Missionary in New Zealand. J. Nisbet & Co., London, 1865.

COLENSO, WILLIAM.

Fiat Justitia. Dinwiddie, Morrison & Co., Napier, 1871.

COLLIER, RICHARD.

The Plague of the Spanish Lady. Macmillan, London, 1974.

COWAN, JAMES.

The Maori Yesterday and Today. Whitcombe & Tombs, Wellington, 1930.

DAILY SOUTHERN CROSS.

Mr J.C. Firth's Conference with Tamati Ngapora and the King Natives at Orahiri. D.S. Cross Reprint, Auckland, 1869.

ELDER, JOHN RAWSON.

The History of the Presbyterian Church in New Zealand, 1840–1940. Presbyterian Bookroom, Christchurch, 1940.

(ed.), *The Letters and Journals of Samuel Marsden 1765–1838.* Coulls Somerville Wilkie and Reed, for Otago University, Dunedin, 1932.

ELSMORE, BRONWYN.

Mana From Heaven — A Century of Maori Prophets in New Zealand. Reed, Auckland, 1999.

Te Kohititanga Marama, New Moon New World. Reed, Auckland, 1998.

FIRTH, RAYMOND.
   Economics of the New Zealand Maori. Government Printer, Wellington, 1959.
GIBSON, TOM.
   The Maori Wars. Reed, Wellington, 1974.
GOLDMAN, LAZARUS MORRIS.
   The History of the Jews in New Zealand. Reed, Wellington, 1958.
GORST, JOHN.
   The Maori King. Paul's Book Arcade/Oxford, Auckland, 1959. (First published 1864.)
GRACE, JOHN TE H.
   Tuwharetoa. Reed, Wellington, 1959.
GREENWOOD, WILLIAM.
   The Upraised Hand. Polynesian Society, Wellington, 1942.
HADFIELD, OCTAVIUS.
   The Second Year of one of England's Little Wars. William and Norgate, London, 1861. (Facsimile, Hocken Library, Dunedin, 1967.)
HAMMOND, REV. T.G.
   In the Beginning. Methodist Literature and Colporteur Society, Auckland, 1940.
HANKIN, CHERRY A. (ed.).
   Life in a Young Colony. Whitcoulls, Christchurch, 1981.
HAYTER, MAUD GOODENOUGH.
   Folklore and Fairy Tales of the Canterbury Maoris. Otago Daily Times, Dunedin, 1957.
HENDERSON, G.M.
   Taina. Wingfield Press, Wellington, 1948.
HENDERSON, J.M.
   Ratana: The Man, The Church, The Political Movement. Reed/Polynesian Society, Wellington, 1972.
HOCHSTETTER, F. VON.
   New Zealand, Its Physical Geography and Natural History. Gotta, Stuttgart, 1867.
HOCKEN LIBRARY.
   The Maori Population. Hocken Library, Dunedin, 1977.
HOHEPA, P.W.
   A Maori Community in Northland. Anthropology Department, Auckland University, Auckland, 1964.
'HOPEFUL'.
   Taken In: Being a Sketch of New Zealand Life. W.H. Allen & Co., London, 1887.
HOWE, K.R.
   Race Relations in Australia and New Zealand. Methuen, Wellington, 1977.
HURINUI, PEI TE.
   King Potatau. Polynesian Society, Wellington, 1959.
JOHANSEN, J. PRYTZ.
   Studies in Maori Rites and Myths. Munksgaard, Copenhagen, 1958.
KEYS, LILLIAN.
   The Life and Times of Bishop Pompallier. Pegasus, Christchurch, 1957.
KING, MICHAEL.
   Te Puea. Hodder & Stoughton, Auckland, 1977.
LAUGHTON, J.G.L.
   Ringatuism — the Ratana Church. Knox College, Dunedin, 1960.
LAURENSON, GEORGE I.
   Te Hahi Weteriana. Wesley Historical Society, Auckland, 1972.

MCINTYRE, W. DAVID, AND W.J. GARDNER (eds).
Speeches and Documents on New Zealand History. Oxford University Press, Oxford, 1971.
MACKAY, J.A.
Historic Poverty Bay and the East Coast, N.I., N.Z. Author, Gisborne, 1949.
MCKEEFRY, REV. PETER (ed.).
Fishers of Men. Whitcombe & Tombs, Christchurch, 1938.
MCNAB, ROBERT (ed.).
Historical Records of New Zealand, vol. 1. Government Printer, Wellington, 1908.
MANING, FREDERICK EDWARD ('A Pakeha Maori').
Old New Zealand: A Tale of the Good Old Times. Robert J. Creighton & Alfred Scales, Auckland, 1863. (Reprints: Whitcombe & Tombs, Auckland, 1956; Golden Press, Auckland, 1980.)
MARJORIBANKS, ALEXANDER.
Travels in New Zealand. Smith, Elder & Co., London, 1845.
MARTIN, LADY M.A.
Our Maoris. Society for Promoting Christian Knowledge, London, 1884. (Reprint: Wilson & Horton, Auckland, 1970.)
MAUNSELL, ROBERT.
Grammar of the New Zealand Language. J. Moore, Auckland, 1842.
MEADE, HERBERT.
A Ride through the Disturbed Districts of New Zealand. John Murray, London, 1871.
METGE, JOAN.
The Maoris of New Zealand. Routledge & Kegan Paul, London, 1976.
MIKAERE, BUDDY.
Te Maiharoa and the Promised Land. Heinemann Reed, Auckland, 1988.
MITCALFE, B.
Nine New Zealanders. Whitcombe & Tombs, Christchurch, 1963.
MORLEY, REV. WILLIAM.
The History of Methodism in New Zealand. McKee & Co., Wellington, 1900.
NIHONIHO, TUTA.
Narrative of the Fighting on the East Coast 1865–1871. Government Printer, Wellington, 1913.
OLIVER, W.H. with B.R. WILLIAMS (eds).
The Oxford History of New Zealand. Oxford University Press, Wellington, 1981.
POLACK, J.S.
Manners and Customs of the New Zealanders, vols 1 & 2. James Madden/Hatchard, London, 1840. (Reprint: Capper, Christchurch, 1976.)
POMPALLIER, RT. REV. JEAN-BAPTISTE FRANÇOIS.
Early History of the Catholic Church in Oceania. Brett, Auckland, 1888.
POOL, D. IAN.
The Maori Population of New Zealand 1769–1971. Auckland/Oxford University Press, Auckland, 1977.
PORTER, FRANCES (ed.).
The Turanga Journals. Price Milburn/Victoria University Press, Wellington, 1974.
PRATT, M.A. RUGBY.
The Pioneering Days of Southern Maoriland. Epworth, London, 1932.
PURCHAS, H.T.
A History of the English Church in New Zealand. Simpson and Williams, Christchurch, 1914.

PYBUS, REV. T.A.
Maori and Missionary. Reed, Wellington, 1954.
REISCHEK, ANDREAS.
Yesterdays in Maoriland. Jonathan Cape, London, 1933.
ROGERS, LAWRENCE M. (ed.).
The Early Journals of Henry Williams 1825–40. Pegasus, Christchurch, 1961.
ROSS, W. HUGH.
Te Kooti. Collins, Auckland, 1966.
RUSDEN, G.
Aureretanga, Groans of the Maoris. William Ridgeway, London, 1888. (Reprint: Capper, Christchurch, 1975.)
SCOTT, DICK.
Ask That Mountain. Heinemann/Southern Cross, Auckland, 1975.
SERVANT, FATHER C.
Customs and Habits of the New Zealanders 1838–1842. Reed, Wellington, 1973.
SHORTLAND, EDWARD.
The Southern Districts of New Zealand. Longman, Brown, Green, and Longman, London, 1851.
SINCLAIR, KEITH.
A History of New Zealand. Penguin, Harmondsworth, 1969.
The Origins of the Maori Wars. N.Z. University Press/Oxford, Wellington, 1961.
STACK, J.W.
Early Maoriland Adventures. University Press, Oxford, 1937. (First published New Zealand, 1935.)
More Maoriland Adventures. Reed, Wellington, 1936.
Notes on Maori Christianity. Press, Christchurch, 1874.
TAYLOR, RICHARD.
The Past and Present of New Zealand, with its Prospects for the Future. William McIntosh, London, 1868.
THOMSON, ARTHUR S.
The Story of New Zealand: Past and Present — Savage and Civilized, vol. 2. John Murray, London, 1859.
TIKAO, TEONE TAARE.
Tikao Talks: Traditions and Tales Told to Herries Beattie. Reed, Dunedin, 1939.
WADE, WILLIAM.
A Journey in the Northern Island of New Zealand. George Rolwegan, Hobart, 1842. (Reprint: Capper, Christchurch, 1977.)
WAKEFIELD, EDWARD JERNINGHAM.
Adventure in New Zealand, vols 1 & 2. John Murray, London, 1845.
WARD, JOHN.
Information Relative to New Zealand, Compiled for the Use of Colonists. John W. Parker, London, 1840. (Reprint: Capper, Christchurch, 1975.)
WARD, JOHN P.
Wanderings With the Maori Prophets, Te Whiti and Tohu (with illustrations of each chief): Being Reminiscences of a Twelve Months' Companionship with them, from their arrival in Christchurch in April, 1882, until their return to Parihaka in March, 1883. Bond, Finney, & Co., Nelson, 1883.
WEBSTER, PETER.
Rua and the Maori Millennium. Price Milburn/Victoria University Press, Wellington, 1979.
WILLIAMS, FREDERICK WANKLYN.
Through Ninety Years 1826–1916: Life and Work Among the Maoris in New Zealand.

Notes of the Lives of William and William Leonard Williams, First and Third Bishops of Waiapu. Whitcombe and Tombs, Auckland, 1939.
WILLIAMS, WILLIAM.
Christianity Among the New Zealanders. Seeley, Jackson, Halliday, London, 1867.
WILLIAMS, WILLIAM LEONARD.
East Coast Historical Records. Gisborne, 1932.
The Maori Mission Past and Present. Keeling and Mundy, Palmerston North, 1904.
WILSON, C.J. (ed.).
Missionary Life and Work in New Zealand, 1833–1862. Private, Auckland, 1889.
WILY, HENRY E.R.L. and HERBERT MAUNSELL.
Robert Maunsell LL.D. A New Zealand Pioneer. His Life and Times. Reed, Dunedin, 1938.
WINIATA, MAHARAIA.
The Changing Role of the Leader in Maori Society. Blackwood & Janet Paul, Auckland, 1967.
WRIGHT, HARRISON M.
New Zealand 1769–1840: Early Years of Western Contact. Harvard University Press, Cambridge, Mass., 1967.
YATE, WILLIAM.
An Account of New Zealand. Seeley & Burnside, London, 1835.

Articles
ANDERSEN, JOHANNES.
'Maori Religion.' *JPS* vol. 49, no. 196, pp. 513–55.
BINNEY, JUDITH.
'Papahurihia: Some Thoughts on Interpretation.' *JPS* vol. 75, no. 3, pp. 321–31.
BLAKE-PALMER, J.
'Tohungaism and Makutu, Some Beliefs and Practices of the Present Day Maori.' *JPS* vol. 63, no. 2, pp. 147–64.
GADD, BERNARD.
'Teachings of Te Whiti o Rongomai, 1831–1907.' *JPS* vol. 75, no. 4, pp. 445–57.
GUDGEON, LIEUT.-COL. W.E.
'Maori Religion.' *JPS* vol. 14, no. 55, pp. 107–30.
'Maori Superstition.' *JPS* vol. 14, no. 56, pp. 167–92.
'The Tohunga Maori.' *JPS* vol. 16, no. 62, pp. 63–91.
HOWE, K.R.
'The Fate of the Savage in Pacific Historiography.' *NZJH* vol. 11, no. 2, pp. 137–54.
IRVINE, JEAN.
'Maori Mysticism in the North.' Peter Davis, John Hinchcliffe (eds), *Dialogue on Religion, New Zealand Viewpoints.* Auckland University Press, 1977, pp. 6–10.
LEWTHWAITE, GORDON.
'The Population of Aotearoa.' *The New Zealand Geographer* VI (April 1950), pp. 35–52.
LYONS, DANIEL P.
'An Analysis of Three Maori Prophet Movements.' I.H. Kawharu (ed.), *Conflict and Compromise*, Reed, Wellington, 1975, pp. 55–79.
MISUR, GILDA Z.
'From prophet cult to established church, the case of the Ringatu Movement.' I.H. Kawharu (ed.), *Conflict and Compromise.* Reed, Wellington, 1975, pp. 97–115.
NGATA, APIRANA T., and I.L.G. SUTHERLAND.
'Religious Influences.' I.L.G. Sutherland (ed.), *The Maori People Today — A General Survey*, N.Z. Institute of International Affairs and N.Z. Council for Educational Research, Wellington, 1940, chapter 10.

OWENS, J.M.R.
'New Zealand Before Annexation.' W.H. Oliver with B.H. Williams (eds), *Oxford History of New Zealand*. Oxford University Press, Wellington, 1981, chapter 2.
'The Unexpected Impact: Missionaries and Society in Early 19th Century New Zealand.' Christopher Nichol and James Veitch (eds), *Religion in New Zealand*. Tertiary Christian Studies Programme of the Combined Chaplaincies and Religious Studies Department Victoria University, Wellington, 1980, pp.13–52.

PARR, C.J.
'Before the Pai Marire.' *JPS* vol. 76, no. 1, pp. 35–46.
'Maori Literacy 1843–1867.' *JPS* vol. 72, no. 3, pp. 211–33.
'A Missionary Library. Printed Attempts to Instruct the Maori, 1815–1845.' *JPS* vol. 70, no. 4, pp. 429–50.

PHILLIPPS, W.J.
'The Cult of Nakahi.' (Letter) *JPS* vol. 75, no. 1, p. 107.

RAURETI, MOANA.
'The Origins of the Ratana Movement.' Michael King (ed.), *Tihe Mauri Ora*. Methuen, Wellington, 1978, pp. 42–59.

SORRENSON, M.P.K.
'Land Purchase Methods and Their Effect on the Maori Population.' *JPS* vol. 65, no. 3, pp. 183–99.

TAREI, Wi.
'A Church Called Ringatu.' Michael King (ed.), *Tihe Mauri Ora*. Methuen, Wellington, 1978, pp. 60–66.

THOMPSON, R.J.
'Christian and Jewish Understandings of the Old Testament.' John Hinchcliffe, Jack Lewis, Kapil Tiwari (eds), *Religious Studies in the Pacific*. Colloquium Auckland University, Auckland, 1978, pp. 69–78.

URLICH, D.U.
'The Introduction and Diffusion of Firearms in New Zealand 1800–1840'. *JPS* vol. 79, no. 4, pp. 399–410.

WALSH, ARCHDEACON.
'The Passing of the Maori.' *TPNZI* vol. 40, pp. 154–74.

WILLIAMS, H.W.
'The Reaction of the Maori to the Impact of Civilisation.' *JPS* vol. 44, no. 176, pp. 216–43.

WILSON, ORMOND.
'Papahurihia, First Maori Prophet.' *JPS* vol. 74, no. 4, pp. 473–83.

WINKS, ROBIN W.
'The Doctrine of Hauhauism.' *JPS* vol. 62, no. 2, pp. 199–236.

WOHLERS, REV. J.F.H.
'On the Conversion and Civilisation of the Maoris in the South of New Zealand.' *TPNZI* vol. 14.

Index

Abel, 186
Abraham, 83, 123–25, 129, 134, 145, 172, 195, 200
Adam and Eve, 63, 73, 186
Adoption, 94
Adultery, 26, 72, 94, 129
Ahuriri, 121
Alcohol, 25, 47, 156, 176, 185, 191
Alexandra (Pirongia), 163
Amalekites, 135–36
Angels, 117, 123, 126, 127, 174, 184, 191–95
Animals (introduced), 46
Apostles, 127, 151
Arawa, 167
Ark (ship), 135, 142–43
Ark of the Covenant, 176–77, 180, 187
Arowhenua, 154–59
Ati Awa, 140, 156
atua maori, 19, 20, 29, 48–50, 64, 80–84, 87–88, 110, 120, 152, 155, 157–58, 198
Atuanui — see God of Christianity
Auckland, 63, 126, 172, 200
Australia, 43, 45, 50, 74, 78, 112

Babel, 185
Baker, Charles, 24, 45, 56, 61, 62, 75, 76, 111
Baptism, 17, 76, 97, 111, 137, 142
Barrenness, 94
Baucke, William, 48, 64, 77, 143
Bay of Islands, 18, 22, 39, 44, 109, 168
Bay of Plenty, 37, 81, 101, 107, 117, 124, 136, 165–70, 182, 187
Beattie, Herries, 79, 155
Benjamin, 74, 95
Best, Elsdon, 82, 83
Beulah, 184–85
Bible (book), 19, 102, 118, 143, 145, 165
Blackout Movement, 114
Brown, A.N., 19, 22, 27, 36, 38, 49, 55, 57–58, 63, 77, 81, 117
Buck, Sir Peter, 195
Buddle, Thomas, 111
Burrows, R., 72
Busby, James, 42

Bush, R.S., 167
Butler, John, 18, 25

Cain, 186
Calendars, 89–90, 96, 181, 194
Canaan, 77, 90, 92, 146, 185
Canaan, N.Z. seen as, 100, 125–30, 185
Cannibalism, 22, 74
Canterbury, 155–59
Carroll, Sir James, 195
Catholic Church, Mission, 20, 25, 26, 59–61, 112, 165
Chapman, Thomas, 24, 26, 38, 61, 112
Chatham Islands, 132–37
Chinese, 144–45
Chosen People, 110, 125, 142, 147
Christ, Jesus, 55, 81, 83–84, 110, 126, 137, 182, 184–86, 192–95
Christ, return of, 117–18, 153, 171, 188, 192, 198
Christian names (see also names, given), 76, 126, 142, 151
Christianity, rejection of, 116–17, 119–22, 125–30, 137–38, 171–74, 187, 194, 198
Christmas, 187, 194
Christs, other, 145, 185–86
Church Missionary Society, 22–26, 33, 50, 59–61, 109, 112, 199
Church of England, 64, 125, 165, 167, 190, 192
Church of the New World, 176
Churches (buildings), 54, 56, 61, 102, 191
Circumcision, 90
Clarke, George, 43, 61
Clothing, 47, 172–73
Cloudy Bay, 22
Colenso, William, 20, 61, 75, 137
Comet, 110, 143, 168
Conversion to Christianity, 17, 18
Cook, Captain James, 42, 45
Covenant of God, 180, 184, 188, 195
Currie, John, 188

Daniel (Hebrew), 76, 89
David (Hebrew), 91, 134, 167, 173, 180–81

Davis, Richard, 61, 119–20
Dead, raising of, 22, 30, 57, 84, 110, 118, 125, 188
Death customs, 90–92, 96
Devil, 20, 62, 87, 95, 111, 112, 118
Diet, 21, 46–47, 142
Disciples, 156, 186–87
Disease, 35, 45–50, 119–20, 125, 142, 155, 195, 198
Divination, 87, 88
Divorce, 94, 97
Dragon, 119–20
Dreams, 87, 89
Du Fresne, Marion, 25
Dunedin, 144

Earthquake, 188
East Coast, 37, 101, 124, 125, 199
Easter, 194
Edward VII of England, 187
Edwards, B.J.F., 153
Egypt, Egyptians, 73, 76, 90, 126, 135–37, 195
Elijah (Hebrew), 26–27
Embalming, 90
End of World, 188
England, 18, 23, 43, 50, 56, 117
English language, 78
Erepeti, 177
Exodus of Israelites, 119, 135–36
Ezekiel (Hebrew), 188

Fairburn, W., 61
Fire from heaven, 118, 126, 134
Fitzroy, Captain, 117
Flood, 176–77, 188
Fox, Major — see Te Pokiha
Fraser, Captain, 156
French, 25–26, 101

Gabriel (angel), 123–24, 126–27, 134
Galatea, 136
Galilee, Sea of, 184
Gate Pa, 56
Gentiles, 142, 194
George IV of England, 43
Gideon, 89, 126
Gisborne (see also Turanga), 107, 185, 187
God of Christianity, 19, 29, 37, 49, 50, 54–56, 77, 81–82, 111, 116, 120, 121
God of Hebrews, 37, 77, 80–84, 92, 96, 100, 101, 110, 125, 126, 137, 142–48, 176, 187, 190–91, 195
Goliath, 91

Gomorrah, 168
Gore-Browne, Governor, 34
Gorst, John, 95
Government (British), 34
Government forces, 54–55, 58
Grace, T.S., 64, 101, 126
Greek language, 73
Gudgeon, W.E., 64, 74
Guns, 36, 39, 43–44, 54

Hadfield, Octavius, 34, 61, 73
Hahi o te Wairua Tapu, 190
Hakopanikau, 116–17
Hall, William, 19, 61
Hamlin, James, 56, 61
Hammond, T.G., 92, 145, 146
Harp, 178–80
Hauhau, 125–30, 159
Hawaiki, 154
Hawea, Lake, 156
Hawke's Bay, 55, 107, 130, 175–81, 182
Heads, preserved, 50
Healing, gift of, 156, 167, 175, 178, 191, 198
Heaven, 95, 111
Hebrew festivals, 103, 136–37
Hebrew language, 72
Hebrews — see Israelites
Hell, 58, 111
Hema, 74
Hepanaia, 124
Hi, Hipiriona, 172
Hi, Remana, 171–74
Hikutu, 109
Himiona Te Orinui, 165–70
Hine-Titama, 84
Hiona, 172–74, 184–86
Hiruharama Hou, 147, 145, 182–89
Hobab, 76
Hobbs, John, 59
Hobson, Governor, 38
Hokianga, 29, 112–14, 121, 123
Holy Communion, 59, 137, 194
Holy Ghost Mission, 190
Holy Spirit, 116–17, 127, 134, 186, 190
Hone Heke, 55, 72, 109–11
Hongi Hika, 18, 43
Horeb, 184
Horopapera, 123
House of Lords (England), 33
Housing, 47
Hursthouse, Charles, 163

Iharaira, 182–89
Ihoa (Ihowa), 82–83, 191

Index

Images, Maori, 88
Impurity, 88, 90, 96
Io, 81–84, 95, 151
Isaac (Hebrew), 83, 134
Isaiah (Hebrew), 187
Ishmael (Hebrew), 72
Israel (country), 117, 184, 200
Israel (Hebrew) — see Jacob
Israel, tribes of, 73–74, 95, 142, 163, 176, 180, 187
Israelites, 79, 119–20, 185–87, 197
Israelites, colours of, 185, 194
Israelites, Maori descent from, 72–84, 95, 100, 194, 199
Israelites, Maori seen as, 72–84, 87–96, 100, 102–103, 125–30, 134–37, 142–48, 156, 167, 173–74, 194–95

Jacob (Hebrew), 73–74, 83, 89–92, 94, 95, 134, 142, 176, 195
Japheth (Hebrew), 126
Jehovah, 37, 77, 80–84, 92, 96, 100, 101, 110, 125, 126, 137, 142–48, 176, 187, 190–91, 195
Jerusalem, 91, 123, 176, 180
Jerusalem, New, 147, 145, 182–89
Jesus — see Christ
Jews, 98
Jews in New Zealand, 23, 78, 100–101, 103, 112, 126, 144
Jews, Maori seen as, 100–103, 112, 121, 125–30, 198, 200
John the Baptist, 185
Joseph (Hebrew), 76, 89, 90, 177–78, 180
Joshua (Hebrew), 173
Judaic law, 72, 88, 89, 95, 150
Judaism, 112, 144
Judgement, 58, 111

Kaitahu, 154–59
Kanana — see Canaan
Karakia Nakahi, 109–114
Karo, Ani, 171–74
Katimamoe, 154–59
Kauri gum, 46
Kemp, James, 61
Kenana Tumoana, 182
Kendall, Thomas, 19, 21, 43, 61, 72–73
Kereopa Te Rau, 54, 124, 126
Kina, 73
King Country, 132, 150–53, 161
King, John, 19, 61, 109
King Movement, 36, 150–53
Kohititanga Marama (Kohiti), 175–81
Kokohinau, 101

Komene, 132
Korito, 177–78
Kororareka, 22, 112
Korotuaheka, 158–59
Kuku, Mata, 172
Kuku, Tame, 172

Lampiler, J., 26
Land, alienation of, 38, 80, 107, 140–48, 171–74, 182–83
Land, confiscation of, 36–37, 182–83
Land, feeling of Maori for, 35–36, 92
Land, sale of, 34–36, 38, 140–48, 161–64, 182–83
Land, sale to missionaries, 60–61, 65
Lands Claims Commission, 61
Laughton, J.G.L., 137, 192
Lazarus, 22
Lee, Professor Samuel, 72
Levites, 92–93, 187
Levy Brothers, 126
Levy, S.A., 101
Life after death, 111
Literacy, 28–30
Lloyd, Captain, 124
Lord's Prayer, 116

Maai, 185
Mahuta, King, 38
Mair, Major W.G., 153
Makaretu, 182
Maketu, 165–70, 173
Makutu, 48, 156, 168
Mana, 48
Mangaaruhe Stream, 176–77
Mangai — see Ratana, T.W.
Mangakahia, 119–20
Mangatawhiti, 176
Maning, Judge F.E., 42, 44, 46
Manna from heaven, 118–19
Maori language, 72–73
Marriage customs, 90
Marsden, Samuel, 19, 24, 38, 50, 61, 72, 78, 81, 92
Martin, Lady M.A., 45, 47
Maru, 82
Mary (mother of Jesus), 137
Matahi, 188
Matarawa, 117
Material goods, 18, 19
Matthews, Richard, 61
Maui, 73, 84
Maungapohatu, 182–89
Maunsell, Beatrice, 78
Maunsell, Robert, 20, 28, 54, 61, 72, 74, 75, 76

Mauri, 48
Melchizedek, 144
Merning, Mr, 23
Messiah, 117, 184–85
Methodist Church, 190, 192–94
Michael (Angel), 116, 123
Midianites, 126
Millennialism, 145, 164, 171, 175–81, 185, 187–88, 197, 198
Miracles, 84, 110–11
Mission teachers (Maori), 62
Missions, poor relations between, 25–27, 59–61
Missionaries attitudes to Maori culture, 19–21, 62–63
Moeraki, 59
Montefiore, Joseph, 78
Moses, 76, 90, 110, 117, 125, 127, 134–38, 142, 144, 145, 156, 173, 184–85, 195, 200
Motiti Island, 165–70
Mount Eden jail, 172

Nakahi, 109–14
Names, given (see also Christian names), 94
Native Land Court, 35, 36, 46, 49
Nazirites, 185
New Moon, 176, 180–81
New Testament, 74–80, 98, 100, 125–30, 138, 163, 167, 172–74, 184, 188
New Testament, translation of, 74–75, 80
New Year, 136, 167
New Zealand Company, 34
Newsham, Mr, 163
Ngakuku, 77
Nga Puhi, 38, 97, 109
Ngarara, 110, 134
Ngata, Sir Apirana, 195
Ngati Apa, 190
Ngati Kahungunu, 175, 182
Ngati Kinohaku, 161
Ngati Maniapoto, 161
Ngati Raukawa, 190
Ngati Tuwharetoa, 27
Ngati Pikiao, 168
Nihoniho, Tuta, 89
Niu, 88, 127, 140
Noah, 73, 74, 129, 142, 144, 145
Northland, 18, 19, 27, 28, 107, 171–74

Ohaeawai, 111
Ohau, Lake, 158
Old Testament, 74–80, 82–84, 95, 100, 102–103, 110, 118–19, 125–30, 134–38, 142–48, 150–53, 155–59, 163–64, 167–68, 172–74, 180–81, 184, 186–88, 194–96, 198–200
Old Testament, translation of, 74–75, 80
Omanaia, 114
Omarama, 158–59
Omens, 87, 89, 118, 195
Opotiki, 54, 101, 124, 125–26
Otago, 45, 59
Otaki, 29
Otumoetai, 72

Pai Marire, 89, 101, 123–30, 132–34, 140, 151, 173
Paihia, 19, 55
Paipeta, Pita, 158
Pakowai, 185
Palestine — see Israel
Pangari, Aporo, 172
Pangari, Kokou, 172
Pangari, Maria, 171–74
Pangari, Wiremu, 172
Papahurihia, 109–14, 136
Papakutu Pa, 29
Paparata, 55
Papatuanuku, 35, 92
Parewanui, 190
Parihaka, 92, 140–48, 161, 171, 173, 191
Passover, 137
Patara, 101, 124
Patuwai, 168
Paul (Apostle), 116
Penetana, 109
Peura (Beulah), 184
Philistines, 91, 126
Pinepine, 184, 187
Pipiriki, 57
Pirikawau, 35
Piripi, 155
Polack, Joel Samuel, 18, 78, 90, 93–95, 112–13
Polygamy, 18, 39, 93, 97, 129, 187
Pomare, Sir Maui, 195
Pompallier, Bishop, 20, 25, 26, 73
Population, 42
Potatau, King, 151
Poverty Bay, 124
Priesthood, Hebrew-Maori, 93
Prophecy, 88, 136, 168, 171–74, 175–81, 184, 187–88
Prophets, Hebrew, 76, 85, 96
Prophets, Hebrew-Maori, 117, 125–30, 134–38, 144–48, 155–59, 167, 180, 188, 194–95, 198–200

Index

Prostitution, 43
Puckey, W.G., 61
Puniho, 146
Putahi Pa, 175

Queen of Sheba, 187

Rangiaowhia, 54, 125
Rangihoua, 109
Rangiriri, 125
Rangitukia, 199
Rapaki, 155
Ratana Church, 190–96
Ratana, Tahupotiki Wiremu, 159, 190–96
Raukatauri, 124
Red Sea, 117, 126
Remana Hi, 171–74
Reptile, 110, 134
Richmond, Christopher, 61
Riemenschneider, Johannes, 28
Rihara Te Reke, 165–70
Rikirangi (Arikirangi) — see Te Kooti
Rikiriki, Mere, 190, 195
Ringatu, 132–38, 165, 167, 181
Rites of passage, Hebrew-Maori, 90–91
Ritual practices, 90–92, 146
Rotorua, 92, 168
Rua Kenana Tapunui, 182–89
Ruakituri Valley, 177
Ruapekapeka, 55
Ruatahuna, 136
Ruatoki, 136
Rura, 151

Sabbath, 24, 55–58, 62–63, 76, 96, 103, 112, 116–17, 136, 167, 171–74, 187, 194
Sacrifice, 26, 90, 171, 172–73
Sacrifice, human, 92, 93, 123, 144, 167
Salvation, 97
Samson (Hebrew), 126
Samuel (Hebrew), 135, 184
Sanskrit, 73
Satan — see Devil
Saul (Hebrew), 91, 135
Scriptures, dissemination of, 28, 59, 74–75, 80
Scriptures, interpretations of, 57–59, 111
Scriptures, power of, 30, 39
Scriptures, published in Maori, 74–75, 80
Selwyn, Bishop, 54, 60, 74
Serpent, 88, 109–10, 112
Serpent, brazen, 112, 120, 127
Servant, C., 89
Settlement policy, 33–36, 40

Settlers, 19–23, 33–35, 62, 140
Sex, premarital, 25, 129
Shem, 74, 124, 126, 144
Shepherd, James, 62
Shortland, Edward, 59
Slavery, 27, 39, 93, 97, 123
Social organisation (Maori), 39–40, 49, 53, 92, 94, 97
Sodom, 168
Solomon (King), 89, 129, 176, 185, 187
South Africa, 35
Spiritism, 114, 119
Stack, James A., 38, 56, 199
Stack, James W., 24, 40, 55, 61, 154
Storytelling, 76–78
Synagogue, 144

Tabernacle of Israelites, 180
Tamakihikurangi, Renata, 55
Tamati, Matenga, 175–81
Tamihana, Te Tiu, 101, 130
Tamihana, Wiremu, 53, 150–51
Tane, 84, 95, 152
Taniwha, 110, 142
Tapu, 20, 48, 53, 80–81, 87–88, 94, 97, 155–59, 172, 176–77, 185, 187
Taranaki, 23, 37, 53, 59, 101, 107, 116–17, 121, 123–30, 140–48, 159, 161, 171, 190–96
Taranaki (mountain), 159
Taratoa, Henare, 56
Tarawera, eruption of, 136, 168
Tareha, 97
Tariao, 150–53, 165
Tattooing, 94–95, 129
Taupo, 27
Tauranga, 26, 54, 56, 72, 117
Tawhiao, King, 150–53, 161, 167
Taylor, Richard, 49, 61, 72, 81, 82, 112, 116–17, 121
Te Ahuahu, 111
Te Aroha, Reihana, 72
Te Atua Wera, 109–114, 121
Te Awaitaia, 97
Te Heuheu, 27, 39, 81
Te Kai, 57
Te Karauna (The Crown), 178
Te Kemara, 60
Te Kooti, 132–38, 167–68, 175, 181, 182–85, 190
Te Kuiti, 163–64
Te Kumi, 161–64
Te Kuru, 29
Te Mahuki Manukura, 161–64, 191
Te Maiharoa, 154–59, 190

215

Te Pirikawau, 35
Te Pokiha Taranui, 167–68
Te Puni, 62
Te Rauparaha, 44
Te Taonui, 26
Te Teko, 101, 136, 137
Te Turuki — see Te Kooti
Te Ua Haumene, 100, 123–30, 140, 151
Te Uira, 163
Te Waharoa, 36, 44, 58
Te Waharoa, Wiremu Tamihana, 53, 150–51
Te Wherowhero, 37, 44
Te Whiti-O-Rongomai, 28–29, 140–48, 161, 164
Te Witu, 118–19
Tekapo, Lake, 155
Tekau-ma-rua, 161–64, 191
Temple of the Lord, 123, 175–81
Temuka, 154
Thames, 72
Tikanga Hou, 116–17
Time, measurement of, 89–90, 96
Tohu Kakahi, 140–48, 161
Tohunga, 39, 49, 54, 56, 89, 92–93, 96, 110, 113–14, 154–59, 165, 191, 195, 198
Trade, 19, 20, 22–23, 43–44, 47, 49, 78
Treaty of Waitangi, 26, 37, 60, 65, 72, 192
Trinity (Christian), 116, 186, 191–92
Tuahiwi, 155
Tuhaha, 156
Tuhoe, 182–86
Turanga (see also Gisborne), 101, 121, 132
Turner, Nathaniel, 77
Turton, H. Hanson, 58–60, 72, 117
Twelve, number, 95, 137, 161

Uenuku, 37, 152
Upper Waihou, 171–74
Urewera, 46, 182, 185–89
Uruao, 154
Utu, 89, 96, 101

Victoria, Queen of England, 145
Visions, 118, 144, 158, 171, 182, 190, 195, 200
Volkner, C.S., 54, 101, 124–26

Wade, William, 21, 28, 61
Wahi Tapu, 119
Waihou, 171–74
Waikaremoana, Lake, 176, 184
Waikato, 27, 54–55, 107, 124, 130, 161, 167

Waikokopu, 177
Waikouaiti, 28
Waima, 114
Waipaoa River, 185
Wairoa (Hawke's Bay), 121, 175–81
Wairoa (Northland), 24
Wairuarua, 119
Waitaki River, 157, 158
Waitangi, 60
Wakefield, Edward Jerningham, 34, 39, 57, 61, 62
Wakefield, William, 34, 62
Walsh, Archdeacon, 44
Wanaka, Lake, 156
Wanganui, 38, 46, 57, 100, 125, 126, 151
Waokena, 58, 60
War, customs of, 91–92
War, inter-tribal, 39
War, Maori-Pakeha, 54–56, 65, 89, 101, 132–38, 140–48
Ward, John, 78
Warea, 116–17
Warren, John, 78
Watkins, James, 28, 38–39
Wesleyan Mission, 17, 25, 26, 59–61, 113
Whakaari (White Island), 187–88
Whakapa rite, 90
Whakatane, 101, 136, 168
Whalers, 22, 43
Whare wananga, 82, 94
White Cliffs (Pukearuhe), 163
White, John, 100, 113, 125, 126, 151
White, William, 76
White clothing, 172–73
Whiteley, John, 61, 77, 123
Wi Maruki, 101
Wilkinson, Mr, 163
Williams, Henry, 20, 23, 28, 29, 54, 58, 61, 62, 63, 89, 97, 109, 112
Williams, John, 73–74
Williams, William, 26–27, 28, 36, 38, 56, 75, 101, 121, 125, 132
Williams, William Leonard, 38, 137
Wilson, J.A., 92
Woon, William, 26, 76, 112

Yahweh — see Jehovah
Yate, William, 74

Zerubabbel, 123
Zion, 172–74, 184–86